Women, violence and strategies for action

Women, violence and strategies for action
Feminist research, policy and practice

edited by
**Jill Radford, Melissa Friedberg
and Lynne Harne**

Open University Press
Buckingham · Philadelphia

Open University Press
Celtic Court
22 Ballmoor
Buckingham
MK18 1XW

e-mail: enquiries@openup.co.uk
world wide web: http://www.openup.co.uk

and
325 Chestnut Street
Philadelphia, PA 19106, USA

First Published 2000

A catalogue record of this book is available from the British Library

ISBN   0 335 20370 1 (hb)   0 335 20369 8 (pb)

Library of Congress Cataloging-in-Publication Data
Women, violence, and strategies for action : feminist research,
   policy, and practice / edited by Jill Radford, Melissa Friedberg,
   and Lynne Harne.
       p.   cm.
   Includes bibliographical references and index.
   ISBN 0-335-20370-1 (hardcover). – ISBN 0-335-20369-8 (pbk.)
   1. Women–Crimes against–Great Britain.   2. Sexual abuse victims
   –Great Britain.   3. Women–Crimes against–Great Britain
   –Prevention.   4. Feminist theory–Great Britain.   I. Radford, Jill,
   1947– . II. Friedberg, Melissa, 1953– .   III. Harne, Lynne, 1947– .
   HV6250.4.W65W6615   2000
   362.88'082'0941–dc21
                                                                99–29673
                                                                     CIP

Typeset by Graphicraft Limited, Hong Kong
Printed in Great Britain by Biddles Ltd, Guildford and King's Lynn

This book is dedicated to the memory of Emma Humphreys, feminist writer and campaigner, 30 October 1967 – 11 July 1998.

Contents

Notes on contributors

Claudia Bernard teaches at Goldsmith's College, University of London. Her research interests are anti-racism, gender issues, and feminist pedagogy. She has worked on issues of violence against women and children from a feminist perspective for a number of years, and has published articles on child sexual abuse and feminist research methodology.

Melissa Friedberg is a lecturer in the Social Work Department at Brunel University, Twickenham, Middlesex. She has had a longstanding involvement in violence against women groups and campaigns and is a member of WAPOW (Women Against the Prostitution of Women).

Terry Gillespie is a senior lecturer in criminology, and course leader for the BA (Hons) Criminology at Nottingham Trent University. She is treasurer of the British Sociological Association Violence Against Women Study Group. Terry has published on sexual violence and rape support services and is researching violence against women on the Internet.

Lynne Harne has taught women's studies and social policy at the University of Westminster for a number of years. She is currently undertaking research at the University of Bristol on violent fathers and child contact. She has previously worked as a school governor trainer, policy officer in local education authorities and secondary school teacher.

Marianne Hester is professor of sociology and social policy at the University of Sunderland. She has carried out research into violence against women for the past 20 years. Marianne has always been concerned with the links between women's experiences, feminist theory and political action.

Catherine Humphreys is a lecturer in the Department of Social Policy and Social Work at the University of Warwick. She has undertaken research, writing and teaching in the area of violence against women in the UK and Australia.

Celia Jenkins teaches sociology and women's studies at the University of Westminster and specializes in gender and education. Her current research interest is in prostitution issues and she is a member of WAPOW (Women Against the Prostitution of Women).

Liz Kelly is a feminist researcher and activist. Since 1987 she has worked in the Child and Women Abuse Studies Unit (CWASU), University of North London. She recently chaired a Council of Europe group of specialists which produced a plan of action on violence against women. CWASU are advisors to the British Council on Violence against Women.

Ellen Malos has been active in the women's movement since the late 1960s, and has worked with Women's Aid since the early 1970s. She is a founder member of the Domestic Violence Research Group in the School for Policy Studies at the University of Bristol.

Jill Radford is a feminist, researcher, teacher and activist committed to ending violence against women and children. She worked at Rights of Women for 10 years. In 1996 she relocated to the University of Teeside where she teaches women's studies and criminology.

Tina Skinner's research focuses on feminist strategy, and the relationships between feminist and police services for survivors of rape and sexual assault. She has worked in a women's refuge, and as a voluntary sector consultant on services for women before becoming a lecturer in criminology at the University of Teesside. She is coordinator of the British Sociological Association (Women's Caucus) Violence Against Women Study Group.

Ruth Swirsky is principal lecturer in sociology and women's studies at the University of Westminster. Her research and writing focus on Jewish women's history and prostitution issues.

Emma Williamson has just completed a PhD thesis at the University of Derby. She is the coordinator of the Domestic Violence and Health Network List, which acts as a forum for researchers examining this area of research, and is currently working as a research associate at the School for Policy Studies, University of Bristol.

1 Introduction

Jill Radford, Lynne Harne and Melissa Friedberg

Women, Violence and Strategies for Action continues the project of presenting contemporary feminist research on men's violence arising from discussions in the British Sociological Association Violence Against Women Study Group.[1] Like earlier books in the series (Hanmer and Maynard 1987; Hanmer *et al.* 1989; Hester *et al.* 1996) it introduces some new directions in feminist work, the changing contexts in which it is occurring, and connections between research and activist intervention strategies in feminist struggles.

A central aim is to present recent research findings and theoretical developments in relation to a range of forms of sexual violence including: domestic violence (Malos; Williamson; Hester); sexual harassment (Kelly and Humphreys; Harne); rape and sexual assault (Skinner; Radford); prostitution (Swirsky and Jenkins; Friedberg); pornography (Gillespie; Swirsky and Jenkins); and child sexual abuse (Kelly and Humphreys; Harne; Bernard). Consequently, the book advances the knowledge base surrounding the problem of sexual violence. A number of chapters refer to the way feminist work has placed this issue on local, national and global policy agendas (Kelly and Humphreys; Gillespie; Harne; Malos; Hester; Radford).

Over the last 25 years the subject has been variously named as 'violence against women', 'sexual violence' or 'gender violence'. The politics of naming and definition, an important theme in feminist theorizing, have been central to work in this field, shaping the development of research and knowledge creation. Feminist definitions, grounded in the experiences of women and children, have developed with the growth of feminist knowledge and understanding, as an outcome of research.

Earlier research named the problem as 'violence against women'. While it signifies the gendered nature of the violence, a limitation of this early concept was its failure to specify any connection with the abuse of children, although the interconnectedness of woman and child abuse has been a longstanding theme of feminist analysis. In this volume contributors explore this inter-connectedness from a range of standpoints.

Gillespie's examination of computer pornography (Chapter 4) identifies one connection in the massive growth of pornography which records and celebrates violence and abuse of women and children on the Internet, whether real or virtual. She also problematizes the ease of access to this material by children in the computer age.

While computer pornography is a relatively new issue, Harne (Chapter 7) records that concern about sexual violence in schools is an issue around which feminists have made significant interventions since the 1980s. However, her research indicates that, as we approach the millennium, sexual harassment and sexual abuse are being downplayed, and inadequately addressed in education policy. This she argues is a consequence of postfeminist notions that equality has been achieved, which has prompted something of a backlash against school provision for the girl child.

Friedberg (Chapter 6) highlights another link between sexual violence against girls and women in exploring the routes from care homes to prostitution. There are complex and interrelated issues connected to girls' and women's involvement in prostitution which were not only not addressed by the care system but exacerbated by it; e.g. girls' involvement in prostitution while in care which continues into their lives as women.

In an examination of the dilemmas facing women as mothers of children who have been sexually abused, Bernard (Chapter 8) explores how the sexual abuse of children impacts on women as mothers and partners of abusive men. Her chapter, which centres on the experiences of black mothers, criticizes the partiality of analyses which neglect racism and fail to recognize how women's experiences are structured through racism as well as sexism. For black women, protecting their children from racism as well as sexual violence poses complex and sometimes apparently contradictory dilemmas around divided loyalties which influence their help-seeking strategies. The Report of the Inquiry into the murder of Stephen Lawrence (Home Department 1999) demonstrates yet again the high levels of racism both in white communities and statutory agencies, which may seriously compromise them as sources of support.

Liz Kelly's (1988) concept of a 'continuum of sexual violence' represented a significant theoretical shift. Rather than focusing on the different forms of violence and abuse as discrete issues, the continuum recognizes commonalities between them in women's experience and theoretically as forms of violence underpinning patriarchal power and control. Developed to facilitate theorization of these commonalities and connections, the continuum is constituted through difference: the different forms of sexual violence, their different impacts, and the different community and legal responses to women, positioned differently, within and between cultures and through history. It illustrates the hollowness of the frequent criticism that radical feminism, in focusing solely on commonalities in women's experiences, offers universalistic explanations. Critics' claims that radical feminism fails to engage with specificity, change and difference in women's experiences and in relation to wider power structures, are misplaced. This anthology, by both including a global dimension and experiences of women and children often excluded from research agendas – black women and girls and women involved in prostitution, for example – further demonstrates that this criticism lacks foundation.

It is the global perspective which, following the Convention on the Elimination of Discrimination Against Women (CEDAW) 1992, has been influential in effecting a more recent shift to the language of gender violence.[2] However all three concepts: violence against women, sexual violence and gender violence continue to hold political and theoretical currency (see Kelly and Radford 1998), and all are used in this volume. Presenting feminist research and activist collaborations at the global, national and local levels carries forward the global feminist aims of 'bringing Beijing home' by illustrating the significance of thinking globally while acting locally in the development of feminist resistance strategies in relation to gender violence.

Changing international contexts

The changed global context, highlighted by the United Nations Fourth World Conference on Women 1995, and subsequent conferences like the 1996 International Conference on Violence, Abuse and Women's Citizenship, Brighton, has resulted in the inclusion of feminist activists and researchers in consultative processes by international bodies and many national and local governments. These initiatives were informed by feminist understandings of and research on gender violence, its nature, impacts, prevalence and critiques of the limited responses on the part of law, police and community.

Both Hester and Radford locate their contributions in the context of developing cross national collaborations in relation to research, law and policy initiatives. Radford (Chapter 12) engages in a comparative analysis of sexual violence, law and feminist activism in India and the UK, while Hester (Chapter 11) explores research and policy development in relation to (primarily) domestic violence in China. These chapters point to the ways sociohistorical specificity shapes the meaning, forms and nature of gender violence and has informed legal, policy and feminist responses. These discussions record the different histories of research and activism in these countries. In India, as Radford illustrates, the history of activism around rape is longer and more continuous than that of the UK, while, as Hester reports, violence against women and children in the home are connected concepts in China. Despite the many differences, both authors highlight the salience of the continuum of sexual violence in relation to developing strategies for resistance and change.

In addressing pornography on the Internet, Gillespie (Chapter 4) has identified a global issue requiring global solutions in relation to regulation and legislation. However, as she indicates, this work is still in its beginning stage in international forums, and is predominantly being conducted within non-feminist discourses. Although some feminists are involved in international collaborations, this is an issue where more feminist engagement is needed if feminist analyses of pornography are to gain influence at a global level.

The difficult question of regulation of pornography generated through prostitution is also tackled by Swirsky and Jenkins (Chapter 5) in the context of local concerns about the promotion of prostitution in London and Brighton's telephone boxes. These authors also review the ways in which feminist research can both be facilitated and constrained by the competing standpoints and positioning of different interest groups.

Changing national contexts

The changed international context has also had an important influence on national governments. Signatories to the Beijing Declaration are now required to report regularly to the United Nations on progress made on 12 'critical areas of concern' relating to the 'advancement of women and the achievement of equality between women and men' as a matter of human rights (United Nations 1996: 33). 'Violence against women' and 'persistent discrimination against and violation of the rights of the girl child' are respectively the fourth and twelfth of these critical areas, and as such are issues centrally included in government reports to the UN. That feminist research and activism features significantly in many national reports is a testament to the widespread influence of feminist work in this area.

While the timing of the Beijing Declaration 1995 meant that, in the UK, it fell to the Conservative government to submit the first national report, the change in government in 1997 marked a significant shift in the political climate in which feminist research and activist interventions are conducted. The election of a New Labour government brought with it both new potential and new contradictions for feminists working in this area. On the one hand, New Labour appears less hostile to feminist interventions than the previous government. In substantive terms New Labour's commitment to 'the elimination of domestic and sexual violence against women' was signified in its consultation document *Peace at Home* (Labour Party 1995). In government, this commitment was reflected in its encouragement of local government initiatives for *Tackling Violence Against Women* (Cabinet Office 1998). So despite the fact that New Labour's promised national strategy is still awaited at the time of writing, in some ways the new political culture appears more favourable to feminist research and involvement in policy making in this area than at any earlier period.

However, as is also becoming increasingly apparent, attempts to eliminate or mediate the impact of gender violence in societies committed to upholding the dominance of patriarchy, white supremacy, heterosexuality and multinational capitalism are not without contradictions. This is evident in New Labour's policy of *Supporting Families* (Home Office 1998) which affords only two pages to the question of domestic violence. The tensions between the stated policy of 'supporting marriage' and dealing effectively with violence against women are unresolved in this document. For example, it endorses the Family Law Act 1996, introduced by the former Conservative government, which simultaneously simplifies the process of applying for injunctions against domestic violence, yet lengthens the time it takes for married women with children to gain a divorce (Hester and Harne 1999).[3] Promoting marriage 'as the surest foundation for raising children' (Home Office 1998: 5) serves to further marginalize children who spend some or all of their childhood outside of that institution, for example, children living with lone parents, children of lesbians as well as those in institutional care. It further strengthens a discourse which can lock women and children into abusive relationships, ironically 'for the sake of the children', as Bernard notes in Chapter 8. As Friedberg (Chapter 6) finds, an ideology which promotes the heterosexual nuclear family as the 'heart of society' (Home Office 1998: 1) impacts negatively on the already difficult experiences of, and further stigmatizes children in institutional care. Although stating that some of the government's proposed changes in Social Services are positive moves, she critiques their limitations in addressing some of the core problems in the care system. Further, *Supporting Families* makes no mention of the recognized problems in the Children Act 1989, which claims to prioritize the welfare of the child, but in practice continues to be interpreted through the presumption that children need contact with violent and abusive fathers, thus compromising their and their mothers' safety. Although New Labour claims to be tackling racism, there is no reference in *Supporting Families* to the problems in immigration law with its notorious 'one year rule' which presents some black and migrant women with 'a stark choice' between remaining with violent husbands or facing deportation (Southall Black Sisters 1995).[4]

While New Labour's commitments around violence against women are indeed welcome, its failure to understand its nature as structural violence rooted in the power relations of patriarchy, heterosexuality and masculinity as currently constructed, inevitably limits its capacity to respond with effective measures, either at the level of law change or in social policy. Kelly and Humphreys (Chapter 2) examine tensions and contradictions arising from shortcomings of recent legislation introduced to secure protection against sexual harassment and child abuse. However both the Protection from Harassment Act 1997 and the Sex Offenders Act 1997 focus on 'stranger danger', and fail to recognize the greater prevalence of these forms of abuse within (former) familial and intimate relationships.

Mirroring this reluctance to engage with what is considered to be the private sphere, is a reluctance on the part of government to engage with sexualized violence. While as is reflected in the work of Malos and Williamson (Chapters 9 and 10), considerable efforts have been made by government bodies and statutory services to address the problem of domestic violence in the UK, issues of sexual assault and sexual harassment have been the subject of less intervention. These issues are still represented as 'controversial', as Skinner, Swirsky and Jenkins, Friedberg, Harne, and Radford all indicate in different contexts.

The questions of coercive sexuality and traded sex seem too close to the heart of the patriarchy for governments and policy makers, anxious to resolve the 'crisis of masculinity', to give serious attention to. This lack of attention disregards the abuse of women involved in prostitution and the impacts of prostitution on women more widely, issues raised by Swirsky and Jenkins, and Friedberg (Chapters 5 and 6). Similar neglect has also characterized responses to sexual harassment and sexual assault, issues which have declined in prominence in the UK (Harne, Chapter 7; Radford, Chapter 12).

Kelly and Humphreys (Chapter 2) emphasize the importance of recognizing the changed political context which has opened new doors to collaborative working with state agencies and national government, but note that strategic thinking is necessary if this is to be achieved without losing sight of feminist visions and theoretical understandings of sexual violence as central to the power relations underpinning patriarchal control.

Changing local contexts

Feminist engagement with multi-agency collaborations at the local level has a longer history (Skinner, Malos, Williamson). Yet as all three note, multi-agency alliances can also generate tensions. Political clarity and strategic engagement are needed in sustaining a feminist influence in the development of service provision. Malos, in her review in Chapter 9 of the structure, organization and working practices of multi-agency domestic violence forums, attempts to analyse what makes for good practice and how it can be evaluated. She opens by posing some complex questions for feminists responding to the challenge of finding strategies for working collaboratively with local government and statutory agencies, positioned within bureaucratic and hierarchical structures, and operating within professional rather than feminist discourses.

Similar issues are raised by Skinner in Chapter 3, who also in the context of inter-agency consultations around rape and sexual assault, raises important theoretical questions about the nature of feminist strategies and tactics, and the criteria used to evaluate their efficacy in terms of both long-term progress towards the realization of feminist visions, as well as short-term gains in terms of achieving beneficial change for women and children. Like Kelly and Humphreys, she points to the need for feminists to reflect on how the changed political context impacts on the development of strategy and tactics in feminist activism.

Changing academic contexts

The work presented here has also been conducted within a changed academic climate. In the UK, research around gender violence, despite its contemporary global influence, has been labelled controversial and marginalized since the 1970s. In the late 1980s new challenges emerged from the postmodern/ poststructuralist domination of contemporary social theorizing 'which presents a false dichotomy between radical social constructivism and various forms of universalism and essentialism' (Mellor 1997: 7). Advocates of the post-it discourse, for example, have joined with the more traditionally reactionary forces in promoting the agendas of men's movements, in an attempt to mount a more sustained attack on the substance and content of feminist research in relation to male violence (see Burgess 1997; Featherstone and Trinder 1997). With the support of the mass media, these challenges have recreated a political climate unfavourable to feminist analysis and research.

The impact of a changed academic and research context is a primary focus of Williamson, and Swirsky and Jenkins (Chapters 10 and 5). These chapters identify how academic concerns with scholastic achievement, income generation and research ratings impact on feminists as academic researchers. Both chapters explore how the changed academic context of the late 1990s aggravates already complex relations of accountability. Williamson explores the ways collaborative working with an inter-agency domestic violence forum and voluntary sector women's organizations raise additional demands in relation to accountability of the research process. She articulates some of the complexities and ethical questions this raises for a research student simultaneously required to meet academic criteria of scholarship and excellence and be accountable to community-based women's organizations. Swirsky and Jenkins discuss similar ethical and political dilemmas in the context of contract research sponsored by a private sector company and a local authority relating to prostitution, a subject which continues to be controversial within feminism and wider society.

Conclusion

All contributors engage with the research, politics and process, contributing to debates around the nature of feminist research methodologies in the context of feminist activism. From a range of research locations and contexts spanning the local to the global, contributors identify the challenge of holding on to feminist visions in research, policy interventions and activism with a view to realizing the feminist aim of making the kind of changes that matter to the lives of women and children. The chapters demonstrate that working simultaneously towards the longer term goal of eliminating sexual violence and the shorter term aim of generating beneficial changes in legal protection, provision of appropriate services and in prevention policies within patriarchal structures involves dealing with difficulty and contradictions. However, it also demonstrates that contributors, as feminist researchers, are working to develop creative and strategic approaches to the dilemma of reform or transformation traditionally defined by malestream social science as irresolvable.

Notes

1 The British Sociological Association Violence Against Women Study group, its influence, composition and aims, described in Hester *et al.* (1996) continues to meet regularly. It welcomes new members committed to furthering its aims of making links between feminist activists, academic researchers and policy makers, and producing research which will make a real difference to the lives of women and children within anti-racist and anti-oppressive practice.

2 CEDAW (1992) stated that the general prohibition of gender discrimination includes:

> gender based violence – that is violence which is directed at a woman because she is a woman or which affects women disproportionately. It includes acts which inflict physical, mental or sexual harm or suffering, threats of such acts, coercion or other deprivations of liberty.

CEDAW affirmed that violence against women constitutes a violation of women's human rights.

3 The implementation of Part II of the Family Law Act, which includes clauses lengthening the time it takes to get a divorce, has been postponed by the government owing to opposition by those seeking a divorce.

4 The government has since announced some concessions to the One Year Rule, whereby women experiencing domestic violence within the twelve month period may be allowed to remain in this country, if there is an injunction, a criminal conviction or a police caution against their partner.

References

Burgess, A. (1997) *Fatherhood Reclaimed: The Making of the Modern Father.* London: Vermillion.

Cabinet Office (1998) *Tackling Violence Against Women: Better Government for All.* London: Central Office for Information.

CEDAW (1992) *Violence against Women*, general recommendation 19 (11th session). UN Doc. CEDAW/C/1992/L.1./Add. 15. Vienna: United Nations.

Featherstone, B. and Trinder, L. (1997) Familiar subjects? domestic violence and child welfare. *Child and Family Social Work*, 2(3): 147–160.

Hanmer, J. and Maynard, M. (eds) (1987) *Women, Violence and Social Control.* Basingstoke: Macmillan.

Hanmer, J., Radford, J. and Stanko, E.A. (1989) *Women, Violence and Policing: International Perspectives.* London: Routledge.

Hester, M. and Harne, L. (1999) Fatherhood, children and violence: placing the UK in an international context, in S. Watson and L. Doyal (eds) *Engendering Social Policy.* Buckingham: Open University Press.

Hester, M., Kelly, L. and Radford, J. (1996) *Women, Violence and Male Power: Feminist Activism, Research and Practice.* Buckingham: Open University Press.

Home Department (1999) *The Stephen Lawrence Inquiry: Report of an Inquiry by Sir William MacPherson of Cluny*, Cm 4262–I. London: The Stationery Office.

Home Office (1998) *Supporting Families: A Consultation Document.* London: The Stationery Office.

Kelly, L. (1988) *Surviving Sexual Violence*. Cambridge: Polity Press.

Kelly, L. and Radford, J. (1998) Sexual violence against women and girls: an approach to an international overview, in R.E. Dobash and R.P. Dobash (eds) *Rethinking Violence Against Women*. Thousand Oaks, CA: Sage.

Labour Party (1995) *Peace at Home: A Labour Party Consultation on the Elimination of Domestic and Sexual Violence Against Women*. London: The Labour Party.

Mellor, M. (1997) *Feminism and Ecology*. Cambridge: Polity Press.

Southall Black Sisters (1995) 'A Stark Choice; Domestic Violence or Deportation: Campaign to Abolish the One Year Rule. *RoW Bulletin*, Winter.

United Nations (1996) *Beijing Declaration and Platform of Action*. New York: Department of Public Information.

Stalking and paedophilia:
ironies and contradictions in
the politics of naming
and legal reform

**Liz Kelly and
Catherine Humphreys**

In 1997 two pieces of legislation with potentially far-reaching benefits for
the protection of women and children became law: the Protection from
Harassment Act 1997 (PFHA) and the Sex Offenders Act 1997 (SOA). Ironically, the women and children who may be the greatest beneficiaries of
these laws – namely those who are subject to violence and sexual abuse
from men known to them – were rarely mentioned in the media attention
or government consultation papers that preceded the legal reforms. Both
popular and official discourses constructed the issues in particular ways that
undercut and overrode a feminist analysis which had long fought for recognition that the greatest (but not the only) dangers of harassment, violence
and abuse towards women and children lie close to home. This chapter is a
musing on the ironies and contradictions in these processes for feminist
theory and practice.

'Stalking' – old behaviour, new name

The term 'stalking' was created by the US media to name persistent harass-
ment.[1] Both in the US and the UK media representation of stalking has
focused on the celebrity victim and the obsessive stalker; Madonna, Olivia
Newton-John, Princess Anne, Princess Diana, Stephen Spielberg and the
Spice Girls are some of the most well-known examples. The everyday language of harassment did not seem adequate for these larger than life figures.
The fact that in some instances physical assaults had taken place (Monica
Seles, Claudia Schiffer, for example), and in at least one case the obsession
had proved lethal (John Lennon), lent support to a name which evoked

danger more graphically. 'Stalking' served this function and rapidly became the language of choice for the media in naming a broad range of behaviours where the celebrity victim was consistently targeted by someone unknown to, but apparently obsessed by them. It has since become cemented in popular discourse through its use in film and book titles, as well as countless newspaper headlines.

The speed of the adoption of this new language can, in part, be attributed to the fact that the stories played into fertile media territory: the preoccupation with the celebrity and their personal lives. One significant irony here is that the willingness of some elements in the media to go to any lengths to get stories about, and pictures of, celebrities could be said to constitute a form of harassment. This was famously highlighted by Charles Spencer at his sister Diana's funeral, and his sentiments have been echoed before and since by others in the public eye. In fact, this tension was noted in the government white paper issued before the drafting of the PFHA (Home Office 1996a). The key task was to draft legislation broad enough to encompass the myriad ways in which harassment occurs, while not making illegal legitimate forms of the same behaviour – journalism was raised as a case in point.

A further media preoccupation in the UK in 1996 was the widespread reporting of cases in which the inadequacy of current legislation in providing a remedy for stalking was exposed. All these cases involved non-celebrity female victims who hardly knew the men who were harassing them. The exception to this rule was a much-publicized case in which a man was harassed by a woman; Robert Fine, a university teacher, claimed he was repeatedly harassed by a former student. The key themes in these stories were: the innocence of the victims; the deviant obsession of the stalker; the damaging impacts of repeated harassment; and the need for legislative reform.

The attempted prosecutions relied on an extension of the definition of grievous bodily harm to include causing serious psychological damage. Perry Southall (October 1996) won her case against Clarence Morris on the grounds that she was suffering marked physical and psychological impacts as a result of daily harassment by a previously convicted rapist with a history of mental illness. The judge had Morris detained in a psychiatric hospital. Similarly, the courts recognized 'mental anguish' as a form of grievous bodily harm in the cases of Tracey Stant (March 1996) and Louise Wilson (March 1996). The men who stalked them were both found guilty and jailed.[2]

Charlotte Sell's case (March 1996) was dismissed in spite of years of regular harassment. Margaret Bent (September 1996) was similarly unsuccessful in her case against Dennis Chambers. She had been threatened with a knife, constantly followed, telephoned up to 10 times a day, and her stalker had even registered his car in her name and run up a series of parking fines. The legal problems in the two unsuccessful cases were proving intent on the part of the man, and the necessity of being able to present evidence of severe psychological damage to the women (see Lawson-Cruttenden and Addison 1997: 7). The harassment alone was not actionable; it could only be a criminal offence if women could prove a particular form of psychological damage which could be recognized in law as a form of bodily harm. So women who resisted, who strove to find strategies which enabled them to continue to live their lives in spite of the threatening presence, effectively had no remedy in law.

Interestingly, Robert Fine, like Margaret Bent, continued to work and maintain a semblance of normality in a life in which harassment featured almost daily. Unlike most of the women, he managed to win a claim of £5000 for damages and costs to cover his legal fees. His case was not pursued through criminal law, and he therefore did not have to provide evidence of psychological damage. Rather the damages claim was part of a civil law nuisance case. He has since benefited financially in another way, through proceeds from a book based on his experiences (Fine 1997).

The problem with the media reporting – which transformed into a concerted campaign for legal reform – was not so much what was said, but what was left out. Research both in the UK and internationally shows that the majority of harassment occurs in the context of domestic violence – like many other forms of violence against women, the most significant threat is from known men, rather than strangers or acquaintances. Graham (1996) puts the figure at 80 per cent of stalking cases and Shaum and Parrish (1995) argue that these are often the most lethal cases. A third of police calls in domestic violence come from separated women who are being harassed by ex-partners (Kelly *et al.* 1999). A US study of protection orders for domestic violence (Harrell and Smith 1996) found that 57 per cent of those instructed by the court to stay away from their victims contacted them, and continued to harass them. The UK National Anti-Stalking and Harassment Helpline (NASH) report that 95 per cent of those using their service were women, a proportion also evident in data produced by the UK police to support the need for legal reform (Wallis 1996). That harassment/stalking is a form of gender violence – the majority of victims being female and offenders overwhelmingly male – was also underplayed, if not absent, in the media reporting.

The media constructions had an uncanny similarity to academic discourses on stalking. The literature is overwhelmingly psychological and relies on typologies; the three main categories are outlined in Table 2.1 (see also McAnney *et al.* 1993; Reid Meloy 1996).

For our purposes, the most important feature of this literature is the fact that, in both academic and media constructions, the most common context in which ongoing harassment occurs is at worst invisible, or at best referred to in passing. The concepts of stalking and stalkers developed within this exclusionary framework. Interestingly, in contrast to both these constructions and the title of the white paper, the eventual legislation uses harassment as the central concept.

The authors explored this separation of harassment and stalking with a group of women who work in the area of domestic violence at the 1997 Women's Aid Federation of England annual conference. In the context of a workshop on the potentials of the PFHA, participants were asked how they

Table 2.1   Academic typologies of stalkers

Type	Main features
Erotomaniacs	Either male or female strangers who imagine themselves to be in love with their target. They suffer from 'delusional thinking'.
Sociopaths	Predominantly men with criminal records for other kinds of anti-social behaviour. This group often targets a particular 'type' of woman (and in some definitions children are included).
Current/Former intimates	Largely men targeting former female partners. In some typologies this group does not appear at all – in all it is residual.

understood the two terms. 'Harassment' was associated with: broadness; happening to everyone; being a nuisance; short term and more public; and not necessarily a serious offence. 'Stalking' on the other hand was seen as: escalating; dangerous; secretive; sinister; fear-inducing; deliberate; specific to a relationship; holding connotations of prey; happening to others; involving power/pleasure on the part of the stalker; and less inclusive than the term harassment.

A discussion ensued in which the wider implications of naming were explored. Most participants expressed a preference for 'stalking', despite acknowledging that women suffering domestic violence would be less likely to identify with the term. Naming the *seriousness* of the behaviour was more important to this group of women's advocates than a more inclusive name.

This outcome surprised us, and reflecting on why, highlighted the complexity of naming and the issues of language appropriation for feminists. There are multiple purposes and processes involved in naming, and they can be in tension with one another. Prioritizing the establishment of the seriousness of the violations women and children endure may lead to different conclusions than seeking to enable women and children to name their own experiences as forms of abuse. In our view the former orientation would favour the name 'stalking' and the latter 'harassment'.

Change the name, change the law

There are further layers in the naming process, which raise complex strategic questions for feminists interested in legal reform and policy change more broadly. 'The stalker' has been constructed as the deviant other, someone unknown, or hardly known to the victim; the emphasis on distorted thinking and obsessional behaviour makes them relatively easy to label as 'mentally ill'. In both academic and popular representations this model has overridden feminist analysis which emphasized the frequency of violence women experience from men known to them – 'ordinary' men, rather than an aberrant minority. Feminists have long sought to name the domestic nature and the prevalence of gender violence, and after almost three decades many assumed that this particular battle had been won.[3] However, the fragility of this shift is demonstrated by the rapidity with which the 'stranger danger' discourse has been reasserted.

Nevertheless, the picture contains within it some interesting paradoxes. No commentator writes about the PFHA without mentioning how quickly this legislation was drafted and enacted (see, for example, Lawson-Cruttenden and Addison 1997); the entire process took less than two years – astonishingly rapid, particularly when contrasted with the years of consultation on the changes to civil injunctions which were specifically tailored for women and children escaping situations of domestic violence in the 1996 Family Law Act.

Although women attempting to free themselves of violent men can use the provisions of the PFHA, it is worth speculating whether the legislation would have had such a smooth movement into law had it been seen to be targeting former partners (and especially husbands). Did the fact that the perpetrators were understood to be a small group of 'deviants' or strangers, enable the creation of the alliances across the media and political parties, which in turn were critical to the speed of legal reform? From a perspective which recognizes the extent of harassment within domestic violence, the legislative process appears bizarre since within a few months two new statutes covering similar areas were enacted, which have different legal processes and non-comparable penalties. The fact that known men were marginal to the discussion of the PFHA (while seen as central to the Family Law Act 1996 [FLA]) is evident in a revealing comment in the government white paper; the estimate was that only 200 criminal cases a year would be brought under the new harassment law.[4]

Both the PFHA and FLA contain provisions for civil protection orders (Band 1996), and both seek to make these more effective than they have been previously. The crucial difference is that the PFHA creates two new criminal offences, and takes the radical step of linking civil and criminal law.[5] Judges are strongly encouraged to accompany any criminal conviction with a restraining order (a civil remedy). This is a welcome, if all too rare, example of 'joined up thinking' within the legal system; the inadequate understanding within the criminal justice system of the need for ongoing protection has deterred many victims of interpersonal violence from pursuing criminal cases or left them vulnerable to additional abuse where conviction has carried a derisory sentence (Harrell and Smith 1996).

There are several other advantages of the linkage for women, particularly when criminal charges are laid: it limits the number of court appearances they have to make; the provisions are more inclusive than the FLA, which only applies to those who have at some point cohabited; claims for damages can be attached to cases under the harassment legislation; and the provisions in the PFHA mean that women not eligible for legal aid do not have to pay legal costs to obtain a protection order.[6]

The possibility of connecting the different goals of criminal and civil justice – the former to address an offence that has taken place, the latter to protect against potential future attacks – has some obvious advantages. However, legal commentators, such as Lawson-Cruttenden and Addison, view the linkage as 'unprecedented' and note that 'it seems unfortunate that the government should have muddied the waters in this way by mingling the civil and criminal law' (1997: 9). The principle of linking the two arms of law is not, however, a revolutionary act, as it is already being practised in other jurisdictions, for example, Australia, Cyprus and Ireland.

What remains to be seen is how far the potential benefits of the PFHA will be used to assist women and children escaping domestic violence. Training programmes on the new legislation have often failed to address the PFHA, concentrating almost entirely on the FLA. In some areas practitioners seem to have been alert to the benefits of the harassment law; for example in one court in the Midlands the PFHA has been used three times more often for women escaping domestic violence than the FLA and convictions were secured in the majority of cases. In other areas police officers working in domestic violence units have commented that they are only using the PFHA for the most 'serious' cases because they were concerned that 'overuse' may result in the loss of its benefits.[7]

One of the contradictions for feminists is that in many ways the PFHA potentially offers more effective protection for women and children escaping domestic violence than the legislation which has conventionally been designed to address this problem. The swift introduction of the harassment legislation was probably only made possible by the 'non-naming' or the invisibility of harassment by ex-partners. Would a strong feminist voice alongside the media campaign have been counter-productive? And if so, what does this reveal about the contradictions inherent in both naming and remaining silent about the uncomfortable and threatening presence of violence in the family?

Within this sits another contradiction; it has been a central element in feminist activism to name violence against women and children (Kelly 1988), and to name it in ways which more accurately reflect women's experience. Naming has never been only about which words are preferable, but how words carry and convey meaning within discourses which function to extend or limit understanding. Where words draw on non-feminist discourse, especially discourses which are unsympathetic to feminist analysis, much more is at stake than preferring one word to another. How perpetrators are constructed within the naming process offers one of the most revealing examples. We have already outlined how 'stalkers' were defined as an aberrant minority, fundamentally different and 'other' from most men; the second example of legal reform offers an even starker example of resistance to feminist naming of ordinary men as perpetrators of child and woman abuse.

The return of the paedophile

During 1996 just prior to the passing of the Sexual Offenders Act 1997 the term 'paedophile' became ubiquitous in the naming of those who commit sexual offences against children; it replaced all of the other names which were commonly used – child abuser, child sexual abuser, child molester and child rapist. So dominant has this word become that it is now frequently used as an adjective. The list that follows are examples noted in media reporting during 1997: paedophile crime; paedophile material; paedophile murder; paedophile videos/photos; paedophile pornography; paedophile couple; paedophile record. The function of the word in these examples serves to replace previous language such as sex murders or child pornography and/or to make shorthand reference to a set of assumed meanings. A more recent example was in a 1998 *Newsnight* report; it designated a woman campaigning against the settlement of a released sex offender in her neighbourhood as an 'anti-paedophile campaigner'.

This shift in public discourse has taken a different form to that in stalking; rather than a new construction, what occurred here was the rehabilitation of an old one. It is more than a little ironic that this clinical term, which had fallen into considerable disrepute within the study of sexual abuse in childhood, could so swiftly and thoroughly replace a whole range of other concepts. Paedophile and paedophilia have become a shorthand for a particular construction of those who sexually abuse children, which carries within it a range of assumptions and images, almost all of which serve to undercut not just feminist analysis but the knowledge base on sexual abuse which has been built over the last two decades (see Kelly 1996 for more detailed discussion).

Immediately the word paedophile is used, we move away from the recognition of abusers as 'ordinary men' – fathers, brothers, uncles, colleagues, neighbours – and are returned to the more comfortable view of them as 'other', a small minority who are fundamentally different from most men. The fact that they have lives, kinship links and jobs disappears from view in the desire to focus on their difference. This in turn enables sensationalist representations of sex offenders as monsters and beasts, and paedophile now evokes such meanings whether it is used in tabloid or apparently more quality reporting.

Because the term paedophile draws on a pre-existing discourse there are further implications. At the level of explanation attention shifts from the centrality of power and control to notions of sexual deviance, obsession and addiction. 'Paedophilia' returns us to the medical and individualized explanations of sexual violence which we have spent so much time and energy attempting to replace. Rather than sexual abuse demanding that we look critically at the social construction of 'normal' masculinity, male sexuality and the family, the safer terrain of 'abnormality' beckons.

The separation of 'paedophiles' in much of the clinical literature on sex offenders, not only from men in general but also other men who sexually abuse, has involved the presumption of difference. Similarities – in the forms of abuse, in the strategies abusers use to entrap, control and silence children – are ignored. Thus fathers, grandfathers, uncles, brothers who abuse are hardly ever suspected of being interested in the consumption of, or production of child pornography, nor are they thought to be involved in child prostitution. This in turn means that investigations of familial sexual abuse seldom involve either searches for, or questions about, these forms of abuse. This contrasts with what we know from adult survivors who tell of relatives showing them pornography, expecting them to imitate it and being required to pose for it. Some also tell of being prostituted by relatives. A significant proportion of organized networks are based in families (Kelly *et al.* 1995).

Unlike child abuser or child molester, the word paedophile disguises rather than names the issue, focusing our attention on a kind of person rather than kinds of behaviour. If we think about the two most publicized cases in Europe in the late 1990s, complex issues and questions emerge, which the simplistic discourse of the 'paedophile' disguises. Fred West was married and fathered at least six children, he abused his own children, befriended others, and abducted some young women. The case occupied the news for months in the UK, as a gruesome and macabre catalogue of horror was revealed as real. The crimes he and his wife Rosemary West committed against a large number of young women (and at least one adult woman – his previous wife) challenge simplistic constructions of both familial abusers and the paedophile. Marc Dutroux was also married, had two young children and, with accomplices, kidnapped, sexually abused and murdered a number of young Belgian women. When the case came to light in August 1996 it prompted outrage and raised serious questions about both the investigation and now societies should respond to sex offenders (see Kelly 1997/8). Both these men have been defined in popular discourses as 'paedophiles', yet neither fit the traditional clinical profile which is based on an exclusive sexual attraction to children.

These confusions have created a context in which differential policy approaches are proposed in relation to 'paedophiles' – such as life licenses, indeterminate sentences and denial of any contact with children – which would cause outrage if they had been proposed in relation to sexually abusive fathers.

Old name, new law

A fascinating parallel with the emergence of 'stalking' is evident if we look at recent and proposed legal reform with respect to sex offenders. The Sex Offenders Act 1997 (SOA) had an even more hasty passage into law. The likely loss of the Bill in the run-up to the 1997 general election was prevented by a concerted media campaign which bounced the political parties into ensuring that the legislation was enacted. What the media highlighted prior to the reform – and unlike harassment stories they have continued to report – were the limited powers available to the criminal justice system in tracking and managing convicted sex offenders. These concerns were echoed in many communities by public protests at the resettlement of convicted offenders in local communities (these have, if anything, increased since the legislation was passed). Outrage frequently elided a number of connected but separate issues: sentencing of sex offenders; the limitations on supervision postrelease; continuing risk; and where sex offenders who have served their sentences should live. Absent from these debates were the equally important issues of the underreporting and underprosecution of sexual abuse, and the limited use of existing powers in responses to convicted offenders (see Kelly *et al.* 1998 for a detailed overview of policy on sex offenders).[8] Most crucially the fact that children are most at risk from men already known to them, men who are part of their family and community networks, was almost entirely lost (Kelly *et al.* 1991) as yet again a 'stranger danger' discourse was reasserted.

Contrary to public pronouncements, the SOA is an extremely limited piece of legislation. It requires those who have been convicted or cautioned (where there was an admission) of a range of sex offences to register (for varying lengths of time, depending on the length of their original sentence) with the police when they are living in the community. The registration requirements are that the individuals give accurate information on their name (and other names they use) and where they live; they are also required by law to report any changes in these pieces of information to the police. The SOA neither mandates (as some similar laws in the USA do) nor disallows wider notification, but the guidance notes from the Home Office (Home Office 1997) make clear that information should only be extended to agencies outside the criminal justice system in exceptional cases, and on a case by case basis. Notifying the wider community is expected to occur only in a tiny minority of cases. The register has become known as a 'paedophile register', yet the act refers to sex offenders and includes rapists.

The most obvious irony in this reform process was that the individuals likely to be perceived as the greatest danger – sex murderers of children – are not covered at all by the SOA. The law was drafted hurriedly and in its draft version included all the crimes conventionally designated as 'sex crimes'. During the consultation process the futility of including prostitution offences under which those working as prostitutes are prosecuted and those used to prosecute gay men for 'cottaging' was pointed out by a range of interest groups. The absence of sex murderers, who will have been convicted under homicide law (or in rare cases other forms of assault against the person) was also raised. The former comments resulted in a number of sexual offences being excluded from the eventual law, whereas the latter comments were ignored.

The SOA has been represented by the then Minister of State, Alun Michael, as one part of a series of measures to address the issue of sex offenders, and those who abuse children in particular. The limited range of the SOA – it only applies to those serving sentences when it was enacted and anyone convicted of the designated offences subsequently – has been addressed through provision for Sex Offender Orders made in the Crime and Disorder Act, 1998. The police are now empowered to apply for orders designed to restrain the behaviour of known offenders who are thought to constitute a grave risk to children. The kind of limitations envisaged are orders which restrict access to children's playgrounds or the area surrounding schools.[9] Still under discussion are proposals by the previous government to make it a crime for those convicted of sexual offences against children to apply for a job which would involve direct contact with children (Home Office 1996b). The fact that both have extensive implications for familial relations has been studiously ignored by politicians, policy makers and the media.

The proposed measures for prevention and protection are based upon limiting access of known sex offenders to children, particularly previously targeted victims. An anomaly is obvious when men who abuse their own children are considered. On two occasions one of the authors has raised the contradiction between these new policies with respect to sex offenders and the rulings of judges in civil childcare cases with senior Labour Party politicians.[10] On each occasion the individuals concerned admitted they had not considered these implications. Thus although 'paedophile' has become an inclusive term for child sexual abusers, familial abusers are excluded from its remit.

Recent debates about community notification (when and in what circumstances communities should be informed that a convicted sex offender is moving into/living in their area) is yet another illustration of how the stranger danger discourse has taken hold. Sections of the tabloid and local press usurped both the debate and government policy by taking it upon themselves to inform communities and fan a kind of vigilante citizenship as a pretext for child protection.[11] Community protests – often led by women anxious to protect their children – have echoed this concern about the danger of 'outsiders' moving into neighbourhoods. The tragic irony is that this emphasis is likely to result in less rather than more protection for children, since the dangers which are close to home from 'insiders' virtually disappear.

A more informed debate about both the principles of community notification and its limitations might have raised the following issues:

- the danger of presuming that community notification is sufficient protection for children. It will only apply to the tiny minority of sexual abusers who are convicted of an offence, and even were it to be introduced it is likely to be limited to those deemed the greatest 'risk';
- the unreliability of current models of risk assessment, and the bias inherent in most of them whereby men who abuse their own children are invariably defined as 'low risk';
- the uneven implementation of the responsibilities on criminal justice agencies to inform victims of the intended release of their abusers, and to be consulted about both their parole conditions and where they are resettled;[12]

- the potential of models of community notification developing in the USA and Canada where it is used as a form of public education. Community meetings, often well attended, are organized in which considerable stress is placed on the fact that there are abusers living in the community, but who have, as yet, not been reported. The message given is that by concentrating attention solely on a stranger moving into a community, or an individual returning following serving a sentence, creates less, rather than more, protection for children (see Kelly *et al.* 1998 for more detailed discussion);
- what kinds of public policy can be developed with respect to those men who professionals (and sometimes even they themselves) regard as a continuing risk to women and children?

Instead, the image of paedophile as stranger has informed the development of these new responses, neglecting the indisputable fact that children are most at risk from men that they know. The policy and popular agenda has shifted from the central issue of the extent of sexual abuse which raises questions about both the family and masculinity, to a minority of incidents which are reported and prosecuted, centring public concern on a small number of identifiable 'deviants' who can be targeted and shunned.

Possible ways forward amidst ironies and contradictions

Detailed exploration of how policy agendas are constructed, and specifically how feminist perspectives are included and excluded is an area of study and activism that deserves more attention. The processes we have outlined highlight the importance of naming and definitions. Two very different legal reforms were enacted: one which seeks to increase protection for adult women through providing new and better remedies in criminal and civil law; the other using measures in relation to convicted sex offenders to enhance protection, especially of children. The critical themes which connect these two pieces of legislation highlight ironies and contradictions that require serious consideration if the trenchant feminist research and analysis which has had some influence in the past, is to remain a strong force for change in the future.

Most significantly the difficulty of the task needs to be recognized. At the heart of feminist perspectives are a number of unpalatable messages. Women and children are most at risk from men that they know; woman and child abuse is routine and everyday rather than rare and 'deviant'; the violence is gendered, with men the vast majority of perpetrators; and no community or class is immune. These ideas (facts) were in considerable tension with the previous government's agenda, and continue to be in tension with the policy framework of the new populist government, strongly supported by a conservative media constantly in search of a new spin. The key messages relevant to this discussion which have, thus far, been promoted by the Labour government include: that violence is widespread, but danger is located away from the home; the two-parent heterosexual family is to be defended as a safe and protective institution; it is the erosion of the nuclear family which is at the heart of the breakdown of community; men are increasingly alienated, their masculinity undermined by the changing position of women. The contrast and surface incompatibilities between feminist and government perspectives provide specific and difficult challenges for feminist and women-centred organizations.

Within this particular political and socially conservative milieu, feminist discourses can be speedily overridden. The swiftness with which popular and professional discourse has returned to a 'stranger danger' framework reveals how fragile – and resisted – acceptance of the knowledge that women and children are most at risk from men who they know is, and how easily research based on survivors' stories can be ignored.

The absence of a strong feminist voice in the debates and campaigns which preceded both of the legal reforms we have explored was marked.[13] There are salutary lessons here if feminist organizations are to have a role, not just in responding to but in setting future policy agendas. We offer what follows as the beginnings of a conversation about some of the strategic challenges which face us at the end of the 1990s.

Perhaps most crucially, key feminist ideas must be consistently reiterated. This calls for a certain kind of vigilance, not only to take every opportunity to participate in the creation of popular discourse, but also to notice the way popular discourse enters feminist perspectives. Language and naming play a key role in the construction of ideas and understandings, and there are dangers in participating in the further cementing of the terms 'stalking' and 'paedophilia' in public discourse. It is incumbent upon feminist researchers and women's advocates to continue to point out to policy makers, practitioners and the media how these words function to misrepresent the dangers women and children face. The ways feminists engage in these contests over meaning need to be varied and wide-ranging, and will include various combinations of the following strategies:

- forming temporary alliances with organizations and sections of the media where there are common interests, if not common philosophies. The irony that the PFHA was passed with little feminist input, yet the legislation fits central aspects of a feminist agenda, should not be lost. The media has become even more powerful not just in marshalling public opinion, but also in directly influencing policy agendas and decisions (as the two reforms we have discussed in this chapter illustrate). While feminist mistrust of the media is justified, it is also clear that developing media savvy is increasingly necessary for any organization interested in social change. Justice for Women is an example of a feminist campaign that has developed a sophisticated relationship with the media (see Bindel *et al.* 1995);
- if feminist perspectives are not to be marginalized, we need to find ways to accommodate more effectively the range of relationships in which abuse

takes place. This means neither underplaying, or leaving as residual, stranger assaults, nor allowing known 'ordinary' men to be let off the hook. By encompassing the continuum of sexual violence (Kelly 1988) we would be better placed to point up the contradictions in how some men are being held accountable for their behaviour while others escape public censure;

- to have a public voice with respect to policy agendas, feminists and women's organizations need to be in a position to react swiftly, and to distil complex information into a number of clear and simple messages. Community notification is an interesting case in point. This idea has taken hold since 1998, and most of the public protest in favour of it has involved women. Yet there has been little feminist comment to inform the debate at either national or local levels;

- almost two decades of an unsympathetic government created a sense of futility in the traditional routes for policy reform, such as lobbying politicians and policy makers. As a consequence the links between women's organizations and decision makers are weak. The Labour government appears interested in consultation, while unresponsive to certain kinds of pressure – such as making demands – which it views as belonging to the confrontational politics which typified work with the previous Conservative governments. This reality demands both a renewed interest in making direct contact with policy makers, while finding new forms of communication which invite dialogue and keep feminist concerns on the policy agenda.

In summary, the recent legislative changes explored in this chapter illustrate that even the most simple and basic issues which feminists have placed on political and policy agendas can be displaced. The extent to which this continues to happen depends crucially upon whether there is a more concerted feminist engagement in public policy debates. Feminist activism has always required a complex positioning – finding acceptable routes to engage on the inside with those who have the power to make a difference at more than the individual level, while retaining the critical perspective of outsiders. We need to take our abilities to negotiate these spaces more seriously, and begin recording and reflecting upon successes and failures – our own, and those of feminists across the globe.

Notes

1 For the purposes of this chapter the terms stalking and harassment will be used interchangeably.
2 Though Tracy Stant's protection order continued after her harasser was released from prison, this did not deter him. He has been again charged, convicted and jailed for 16 weeks for his continued criminal behaviour (*Independent* 5 January 1999).
3 This is not to suggest that the term 'domestic violence' has not been contested by feminists.

4 In fact, the Metropolitan police statistics for London, for the six month period April–September 1998, recorded 2729 claims under the Protection from Harassment Act, but the number involving former partners is unspecified.

5 The PFHA defines harassment broadly as behaviour/s which must have occurred on more than one occasion and which a reasonable person would know, or should know, that the behaviour constituted harassment of another. The criminal offences are a lesser offence of 'causing harassment' and a more serious offence of 'fear of violence' which carries a maximum penalty of five years custodial sentence and an unlimited fine.

6 The cost of an injunction under the FLA for women who do not qualify for legal aid (i.e. have earnings above Income Support level) is currently between £1500 and £2000.

7 These comments were made during workshops at conferences in different parts of Britain.

8 The current estimates are that only 5 per cent of child sexual abuse cases are reported (Kelly *et al.* 1991) and of those reported cases an estimated 5 per cent are prosecuted, only a proportion of which will result in a conviction. The data on reported rapes shows that over a period of 20 years reporting has increased markedly whereas the number of convictions has remained almost the same. Thus in 1977 34 per cent of reported rapes resulted in a conviction, whereas in 1995 the figure was 9 per cent (Kelly 1997).

9 Quite how such orders are to be enforced has not been the subject of much public scrutiny.

10 Currently under civil law 'the best interests of children' are understood to include the presumption of contact with parents, unless incontrovertible evidence that contact is damaging can be put before the court.

11 Examples include the *Daily Record* in Scotland which printed photographs, names and descriptions of convicted offenders, and the *Manchester Evening News* which notified local people of particular offenders (the outcome in one case was that an elderly man was mistakenly identified and severely beaten up).

12 A number of the recent community protests involved parents angry that men were being allowed to move back into the area where the offence/s occurred and where the victim/s still live.

13 The exception here is the Family Law Act 1996. The Women's Aid Federations and Rights of Women put considerable energy into lobbying at all stages of the process. Much of this work, however, took place behind the scenes and was not visible to the wider public.

References

Band, T. (1996) *Blackstone's Guide to the Family Law Act 1996*. London: Blackstone Press.

Bindel, J., Cook, K. and Kelly, L. (1995) Trials and tribulations – Justice For Women: a campaign for the 1990s, in G. Griffin (ed.) *Feminist Activism in the 1990s*. London: Taylor and Francis.

Fine, R. (1997) *Being Stalked: A Memoir*. London: Chatto and Windus.

Graham, M. (1996) *Domestic Violence, Stalking and Anti-stalking Legislation*. Washington DC: National Institute of Justice.

Harrell, A. and Smith, B. (1996) Effects of restraining orders on domestic violence victims, in E. Buzawa and C. Buzawa (eds) *Do Arrest and Restraining Orders Work?* Thousand Oaks, CA: Sage.

Home Office (1996a) *Stalking – the Solutions*. London: Home Office.

Home Office (1996b) *Sentencing and supervision of sex offenders: a consultation document*. London: Home Office.

Home Office (1997) Sex Offenders Act 1997 HOC 39/1997. Sentencing and Offences Unit, London: Home Office.

Kelly, L. (1988) *Surviving Sexual Violence*. Cambridge: Polity Press.

Kelly, L. (1996) Weasel words: paedophilia and cycles of abuse. *Trouble and Strife*, 33: 44–9.

Kelly, L. (1997) Rape: the all patriarchal (and forgotten) crime. Keynote speech at Rape and the Criminal Justice System conference, London, June.

Kelly, L. (1997/8) Confronting an atrocity. *Trouble and Strife*, 36: 16–22.

Kelly, L. with Bindel, J., Burton, S., Butterworth, D., Cook, K. and Regan, L. (1999) *Domestic Violence Matters: An Evaluation of a Development Project*, Home Office Research Study 193. London: Home Office.

Kelly, L., Burton, S. and Regan, L. (1998) Policy on managing sex offenders and debates on community notification, in *Protecting Children: Managing Sex Offenders in the Community*. London: NCH Action for Children.

Kelly, L., Regan, L. and Burton, S. (1991) *An Exploratory Study of the Prevalence of Sexual Abuse in a Sample of 1244 16–21-year-olds*, Final Report to the ESRC.

Kelly, L., Wingfield, R., Regan, L. and Burton, S. (1995) *Splintered Lives: Sexual Exploitation of Children in the Context of Children's Rights and Child Protection*. Ilford: Barnardo's.

Lawson-Cruttenden, T. and Addison, N. (1997) *Blackstone's Guide to the Protection from Harassment Act 1997*. London: Blackstone Press.

McAnney, K., Curliss, L. and Abeyata-Price, C. (1993) From imprudence to crime: anti-stalking laws. *Notre Dame Law Review*, 68: 819–909.

Reid Meloy, J. (1996) Stalking (obsessional following): a review of some preliminary studies. *Aggression and Violent Behaviour*, 1(2): 147–62.

Shaum, M. and Parrish, K. (1995) *Stalked: Breaking the Silence on the Crime of Stalking in America*. New York: Pocket Books.

Wallis, M. (1996) Stalking solutions. *Police Review*, November: 16–17.

Statutes

Family Law Act 1996
Protection from Harassment Act 1997
Sex Offenders Act 1997
Crime and Disorder Act 1998

3 Feminist strategy and tactics: influencing state provision of counselling for survivors

Tina Skinner

Introduction

This chapter critically examines feminist strategy and tactics in relation to state provision of counselling for survivors of rape and sexual assault. The terms strategy and tactics have regularly been used in 1990s feminist texts. Examples include the 1996 Brighton conference Violence, Abuse and Women's Citizenship: Global Strategies for Prevention, Protection and Provision, and calls for more 'coherent and comprehensive strategies' by Foley (1994: 53). However, this has not been accompanied by a detailed (re)assessment of what feminists think about 'strategy' and 'tactics', and how we conceive of feminist action and interaction.[1] In this chapter I seek to critically consider what might be understood by these concepts, and use the (re)definitions to enable a more rigorous analysis of feminist strategizing in relation to counselling services for survivors.

Since 1976 provision of free support and counselling to female survivors has been undertaken by voluntary sector organizations such as Rape Crisis and Women's Aid.[2] However, as the work of Foley (1994, 1996) illustrated, the provision of counselling services through police forces and health authorities is increasing. In 1987 Greater Manchester Police and Police Authority, and Central Manchester Health Authority launched the first sexual assault referral centre (SARC) in Britain, and in 1991 Tyne and Wear followed suit. Both SARCs currently provide counselling, forensic examinations and advice on health issues to male and female survivors. Other police and health authority projects, including Hammersmith and Fulham in London, have since developed, and further projects are being planned elsewhere. Yet most of these later projects differ significantly from the SARC model. The main focus of this chapter is the possible role of feminist action in this apparent move away from the SARC model. In order to do this I draw upon research undertaken from 1994 to 1996 as part of a PhD, in one northern metropolitan county council in the UK.

Context

In the late 1960s and early 1970s male violence started to be seen by many UK feminists as a 'primary controlling force' in the lives of women (Hanmer et al. 1989: 3). The forms of violence they were beginning to identify and speak out about included woman battering, rape, sexual assault, child abuse, sexual harassment, mental torture and murder. As more women came forward, rape within marriage and ritual abuse were added as feminist concerns. Having started to uncover the violence suffered by women, feminist campaigns developed around three interconnected themes: prevention of violence against women, protection of women from violence, and provision of services for women who had suffered violence. Later feminist campaigns also addressed the theme of justice in relation to the treatment of women who experienced male violence, and the decriminalization of male perpetrators.[3] These themes are reflected in the development of feminist services for survivors, and in feminist campaigns to influence state services.

Feminist campaigns to prevent police mistreatment of women date back to the turn of the twentieth century, and were reinstated as a key issue for second wave feminism in the 1970s. The aims were threefold: first to highlight police treatment of women and so expose the patriarchal nature of the police and criminal justice system and its collusion with violent men; to change police attitudes towards women, particularly women who had experienced violence; and to improve services for women. Initially direct action was the primary strategy. At this stage, feminist action tended to raise several issues simultaneously. For instance, Take Back the Night marches highlighted police mishandling of specific cases, as well as broader issues including domestic violence, women's fear of public space, and the trivialization of violence against women by the media and its celebration in pornography (see Fairweather 1979; Hanmer 1989).

From approximately the mid-1980s onwards there was a discernible change in the form of feminist action as direct campaigning began to be complemented with action involving alliances. These alliances were composed not only of feminist groups, but included work and consultation with non-feminist national and local government services and bodies. This form of action has been reflected in feminist local authority women's committees with a view to gaining funding and influence, and for multi-agency forums to discuss issues directly with the police and other state services (see Malos, Chapter 9, this volume).

From the early 1980s change in police response to rape and sexual assault became apparent at the level of policy if not always in practice. This followed an exposé of police attitudes towards cases of rape and sexual assault that occurred in 1982, with a television documentary on Thames Valley

Police. Viewers saw police officers *interrogate* a female survivor, causing public outcry.[4] In the same year Detective Inspector Ian Blair compiled an official report into the investigation of rape. In 1983 the Home Office put forward new guidelines on dealing *sympathetically* with rape cases (Blair 1985; Radford and Stanko 1996). Subsequently, the police developed examination suites for survivors of rape, sexual assault and abuse, training on rape issues for new recruits, and some forces set up special women-only policing units to deal specifically with these crimes. The provision of counselling to survivors has been one of the most recent changes.

Before and throughout these changes feminists have attempted to influence police services. They are often credited as key instigators of police change (see Bindel *et al.* 1995; Radford and Stanko 1996). Yet attempting to influence the police presents feminists with a dilemma: is working with the police necessary to instigate and maintain change, or is it collusion that helps to shore up police patriarchal and professional power to define, 'treat' and/or trivialize women's experiences of male violence (see Hanmer 1989; Dobash and Dobash 1992)? Some feminists also question whether cooperation with state agencies, given their different aims and objectives, threatens the already precarious existence of feminist services like rape crisis groups (see Gillespie 1994; Foley 1994, 1996).

The research

The initial data collection consisted of a telephone and postal survey mapping the provision, uptake, and funding of police/health authority and voluntary sector counselling services for survivors of rape and sexual assault. The survey was administered to services in the six old metropolitan county councils of England. From this one metropolitan county council area, referred to as X, was selected for the qualitative research. It contains a number of districts with autonomous local councils and several large urban areas. It has a relatively high level of voluntary sector provision and funding, four local health authorities, and a large metropolitan police force which has recently developed a counselling service for survivors in conjunction with the area health authorities.

The development of this service can be traced back to 1987 when the police began to publicly discuss the possibility of developing a SARC. However, by the time the project was launched in 1994, they had developed a different mode of service. SARCs are usually hospital-based centres that survivors can visit, and provide full medical and forensic examinations as well as counselling with in-house counsellors and psychologists. The rape and sexual assault counselling service (RSACS) developed in X does not have medical facilities or forensic responsibilities, a centre to visit, and only two full-time staff based at the area police headquarters.

My particular interest in the qualitative phase of the research was the possible role feminist action played in the change from a SARC model to

RSACS. The methods used in this phase were: archival data collection, including women's committee and police authority minutes, policy documentation and newspaper reports; and 40 in-depth semi-structured interviews with voluntary sector and statutory sector providers, including Rape Crisis groups, women's refuges, senior police officers, health authority decision makers and local Labour councillors.

Confidentiality, contestation and 'representation'

Three key issues need consideration in relation to these interviews: confidentiality, contested stories and how I 'represent' those stories. To maintain confidentiality pseudonyms are used for organizations and individuals. Interview quotations are edited to reduce the possibility of individuals being recognized. Some participants did not want interviews to be taped, or said things like, 'Don't quote me on this but . . .' To respect this I have only used the information given in a general sense.

Each story was different to some degree, ranging from discrepancies in how feminists heard about police or health authority plans, to the roles particular feminist groups played in campaign(s). Some of these discrepancies are discussed in the text. Contestation in representations of particular actions does not negate a story's value. 'Representations' (the stories we tell) are political acts in their own right, as important to politics as the actions they seek to describe. How individuals attempt to represent any action will always be negotiated through the information available, representations of other people, motivations for wanting to do a particular representation, and the perceived audiences. Representations therefore are more about the development of an argument, than descriptive 'truth' or factual accounts about what 'actually went on' (Skinner 1998). What I am doing in this chapter – representations of representations – is no less political. Some of the difficulties this entails are discussed elsewhere and will not be rehearsed here (see Borland 1991; Holland and Ramazanoglu 1994; Skeggs 1997). My representations have been driven not by a wish to speak on behalf of those interviewed, but to interpret and analyse their strategies and tactics. Such analysis may be at odds with the interviewees' own interpretations. However, as both Borland (1991) and Skeggs (1997) argue, disagreement does not invalidate either interpretation.

Defining strategy and tactics

Feminist politics has reached an appropriate juncture to reassess the meaning of strategy and tactics. This is not simply a case of tightening up definitions in order to engage meaningfully in academic debate, though this is important. The profile and dynamism of feminist campaigning in the last decade – through Justice For Women, Southall Black Sisters, Zero Tolerance and the establishment of the Rape Crisis Federation of England and Wales, to name a few – requires activists/academics to rethink our understanding of feminist action. My concern is to stimulate debate that will link both academic and activist discussions, take account of the changing nature of feminist action through the 1990s, and begin to strengthen feminism's conceptual base into the millennium. Analysis of feminist action is not new. Previous literature has put forward and analysed radical feminist strategies (Bunch 1987), socialist feminist strategies (Rowbotham *et al.* 1979), liberal feminist strategies, and postmodernist feminist strategies (Bondi and Domosh 1992). I try to delve deeper however, and attempt to define exactly what it is that makes a particular campaign strategic or tactical, and will start this with a basic definition.

Dobash and Dobash approached a similar task in 1992 using Mathiesen (1974). They suggested that feminists need to keep sight of their long-term aims (the vision or visions) while pursuing short-term tactics (see also Radford 1992; Kelly 1992/3). This conceptualization of strategy, containing both long- and short-term aims, is illustrated in the work of Justice for Women. For many campaigners within Justice for Women the vision is of social change, including an end to violence against women (Radford and Kelly 1995). One of the tactical (short-term) aims is to attempt to gain change within the discourses and practices associated with violence against women. This includes changing legal discourses and practices as 'one route to creating social change, within which inequality is both recognized by, and challenged through, law' (Radford and Kelly 1995: 197).

In this mould, a strategy possesses two key components: vision(s) of (and campaigning for) a new alternative future *beyond* currently dominant discourses and practices, and tactical attempts to obtain change *within* dominant discourses and practices (for example, the law and the judicial system). Although tactics may attempt to change discourses and practices they do not in themselves attempt to move beyond them. Thus for Justice for Women change within the legal system is a tactical 'part of a political struggle but neither the totality nor an end in itself' (Radford and Kelly 1995: 186). Only strategy represents an attempt to move beyond.

This definition of strategy and tactics will be used in analysing feminist action in relation to RSACS. However, a tactic (in the singular) is not necessarily conceived of as part of a strategy at the time the tactic originally took place; it may be put into a strategy post hoc. A group or individual may react to a situation on the spot, but only later rationalize and/or develop that action as a tactic within a strategy. This was apparently the case with Justice for Women when they realized the potential usefulness of media coverage to their campaigns and decided to cultivate the media as a 'campaigning tool' (Bindel *et al.* 1995: 68). Further, the tactics of one group can be used in the strategy of another. For instance, though a tactic may well be a part of a particular strategy, it may be used by other campaigns with strategic intent, or incorporated into a strategic framework post hoc.

State provision and feminist action

Police and health authority provision of counselling to survivors in X can be understood as one of several local police responses to the changing pressures outlined above. In March 1989, a report from the Chief Constable was given to the police authority recommending the 'enhancement' of services for rape 'victims' based on the clinical model of the St Mary's Centre in Manchester. Shortly after, the police force in X put forward funding applications to the area health authorities to set up a sexual assault referral centre, having already gained a pledge for 50 per cent of the money from the police authority. These initial applications were unsuccessful in two of the four health authorities. It took four years of further discussions with health authority members, and some very significant modifications in the project model, before all area health authorities agreed funding. Instead of a central multiservice project offering counselling *and* medical services (the SARC model), the resultant project (RSACS) was showcased as a coordinating project that purchased counselling from external (primarily private sector) counsellors.[5]

Feminists became involved in the consultation process for the SARC in 1990, though it is difficult to establish exactly when and how they found out about police plans to develop a SARC. Documentary sources indicate that the police contacted feminist groups and other interested parties outlining their plans and inviting them to a meeting. However, feminists' stories suggest they were only contacted because they had found out about the plans through other means. When the extent of police plans began to emerge, a feminist campaigning group was formed.

The majority of feminist campaigning occurred from 1990 to 1993, prior to the project launch. The main campaigning group formed under the banner of X Women Against Violence (XWAV), and included individual women from many local voluntary sector groups concerned with violence against women, such as Rape Crisis and Women's Aid. Other feminists and feminist groups concerned with violence campaigned independently of XWAV, including local councillors, academics and a local inter-agency project on women and violence.

In the following I explore members' concerns about SARC, the action they undertook, and the extent of their involvement in the modification. My aims are to attempt to establish possible reasons for XWAV's involvement, the way they were involved, and to begin to suggest how this involvement can be interpreted.

XWAV's objections and aims

Concerns voiced by XWAV members about the original SARC model, in interviews, letters and consultation meetings' minutes, included:

- *potential for discrimination*: concern that institutionalized racism and homophobia within the force would be transferred into the appointment of centre staff, and the 'treatment' of survivors;
- *lack of survivor autonomy*: a service connected with the police would pressure survivors to report rape and sexual assault to the police;
- *location of the centre*: accessibility of the centre to women who lived in outlying districts, as well as to women who did not have access to transport;
- *unisex service*: it might cater for both men and women, and a female survivor might be expected to see a male counsellor;
- *voluntary sector funding*: this would be effected by the new service;
- *'only a phase' in policing*: police and health authorities would develop this service, then funding priorities would change and they would drop the service, having diminished or destroyed Rape Crisis's funding, leaving women with little or no service options;
- *inappropriate model of service*: the counselling ethos used would be inappropriate for survivors, and would lead to the medicalization of women and professionalization of counselling; and
- a SARC would *take the politics out of rape and abuse* and shift the focus away from placing the responsibility on the perpetrators and instead focus on restoring survivors to a state of 'normality'.

Funding, ethos and politics appear to have been priority issues in XWAV's campaigning. Members were particularly concerned about the possible effects of a police and health authority service on the Rape Crisis groups in the area. The provision of support and counselling to male survivors had been patchy and problematic, with a Survivors Project existing only intermittently in one city. Here, the new state service was set to fill a significant gap in provision. In terms of women's services, in 1994/5 there were six feminist groups offering counselling to female survivors. Despite this relatively high level of provision compared to national averages for metropolitan areas outside of London (Skinner 1998), these services could not meet existing need and would have welcomed further funding to expand their services. This is highlighted by a member of XWAV:

> We thought: just a minute, Rape Crisis is an underfunded organization, we don't want to see all this money going to a centre such as the St Mary's Centre in Manchester when we feel that Rape Crisis know what women need . . . A lot of Rape Crisis group members have been through the process, they have all suffered in one way or another, and we think Rape Crisis know what they're talking about far more than the police do.
> (interview transcript, 1995)

This is a post hoc representation of XWAV's concerns by an individual member. However, confidential group correspondence, minutes of group meetings and other interviews confirm that this quotation is reflective of group concerns at the time. The underfunding of Rape Crisis groups is a longstanding issue at national and local levels, and members of XWAV thought the funding destined for SARC would be better placed with Rape Crisis.

Not only was there concern that a police/health authority project was to receive funding that could be put to better use by Rape Crisis groups, but also fear that such a service would lead to the reduction of existing Rape Crisis funding through a perceived overlap in services. This was particularly pertinent considering that Rape Crisis groups in the area were dependent on local authority funding and health authority sources. One health authority decision maker stated that they were concerned there would be an overlap which might affect the future funding of voluntary sector services (local health authority representative, interview transcript, 1995).

The concern over loss of funding to Rape Crisis groups was also connected to concerns about the different ethos embodied in the SARC model. One member of XWAV stated:

> Looking at Rape Crisis statistics very very few women actually report rape immediately after it happened; most women are raped by someone they know, which is another reason they don't report it straight away, a lot of rape happens within marriage, within domestic violence situations, and we didn't think it was appropriate; because yes, some women might need hospital treatment, but an awful lot . . . don't. What they want is someone to listen to them and to talk about it in their own words, not to be processed through a system that gives them a shower and a clean set of clothes, a forensic examination and then passes them on to a clinical psychologist. We just thought they'd got the whole ethos of it wrong and that they were looking at rape in an unrealistic way.
>
> (Interview transcript, 1995)

This is a juxtaposing of a feminist Rape Crisis ethos against a non-feminist, medicalized model. While there is not necessarily agreement amongst Rape Crisis groups about all aspects of what constitutes a feminist service, there is some common ground. To begin to discuss what this might be I draw on the 1996 annual report of one of the Rape Crisis groups in my research area:

> X Rape Crisis Group is a feminist organisation. Our aim is to fight back against sexual violence in the following ways:
>
> 1 By providing appropriate and accessible services which include counselling and practical support, as an empowering alternative to psychiatric, medical and social work service.
> 2 The provision of a woman-centred counselling service for survivors of rape and sexual abuse.
> 3 Campaigning and public education in order to break down the myths which surround sexual violence and gain justice for women.
> 4 To value all our members, their different experiences, knowledges and expertise and to work together to oppose oppression in all its forms.
>
> (X Rape Crisis Group 1996: 1)

There are a number of key words and phrases which differentiate their self-defined feminist service from other non-feminist services. These are 'empowering', 'woman-centred', 'campaigning', 'value all our members' and 'oppose oppression'. The word empowering is used to contrast a feminist model of counselling and support with state services and other non-feminist voluntary sector groups. This is illustrated in the fourth point: 'to value all our members'. This means to acknowledge, respect, develop and utilize the skills of those who participate in the counselling and support process, not least the survivors themselves, thus breaking down the client–professional dichotomy. This contrasts with some non-feminist services where the division between service provider and 'client' can be maintained to the extent that the survivor feels she played little part in her own survival.

Point two emphasizes the provision of a woman-centred service offered by women for women. This has been a cornerstone of Rape Crisis groups since the first UK group opened in London in 1976, and continues to be one of the criteria of membership of the Rape Crisis Federation of England and Wales. The third point, campaigning and education, is problematic for many voluntary sector groups because local authority funding is often tied to a no political campaigning clause.[6] This clause does not preclude public education campaigns or training professionals, however. It also does not include campaigning in the form of representation on committees or at meetings, or prevent group members campaigning as individuals. Nevertheless, it remains that any campaigns undertaken in the name of a Rape Crisis group must be undertaken with care.

Feminist groups do not have a monopoly on campaigning. Many voluntary groups, the police and health authorities are involved in public education campaigns orientated around raising awareness and promoting the use of services.[7] What differentiates feminist campaigns, *strategic* feminist campaigns, is that they actually attempt to question (and move beyond) the dominant discourse and practices associated with violence against women to tackle the problem at source, rather than simply clear up at the end. This, it could be argued, is reflected in the phrase 'to break down the myths which surround sexual violence', and in the aim to 'oppose oppression' (X Rape Crisis Group 1996: 1).

The four points that appear in the 1996 annual report are not definitive of what constitutes a feminist service. Another issue associated with feminist Rape Crisis groups is the assertion that not only do women have the ability to survive violence, but also define for themselves what it means to have survived, and be able to go beyond survival towards political action. Many also advocate that there is no prescribed time by which a woman should have 'recovered' and therefore no cut-off point for support and counselling. Other issues seen as important in feminist services include: no pressure to report rape or sexual abuse to the police; and equal access regardless of sexuality, ethnicity, language, class and disability. Such a feminist ethos contrasts with that associated with the SARC model.

A feminist critique of SARC pinpoints two key areas of concern: medicalization and professionalization. Foley (1996) argues that medicalization of rape is not synonymous with the forensic examination that a woman might undergo after a rape, or the medical services that the woman might require. She states that the medicalization of rape is instead: 'a process whereby a social and political issue is redefined as an individual problem requiring treatment' (1996: 172; see also Kelly 1988, 1989). Likewise XWAV's critique was that a SARC would depoliticize rape and abuse. For instance, a medicalized counselling and therapy service would focus on the woman resuming 'normality', normality being seen as synonymous with heterosexual sex. In contrast, a feminist service, would be more inclined to question the notion of 'normality' and accept a woman's response without prejudice (Kelly 1988; Foley 1996).

In light of XWAV's concerns about the funding of SARC and the ethos of the model, their campaign aimed to stop any police initiated service going ahead, or failing that, to significantly modify the model of service to be offered.

The campaign

Having outlined what I identified as the key concerns of XWAV, I turn my attention to tactics. After formation, one of the first things XWAV did was to contact Manchester Rape Crisis Group to discuss the problems the Manchester group had faced since St Mary's opened. Many of the issues raised by the Manchester group were reflected in the concerns outlined above. The initial tactic for XWAV, therefore, was to liaise with other feminist groups and present an apparently united front, locally and nationally.

The second was to participate as much as possible in police consultation, including attending meetings, letter writing, and encouraging telephone enquires from the police. The spirit in which this was done varied from individual to individual and through time, from what has been described by the police as aggressive behaviour and by feminists as 'shouting ... to get views across' (member of XWAV, interview transcript, 1995), to fairly informal friendly discussions with individual police officers.

At one of the later consultation meetings a deal was struck between some feminist campaigners and the police. Moving away from their original aims, feminists conceded to the setting up of the SARC provided that feminist groups could be on its steering committee (including members of Rape Crisis) thus enabling them to have an input on issues such as counsellors' job descriptions. Another tactic, therefore, was to utilize compromise by (apparently) substituting the aim to stop a police initiated service with the aim of having an ongoing input into its development. However, this move was not as coordinated as it appears. Those primarily responsible for the promise of feminist representation on the steering committee were feminists working independently of XWAV. XWAV was relatively unhappy about this compromise because such concessions to feminist involvement can be conditional: appearing to address feminist demands while attempting to silence their dissent.

Seemingly, the most influential tactic of XWAV's campaign was through direct contact with one particular health authority. In the district where the contact appeared to have been most effective for XWAV, communication was actually initiated by health authority workers:

> [A representative of one health authority] would turn round and say, 'Oh you're from Rape Crisis . . . we were a bit concerned about this', and, 'How many women from [this area] would it affect?', and, 'How many women from [this area] would it actually benefit?', and, 'Is that where our money's best spent?' And we said, 'Well we're not convinced about that', and we talked to [the health authority representative] about our fears and what we did and how we were funded. It was not just us, the . . . women's groups talked to the health authority after these meetings on the way out or something like that, in the coffee break, and they seemed to take it seriously.
>
> (member of XWAV, interview transcript, 1995)

Confidential documentary sources also suggest that this health authority made the decision not to financially support the SARC in X because of this Rape Crisis group's comments. By 1993, due to a 'failure to agree a funding formula with various health authorities' (X Police Authority Minute Sheet, 22/01/93), the area police force conceded that 'rather than establish a central unit . . . it would be far more effective to set up a counselling service' with a 'Victim Liaison Coordinator'. This eventually took the form of RSACS. It would appear that feminist action, through contact with health authority representatives, did make a significant difference to police plans.

After the funding difficulties, the police did not maintain contact with members of XWAV interviewed for this research. They proceeded to develop the alternative service (RSACS), omitting to inform XWAV of meetings or changes until just before RSACS was to be launched in 1994. This left feminists involved in XWAV to presume that the battle was over.

> Communication between the police and certainly ourselves at that point was really dwindling . . . energies just became dissipated and information wasn't coming from the police, other than 'it's not going to happen now' . . . The next thing we know we're getting a leaflet about the [RSACS] project.
>
> (Member of XWAV, interview transcript, 1995)

A critical analysis

Assessing the impact of feminist action is not simply a case of matching XWAV's aims with the eventual results. Though one of their aims was achieved (a SARC was not instituted), it does not automatically follow that XWAV greatly influenced this decision. In this section I seek to shed some light on what might have been going on behind the scenes which informs a discussion of whether the campaign can be understood as strategic.

It could be argued that the invitation to feminist groups to participate in the consultation process was extended to legitimate police decision making rather than gain feminist input. As stated, the police initially encouraged feminist participation. In the early stages of the project's development the police sought funding from the health authorities. In order to do this they had to sell their idea to the health authorities, and they set these consultation meetings up to woo them into funding the project. Some of the health authorities appeared to be more sympathetic to the voluntary sector than the police. Thus one method of selling the SARC model to the health authorities was to temporarily co-opt voluntary sector feminists to legitimate the 'consultation' process. After the decision was made not to go ahead with the SARC, the police excluded XWAV from the consultation process. It would appear that the legitimation that 'consultation' with XWAV might have brought was expendable. It is precisely because feminists were vulnerable to exclusion at the whim of the police that their inclusion in consultation was conditional and insecure.

Likewise, it is questionable whether the health authority decided not to fund the SARC project simply on the basis of a single Rape Crisis group's comments (as interviews and confidential documentation suggest). It is possible that the key concerns of the health authority were not the issues raised by Rape Crisis, but finance. It could be argued that the health authority was looking for a reason not to fund, and feminists provided that reason. Thus Rape Crisis may have been used to legitimate a funding decision the health authority had already made or wanted to make.

Members of XWAV were aware that their involvement in consultation was in part being used to legitimate the consultation process and health authority decisions. Nevertheless, they still believed it was important to be involved in order to monitor police proposals and be in a position to influence decision making. Further, though it is likely that feminists were co-opted to legitimate the decision-making processes, it is still possible that they had an impact, although the exact nature of the impact is difficult to discern. What is clear however, is that while state services gained a degree of legitimation, they were also subjected to a sustained feminist critique of their discourses and practices. The outcomes of this critique may not have been seen immediately, but may have an effect if sustained over the longer term.

Beneath these processes, there appears to have been a trade-off. The police and health authority used the fact of feminist involvement to legitimize their decisions. Although aware of possible pitfalls, feminists adopted a tactic of continued involvement because of its potential benefits. These benefits, although not directly apparent, formed part of an ongoing campaign, keeping feminist concerns on the agenda. Although I have raised questions about the effectiveness of feminist campaigning, I am not suggesting it was non-strategic. Its strategic aim lay in the attempt to prevent the political element being taken out of survivors' services. Similarly, as with Justice for Women's acknowledgement that change within the legal system is not the totality, stopping the SARC was not the totality of XWAV's campaign.

The tactical campaigning in this case was fractured. For instance, it was feminists who were not members of XWAV who were most likely to have been responsible for gaining feminist representation on the steering group of the unsuccessful SARC. It was also an individual Rape Crisis group (not XWAV as a collective) that did much of the consultation with one of the health authorities that refused to fund the SARC model. A fractured campaign is not the same as a non-strategic campaign, however. If we understand strategic action as necessarily organic, in that it is able to adapt to and utilize changing circumstances and tactics of other campaigns, then a fractured campaign can still be understood as strategic, if not always ideal.

Conclusion

My particular concern has been with feminist action in relation to state provision of counselling for survivors of rape and sexual assault. Some general reassessment of feminist strategy and tactics can be drawn from this case. First, it is necessary both to be realistic about what feminist action can achieve, and aware of the danger of feminist cooperation being appropriated by state agencies in support of their own, rather than, feminist agendas. However, what may initially appear as pessimistic outcomes, with hindsight can also be seen to contain some valuable strategic shifts towards more long-term goals of preventing violence against women. Feminist actions should not purely be evaluated in terms of short-term achievements. In the long term, co-option may enable continuing feminist influence over the discourses and practices used by the state, and impact upon public as well as institutional perceptions of, and reactions to violence against women. In short, social change does not happen overnight, and short-term sacrifices may bring long-term rewards.

In addition, although feminists often do not work in unity, this does not automatically imply that feminist action is unsuccessful in instigating positive change. Though coordination is desirable, resources, geography and politics can render united campaigning problematic. Nevertheless, flexible tactics with strategic intent are needed at a multitude of levels in order to pursue change within currently dominant discourses and practices, and to attempt to move society beyond those discourses and practices to new alternative(s). Thus, the fractured nature of feminist action could be a root to success rather than a prediction of doom, for the simple reason that a message needs to be conveyed from many angles before it really can be taken on board.

Notes

1 Here I am referring to feminists who are involved in action on violence against women.
2 While I acknowledge that some women who have experienced violence may prefer the term 'victim' as an expression that they are a 'victim of a crime' (Gillespie 1994), and that a woman may first want to feel she has 'survived' before using the term 'survivor', I use the term survivor throughout this chapter. London Rape Crisis Centre state that 'using the word "victim" to describe women takes away our power and contributes to the idea that it is right and natural for men to "prey" on us' (1984:x). The term survivor is used instead to express 'the capacity of women to resist and struggle against' male violence (Gillespie 1994: 37; see Kelly 1988), where the goal is not solely personal survival but also social change (Kelly 1992/3).
3 For example, campaigns by Justice for Women and campaigns around prostitution.
4 This programme was broadcast on 18 January 1982, and was widely reported on during the following two days (Jeffreys and Radford 1984).
5 The counsellors now see both male and female survivors in their own practices, in a location convenient to the survivors.
6 The 'no campaigning' clause relates specifically to party political campaigning.
7 Exceptions here are local authority campaigns inspired by feminists, such as Zero Tolerance of male violence campaigns, which have a political as well as a public education dimension.

References

Bindel, J., Cook, K. and Kelly, L. (1995) Trials and tribulations – Justice For Women: a campaign for the 1990s, in G. Griffin (ed.) *Feminist Activism in the 1990s*. London: Taylor and Francis.

Blair, I. (1985) *Investigating Rape: A New Approach for Police*. London: Croom Helm in association with The Police Foundation.

Bondi, L. and Domosh, M. (1992) Other figures in other places: on feminism, postmodernism and geography. *Environment and Planning D: Society and Space*, 10(2): 199–213.

Borland, K. (1991) 'That's not what I said': interpretative conflict in oral narrative research, in S. Berger-Gluck and D. Patai (eds) *Women's Words: The Feminist Practice of Oral History*. London: Routledge.

Bunch, C. (1987) *Passionate Politics: Feminist Theory in Action*. New York: St Martin's Press.

Dobash, R.E. and Dobash, R.P. (1992) *Women, Violence and Social Change*. London: Routledge.

Fairweather, E. (1979) Leeds curfew on men. *Spare Rib*, 83: 6–9.

Foley, M. (1994) Professionalising the response to rape, in C. Lupton and T. Gillespie (eds) *Working with violence*. Basingstoke: Macmillan.

Foley, M. (1996) Who is in control?: changing responses to women who have been raped and sexually abused, in M. Hester, L. Kelly and J. Radford (eds) *Women, Violence and Male Power*. Buckingham: Open University Press.

Gillespie, T. (1994) Under pressure: Rape Crisis Centres, multi-agency work and strategies for survival, in C. Lupton and T. Gillespie (eds) *Working with Violence*. Basingstoke: Macmillan.

Hanmer, J. (1989) Women, violence and crime prevention, in J. Hanmer, J. Radford and E. Stanko (eds) *Women, Policing and Male Violence*. London: Routledge.

Hanmer, J., Radford, J. and Stanko, E. (1989) Policing, men's violence: an introduction, in J. Hanmer, J. Radford and E. Stanko (eds) *Women, Policing and Male Violence*. London: Routledge.

Holland, J. and Ramazanoglu, C. (1994) Coming to conclusions: power and interpretation in researching young women's sexuality, in M. Maynard and J. Purvis (eds) *Researching Women's Lives from a Feminist Perspective*. London: Taylor and Francis.

Jeffreys, S. and Radford, J. (1984) Contributory negligence or being a woman? the car rapist case, in P. Scraton and P. Gordon (eds) *Causes for Concern: British Criminal Justice on Trial?* Harmondsworth: Penguin Books.

Kelly, L. (1988) *Surviving Sexual Violence*. Cambridge: Polity Press.

Kelly, L. (1989) The professionalisation of rape. *Rights of Women Bulletin*, spring: 8–11.

Kelly, L. (1992/3) Survival was never enough. *Bad Attitude*, December/January: 25.

London Rape Crisis Centre (1984) *Sexual Violence: The Reality for Women*. London: The Women's Press Handbook Series.

Mathiesen, T. (1974) *The Politics of Abolition*. London: Martin Robertson.

Radford, J. (1992) Introduction, in J. Radford and D. Russell (eds) *Femicide: The Politics of Woman Killing*. Buckingham: Open University Press.

Radford, J. and Kelly, L. (1995) Self-preservation: feminist activism and feminist jurisprudence, in M. Maynard and J. Purvis (eds) *(Hetero)sexual Politics*. London: Taylor and Francis.

Radford, J. and Stanko, E. A. (1996) Violence against women and children: the constructions of crime control under patriarchy, in M. Hester, L. Kelly and J. Radford (eds) *Women, Violence and Male Power*. Buckingham: Open University Press.

Rowbotham, S., Segal, L. and Wainwright, H. (1979) *Beyond the Fragments: Feminism and the Making of Socialism*. London: Merlin Press.

Skeggs, B. (1997) *Formations of Class and Gender: Becoming Respectable*. London: Sage.

Skinner, T.N. (1998) (Re)conceptualising feminist strategy and tactic: responses to violence against women. Unpublished PhD thesis, University of Sheffield.

4 Virtual violence?: pornography and violence against women on the Internet

Terry Gillespie

Introduction

I became concerned about pornography and violence against women on the Internet as a result of using the World Wide Web for the first time in 1994 while researching rape support services (Gillespie 1994, 1996). Searching linked web pages, I quickly found sites containing disturbing images and text in relation to rape and sexual abuse, including pornographic material. Around the same time, stories were surfacing in the media about pornographers' and child abusers' use of the Net and attempts by statutory and voluntary organizations to police and regulate the Net, which was widely celebrated as anarchic and beyond regulation. A major concern of this chapter is the prevalence and ready availability of pornography on the Net. A range of evidence is considered, including links between the Internet and sex tourism (Hughes 1996a, 1996b, 1997), together with information from the media demonstrating the global market in computer pornography. In terms of establishing the harmful nature of computer pornography specific issues are addressed, including: access and the ease of availability of Internet sites which reach a wide constituency; the content of computer pornography; the use of women and children in its production; the degree of regulation and control over the use of material, especially with interactive pornography; and the issue of how men relate to computer pornography.

Contextualized historically, computer pornography can be viewed as merely the latest medium for depicting graphic and degrading representations of women. However, the global availability of the Internet raises new problems and issues in relation to sexual violence. These result, in part, from technological innovation and a seemingly insatiable market for pornography based on the abuse of women and children. Feminists have criticized such abuse and exploitation, critiquing pornography as a form of violence against women (Dworkin 1992; Itzin 1993; Swirsky and Jenkins, Chapter 5, this volume), and continue to challenge new forms and representations of violence against women (Butterworth 1996; Hughes 1996a, 1996b, 1997; Kelly and Butterworth, 1997).[1] A crucial issue is the distinctiveness of computer pornography and its continuities with other forms of pornography (Michals 1997). 'Representations' of sexual abuse and violence against women on the Internet are not 'virtual violation' or 'virtual rape'. Rather, they are based in reality, both in the sense that the depictions and images are of *real* women, and may have real effects in terms of the degradation of women generally.

Powerful groups have lobbied against any restrictions or censorship of the Net (such as the Supreme Court's rejection in July 1997 of the Communications Decency Act 1997) in the US, in opposition to the police and government departments who have collaborated with Internet service providers (ISPs) in seeking to regulate indecent and harmful material. The favoured mode is self-regulation by service providers, while various strategies and technologies are being developed, including filtering and rating systems for material deemed unsuitable for minors. However, feminists are sceptical of such developments as they fail ultimately to stop the availability of pornography and material harmful to women (Kelly and Butterworth 1997).

At a more fundamental level this issue can be construed as one of women's rights to freedom from harm and abuse over men's rights to consume pornographic and violent material. As Butterworth has argued, the framework of institutional inequality which underpins pornography cannot coexist with freedom and dignity of the person. Pornography is a violation of women's human rights (Kelly and Butterworth 1997).

There are a number of myths concerning pornography and the Internet. Superintendent Martin Jauch of the Metropolitan Police Clubs and Vice Unit has argued that the 'two most widely held myths about pornography on the Internet [are that] there is very little of it and it is very difficult to find' (Jauch 1998: 14). Jauch argues that neither of these claims stands up to examination, as borne out by the growth and profitability of computer pornography. A further myth relates to the claim that there is a clear distinction between adult and child pornography. For example, Kelly points to research on pornographic videos which showed that three-quarters of a sample of 50 legal Swedish pornography videos emphasized that the women in them were young and virgins (Kelly and Butterworth 1997: 46).

Pornographers have moved to the Net as a means of producing and distributing child pornography which for Kelly 'is nothing more and nothing less than a pictorial record of child abuse' (Kelly and Butterworth 1997: 44). In addition, sexual abusers also use the Net to gain access to children. There is insufficient space to consider all the complexities of legal and moral issues related to child pornography on the Internet. However, this area of Internet pornography is being targeted in relation to the policing and regulation of the Net.

The growth of pornography and the Internet

The British Computer Society defines computer pornography as

> the use of computers and associated techniques in the development, storage, transmission and display of offensive, degrading and threatening material of an explicitly sexual or violent nature.
>
> (Akdeniz 1996)

Such a definition indicates parallels with the liberal definition enshrined in the Obscene Publications Act (1959). This liberal view of pornography has been challenged by feminists; it is in relation to legal regulation that feminist debates on the nature of pornography have been most clearly articulated (Itzin 1993; Edwards 1997).

Mann and Sutton (1998) point to the development of the Internet in the 1970s as a military computer network marked by control and flexibility, which subsequently grew into a global network accessible to the public. In 1998, the Net was available in 150 countries with over 60 million users. By 2000 they estimate that over 100 million computers will be able to access the Net. The Internet incorporates various means of communication including the Web, newsgroups and e-mail.

The World Wide Web, or 'the Web', is the most common means of advertising or publishing information. Web pages are linked to other web pages, thus one pornographic site may be linked to hundreds of other such sites. Specialist magazines advertise hundreds of addresses for pornographic websites. One proclaims 'Everything men want – direct from the Net' (Millar 1997). A typical issue includes a CD-ROM offering more than 300 links to pornographic sites, directory pages including 14 pages of porn-related Web addresses, and reviews of each site.

Newsgroups are accessible through Internet browsers or linked web pages, and enable participants to exchange information and views around topics of common interest. Discussions are posted so that members can read messages left by others. Users are expected to respect the rules of 'netiquette', such as reading the FAQ (frequently asked questions) before joining a group, and ensuring that they don't send messages using capitals (viewed as 'shouting' by Net users). There are well over 200 newsgroups devoted to pornography. Internet service providers are keen to promote newsgroups as they are profitable.

E-mail is a system which enables people to send messages in text or graphic form to other computer users. While increasingly commonplace in academia and business, e-mail is often used by men to harass or stalk (cyberstalking) women on-line either by sending offensive messages (usually anonymously) or unsolicited pornography.

Internet relay chat (IRC) is a form of on-line conferencing that provides instant interaction with other 'chat users' and is totally unregulated. Participants are anonymous and use a nickname, while some create an alternative personality within the chat environment. As Jauch states 'Some are just rather sad people who exist in "cyberspace" and talk about real life (or RL, as they call it) as the alternative existence' (1998: 16). Others, however, use IRC for predatory purposes, such as child abusers who establish contacts with children. The *Which? Report on the Internet* (Consumers Association 1997) found several examples of users accidentally accessing pornographic material. In one case a 14-year-old girl had switched from a live Internet chatroom into a 'sideroom' (where users move out of the chatroom to communicate one-to-one on e-mail) where she was asked sexually explicit questions. Other participants reported finding pornographic related material when searching for other topics, a common experience when using the Net.

Multiuser domains (MUDs) are popular with players of fantasy games. They are

> vivid text based virtual environments, divided into rooms or areas that you can move around in . . . MUDs allow you to participate in the action and help determine the outcome of a scene.
>
> (Senjen and Guthrey 1996: 121, 123)

MUD users create stories, frequently sexual or pornographic in content, in which anyone (usually male) can participate. In at least one MUD, players can engage in such activities as 'virtual sex' and 'virtual rape' (Spender 1995).

Pornography is big business. New technologies are rapidly being developed on the Internet, driven to a great extent by the demands of the computer pornography industry which, in turn, argues that they are meeting the needs of consumers for more 'interactive' material. According to Lillington (1998), Internet pornography is in the top five industries investing in new computer technologies. Consumers spent $137 million on US websites in 1997, and it is estimated that this figure will treble by 2001. One-third of all web users have accessed a sex site. There were estimated to be 10,000 pornographic sites on the Web in 1997, including explicit hard-core material. One site alone is accessed over 5 million times a day and has 22,000 subscribers who pay approximately $15 per month for access to over 15,000 pornographic images.

It appears that with the advent of computer pornography, consumers want more explicit hard-core material than is available in sex shops. In a study conducted in 1996 by Carnegie-Mellon University, it was found that cyberporn was more graphic, violent and deviant than other pornographic material. The survey of 917,410 images downloaded 8.5 million times by consumers in 40 countries found 83.5 per cent of images posted on the Net were pornographic. Disturbingly, 50 per cent of nearly 6 million downloads of computer pornography were related to images of children or adolescents (Krum 1996).

'Virtual sex' and 'virtual reality'

The area that is causing most interest within the computer pornography industry, and which is estimated to become the most profitable is 'virtual reality', variously termed 'interactive sex', 'virtual sex' or 'cybersex'. As a result of a steady decline in sales of 'top shelf' pornographic magazines, publishers have switched to the Internet to sell 'interactive' pornography. Websites offer live chat with 'models' together with catalogues of 'erotic' photographs. Consumers can already download 'live sex' videos on payment by credit card. For example:

> Customers typically pay $49.95 for 30 minutes to talk by phone or keyboard to strippers and sexual performers who are paid about $20 an hour. Men (this is typically a guy thing) can communicate their most profound thoughts and suggestions to the nude dancers, requesting specific gyrations and acts.
>
> (Sussman 1997)

It is envisaged that before long a computer user could be linked by a body 'glove' to another computer and engage in 'interactive sex'. This 'virtual' experience has been referred to as ' "teledildonics", the ability to interact not just visually but through touch with a 3D computerised playmate' (Lillington 1998). Indeed, one major company is working with manufacturers to develop the technology 'of neural and sensory interfaces' (Sussman 1997), or 'virtual sex' as it has become known. For Butterworth (1996: 318),

> What is . . . likely is that 'virtual sex' would lead to a whole new era of prostitution – women paid to have 'virtual sex' with men . . . Women have been exploited by technology in the service of male sexuality since the camera was first invented.

Feminist critics of computer pornography argue that 'virtual violence' and 'virtual rape' have real effects, and as such constitute violence against real women. They refute the notion that computer pornography is not harmful material that acts as a 'safety valve' for male users, deflecting them from acting out their fantasies on real women. For example, Butterworth argues that 'virtual sex' would not be 'safe' sex as it shapes and reinforces men's beliefs about women's sexuality: 'through the propaganda of pornography. . . . Any technology which promises to lead to an expansion of the sex industry cannot be safe for women' (1996: 318–19).

Butterworth (1996: 317) further states that

> Interactive pornography means that the consumer is no longer just the consumer, he is, in a sense, the producer as well. Not content with gazing passively at images of women, he can now 'enter into the fantasy' by directing the action.

For Dale Spender (1995: 220) it is

> the 'realness' of the new porn which makes it so very different from anything that's been around before. As with every other type of information in cyberspace the viewer/user becomes a participant; a 'doer' of pornography rather than an observer of it.

This 'interactivity' reinforces harmful notions about male dominance and female subordination in the wider society. Indeed it was only a matter of time before television drama exploited the theme of virtual violence. The psychological thriller *KillerNet* (Channel 4, May 1998) focused on the 'virtual stalking' and (eventual) murder of a woman. A psychology student is depicted researching for the computer game KillerNet, and refers to Peter Sutcliffe among other notorious killers of women. When entering the required information he is informed, 'Congratulations, you have killed your victim. Move on to stage three'. The game then allows him to select a real victim.

While the thought of future technologies and cybersex may be alarming, it is important to recognize that women are already being abused on the Internet as in other areas of social life. There have been many reported cases of sexual assault on women by men they have met through the Net. Further, women who use the Net are increasingly finding themselves subject to sexual harassment. The fact that this abuse occurs on-line does not make it any less frightening for those who encounter it. For example, while exploring Internet chatrooms Debra Michals (1997) found one entitled 'Rape Fantasy' where a gang rape was being enacted 'virtually' and brutally by five men. When she posted a message to complain she was 'flamed' with angry responses from males using the chatroom.[2] She found this not uncommon experience both violating and terrifying:

> Given the number of actual rapes that are committed . . . this on-line behaviour obviously mimics real life. But what effect does it have on us in both our real and virtual lives? . . . Women on the receiving end of this graphic sexual violence on the Net have indeed reported being traumatized by the experience. While many may turn off their computers or leave a chat area if they feel attacked, they often have trouble shaking the memory that a stranger at a far-off computer terminal wanted to hurt them.
>
> (Michals 1997: 69)

Michals goes on to point out that

> For young people still learning the difference between fantasy and reality, the lessons may well be that violence is a normal part of male behaviour, that for men sexual domination is erotic, and that for women passivity and a willingness to be victimized are the rule.
>
> (1997: 70)

Reinforcing this view Kelly has stated 'What [also] concerns us is how widespread the function of pornography is, for how many young men it is effectively a form of sex education or perhaps more accurately sexist education' (Kelly and Butterworth 1997: 46).

A number of 'men of good faith' (Kelly and Butterworth 1997) have written about their use of pornography and its influence on notions of masculinity and sexuality (see, for example, Brod 1990). Robert Jensen (cited in Kelly and Butterworth 1997) admits that pornography was central to his sexuality and that it encouraged him to objectify women. For Kelly, Jensen 'has no doubt, nor do we, that pornography is directly and indirectly implicated in some men's acts of sexual violence' (1997: 46).

This view is supported by those who police and regulate the Net. Dr Alan Harding, head of the Sentencing and Offence Unit at the Home Office, points to the association between pornography and sexual violence while acknowledging that it is difficult to prove a causal link. It is known, for example, that adult pornography is used in the grooming process by child sexual abusers (Harding 1997). Further, Martin Jauch, who deals with pornography on a daily basis, has noted that the material on the Net is 'just as nasty' as that found in video or magazines, often involving the exploitation of women and children. Jauch claims to have uncovered material where it is clear that women are coerced into taking drugs before being tortured, for example, having their breasts burned with a cigarette (Jauch 1997).

The Internet and violence against women – cases

As indicated, there have been a number of cases reported, mostly in the US, where men have met women through the Net, known as 'off-line dating', and gone on to abuse them. One case involved the sexual assault and kidnapping of a young woman, while another ended in murder. For example, in 1996 in Baltimore a 45-year-old man, Robert Glass, killed a woman he had met through contact on the Internet by strangling her after sexually torturing her. Glass claimed that by engaging in erotic e-mail exchanges with him for some time prior to her murder the woman had 'consented' to her murder. In another case in the US, a 50-year-old male assumed the identity on-line of a 21-year-old woman in an attempt to hire someone to rape and sexually mutilate his wife (Fowler 1997).

In another widely reported case, a 30-year-old male postgraduate student from Columbia University, Oliver Jovanovic, was charged with 11 counts of sexual assault and the kidnapping of a 20-year-old student he had met on-line. The woman was subjected to 20 hours of assault and abuse by Jovanovic, who again claimed that she had 'consented' to the ordeal on the basis of previous e-mail exchanges. It transpired during the trial that at least 12 other women had been subject to e-mails from Jovanovic of a sado-masochistic and violent nature (Krum 1997). According to Krum (1997), 'American police speculate that there are many more cases of abuse resulting from "off-line" dating, but victims are often too embarrassed or too traumatised to come forward'.

Much of the coverage of these cases focuses on the degree of 'consent' given by the women in e-mail exchanges prior to meeting their abusers. In relation to these cases, it appears that the men involved have sought to excuse their violent and abusive behaviour by blaming the victims. This kind of justification is typical in cases of rape and sexual assault off the Net, and further serves to highlight the false distinction between 'virtual' and real consent to sexual abuse. It appears that the anonymity of the Net leads some men to think that they can act out their violent fantasies in real life. According to Fowler (1997),

American psychologists have already investigated what they call the 'Mardi Gras phenomenon', in which surfers of the Net feel they are wearing a mask and can act anonymously and speak with impunity.

Sexual harassment and 'cyberstalking' on-line

In addition to cases of physical and sexual violence against women by men who have used the Net as a means of access, there are countless cases documented on-line of the sexual harassment and 'cyberstalking' of women. Colin Gabriel Hatcher, co-founder of CyberAngels, an 'Internet safety organization' based in the US, states that:

> The truth of the matter is that on-line stalking is just as frightening and distressing as off-line stalking – and just as illegal too . . . Both men and women can be stalked on-line, but the majority of victims, as off-line, are female . . . Likewise, most cyberstalkers are male.
>
> (Hatcher 1997)

In another case in the US a male student was prosecuted for posting a 'fantasy' on the Internet concerning the rape of one of his fellow students. According to Butterworth:

> Women have been harassed, threatened and blamed in newsgroups and via e-mail just because they are women. In the book *Nattering on the Net* [Spender, 1995] is a case of a woman who received an anonymous Valentine's Day message saying that she would have her throat cut and be sexually assaulted. The author drafts parallels between this kind of behaviour and other forms of sexual harassment, behaviour which is designed to stake out territory and exclude women.
>
> (Kelly and Butterworth 1997: 47)

In reflection on how women are blamed or held responsible for men's violence in daily life some websites are now offering women (albeit well-meaning) advice on dealing with 'flame war abusers'(those who post aggressive or threatening messages to Net users) and 'cyberstalkers'. For example, the CyberAngels website offers the following strategies to women for dealing with on-line harassment. On dealing with 'flame war abusers':

> Their attempts to 'hit' on a female user will be clumsy and crude – but be careful how you turn them down, as they are highly sensitive to rejection and humiliation, and you can begin a vendetta against yourself if you publicly humiliate this kind of person.

On dealing with 'cyberstalkers':

> To protect yourself against cyberstalkers it is important for you to know what makes you attract their attention in the first place . . . The typical cyberstalking target is the inexperienced user, and most targets (80%) in our experience are female.

Hatcher goes on to advise women:

> It follows that the best way for a user to empower themselves and protect against on-line stalking and harassment is to learn Internet netiquette, [be] cyberstreetsmart and gain technical mastery of their Internet technology. This is the essence of proactive cyberspace self-defense, since it makes the user less 'attractive' as a target to a potential cyberstalker.
>
> (Hatcher 1997)

This website also offers a somewhat spurious explanation for men's violence to women on-line, namely 'love obsession':

> Love obsession stalkers are usually highly jealous and possessive people. This is why so many love obsessions end in violence. When the stalker finally realizes that he cannot have the object of his desire, he may in a rage decide that if he can't have you then no one else will either. Likewise, on-line love obsession stalking can easily become malicious, when the NO finally sinks in. *Death threats by mail or through live chat messages are a common escalation in on-line love obsession stalking.*
>
> (my emphasis)

The message for women would appear to be that they have no place on the Internet. Should they risk going on-line, they are held responsible not only for their own safety but also for men's abusive and harassing behaviour. Flaming and cyberstalking are frequently excused on the grounds of the inexperience of the novice (female) Net user rather than being viewed as yet another form of violence against women. At the time of writing there have been no prosecutions in the UK for cyberstalking. However, this may change with the introduction of the Protection from Harassment Act (1997).

Trafficking of women on the Net

Another area in which men are exploiting and abusing women on-line is in the global trafficking of women on the Internet. Donna Hughes (1996a, 1996b, 1997) has researched the growth of sex tourism on the Net and found that:

> Promoters of sex tours are pimping women's bodies and sexuality throughout the world on the Internet. This international communication network of computers is being used to sell women to a global market of men, mostly from industrialised countries.
>
> (1996a: 71)

Examples of openly advertised websites include those offering sex tours, mail order brides, brothels, strip bars and escort services. Often the same women appear on sites for mail order brides and brothels, suggesting that the sale of women on the Net is an organized industry in some countries which have come to rely on the sale of women's bodies as their cash crop (Hughes 1996a: 74).

Men use newsgroups to provide descriptions of sex tours together with pornographic details of their encounters with particular women, often using misogynistic and sadistic language. Reinforcing Kelly's argument that there is frequently a false distinction made concerning the exploitation of women and children in pornography, Hughes points out that: '[Though] the average age of prostitutes in Bangkok is so young that most of it is by definition child sex abuse, the cyberpimps publish information on where to find very young girls' (1996b: 4). Further,

> Numerous accounts by human rights groups have revealed that many of the girls and women in Bangkok's sex industry are virtual slaves. The men who buy them know that. Their comments prove that.
>
> (1996b: 4)

For Hughes, a member of the Coalition against Trafficking in Women who support the Beijing Declaration (Fourth World Conference on Women, 1995) calling for an end to the sexual exploitation of women through trafficking and sex tours, states

> the entrance and growth of the sex industry on the Internet is a symptom and evidence of the harm that is being done to women. The primary harm is the sexual exploitation of women and abrogation of their human rights.
>
> (1996a: 74)

The policing and regulation of the Internet

It is precisely the global nature of the Net that has led to concerns about the effectiveness of legislation in controlling pornography on the Net. As yet, laws on pornography and obscenity are not harmonized, although governments are working towards this goal. The policing of the Net is rendered problematic due, in part, to reasons of jurisdiction.

Legislation, censorship and 'civil liberties'

Internet service providers and web page owners may commit an offence in providing illegal material for display or downloading via a web page or a link from a web page. Charlesworth (1996) points out that even browsing the Web may be an offence if displaying or downloading illegal material. The distribution of computer pornography is covered by various pieces of legislation in the UK. These include: Section 43 of the Telecommunications Act (1984); the Obscene Publications Act (1959); and in the case of child pornography, new legislation under Sections 84–87 of the Criminal Justice and Public Order Act (1994) aimed specifically at computer generated and distributed pornography (Charlesworth 1996: viii).

Most of the discussion on the policing, regulation and censorship of the Net in the UK focuses on the Obscene Publications Act (1959) which refers to material 'likely to deprave and corrupt'. According to Alan Harding, 'One concern is that [the Act] is not an exact predictor of where the line should be drawn' (1997: 41), and further, the line has shifted over time. However, in relation to computer pornography, the police point to Section 2 of the Act which covers more violent pornographic material such as that increasingly being distributed via the Net and which carries the threat of imprisonment (Dewe Matthews 1998). In the UK, pornographic material on the Net is subject to the same legislation as other media; an Internet service provider is as liable as a magazine publisher (Harding 1997).

As in the UK, European Ministers have focused on the role of the private sector in regulating illegal and harmful material on the Net (Harding 1997; Mann and Sutton 1998). The EC Green Paper on *The Protection of Minors and Human Dignity in Audio-Visual Information Services* is concerned about such content, particularly in relation to its impact on children, and proposes the use of filtering and rating systems to regulate harmful or illegal content.

Feminist critics such as Edwards (1997) and Kelly (Kelly and Butterworth 1997) have highlighted the inadequacies of current legislation in the UK, while in relation to the EC Green Paper, for Kelly the 'protection of human dignity' needs to be considered in the wider context of the degradation of women in pornography (Kelly and Butterworth 1997). While there is a need for effective legislation, this should not be based on values of obscenity, taste and decency, but on harm and gender inequality.

For example, in considering the issue of censorship, Kelly refers to Andrea Dworkin and Catherine MacKinnon's attempts to make pornography unlawful in the US. There is a legal argument that pornography libels women. This refers to the power of pornography as a form of speech. The Dworkin and MacKinnon Ordinance in the US resulted in the Supreme Court concurring with feminist analysis of pornography as a systematic practice of exploitation and degradation which harms women's opportunities for liberation (Kelly and Butterworth 1997: 46).

Nevertheless, the Ordinance was subsequently overturned by the Supreme Court in response to pressure from civil libertarians and those with an interest in the pornography business. There are parallels here with the recent decision in the US to overturn the Communications Decency Act (1997), almost as soon as it was passed, in response to similar pressure from civil libertarians who claim that the Internet is one of the last bastions of 'free speech'.

However, as Kelly and Butterworth have argued, from a feminist and human rights perspective, freedom for some groups is predicated on the abuse of other groups, and pornography on the Internet can be seen as a violation of women's human rights. The solutions should not centre on enabling individuals to avoid pornography or suggesting that one should avert one's gaze (Kelly and Butterworth 1997). Rather, the solution, at least in part, should centre on effective policing and regulation of the Internet.

Policing the Net

Government departments, regulatory bodies, Internet companies and service providers have, to date, been most concerned with the production and distribution of child pornography on the Internet. However, the Metropolitan Police Clubs and Vice Unit has also identified the trafficking of women and the licensing of the sex industry in the UK as priorities (Jauch 1997). Further, as indicated, adult pornography is a concern when used in the commission of serious offences such as its use by 'paedophiles' to desensitize children in child pornography. The British police also recognize the need 'to combat other forms of pornography and violence on the Internet' (Reynolds 1997: 57).[3]

Superintendent Martin Jauch points out that the Net presents new problems, for example, live strip shows and 'live child abuse, in real time and on video conferencing from somewhere in the third world' (1997: 28). In response to these problems, the police have produced a handbook for dealing with computer pornography which has been circulated to all police forces in the UK.

One of the difficulties of policing the Net is the issue of jurisdiction. For Jauch, 'We already know that we can neither "control" nor "police" the Internet in the normal sense of those words' (1998: 14). A lot of the pornography that would be considered illegal in the UK is outside the jurisdiction of the British police.

According to Reynolds, pornography often depicts serious sexual crimes of violence (1997). This view echoes that of feminist critics. Reynolds argues that when someone is viewing child pornography they are viewing the scene of a crime. The problem for the police is in determining where the scene of the crime is located. Nevertheless, the British police have prosecuted those involved in organized child pornography in international, multijurisdictional investigations, most notably in the case of Operation Starburst in 1995, and the Operation Cathedral investigation of the 'Wonderland' paedophile ring in 1998. Mann and Sutton (1998) predict that 'jurisdiction hopping' to find the most favourable country for a successful prosecution, may become more frequent.

For Jauch, at the sharp end of investigation into computer pornography, while the Internet presents difficulties for effective policing, these are not insurmountable. There is a need for legislation and an international level of enforcement: jurisdictional problems are no different from those that have been confronting us for years in terms of international complex fraud (1997: 30). Evidence presentation needs to be forensically sound and understood by the courts and jurors in order to secure a conviction.

In the UK, the policing and regulation of the Net has followed a multi-agency approach. This has included the setting up in 1996 of an interdepartmental working group on obscenity which includes government departments, the police, customs and excise and Internet service providers. The group formulated 'Safety Net' proposals, including further action to be taken in policing the Net, the self-regulation of Internet service providers and the establishment of the Internet Watch Foundation. As self-regulation is the favoured approach of governments in Europe, technologies have been developed to filter and/or rate material on websites and newsgroups.

Self-regulation

Technologies

In response to the threat of increasing government regulation, the larger Internet companies and service providers have joined forces to develop PICS (Platform for Internet Content Selection), a detailed rating system for the Net which grades material from 0 to 4 under four categories – sex, violence, language and nudity (Hargrave 1996: 13). According to Jauch, however,

> we do not accept that illegal material can be rated. Illegal material is illegal material and that's the end of it. We will take action if people refuse to move that from their sites.
>
> (1997: 30)

Further, the rating of illegal material clearly does not cover much of the pornographic material legally available on the Net.

Another technology which has been developed, in this case for use by consumers, is filtering software. Filtering packages are designed primarily for concerned parents to control their children's access to unsuitable websites. This software has been available for some time and is sold with titles such as Net Nanny, Surf Watch and CyberSitter. However, such technological 'fixes' do not address the more fundamental problems associated with the growth of pornography on the Net.

Feminist writers have been critical of the notion that the Net can be effectively regulated through technological innovations alone. For example, Edwards argues, in relation to the self-regulation of pornography on satellite television and on the Internet, that labelling and rating systems for classifying content do not go far enough:

> There is also the unintended consequence that self-regulation at the point of 'service providers' and 'users' may result in a laissez-faire market-place permitting a greater promulgation of pornography on the Internet on the basis that it is, after all, up to parents to regulate.
>
> (1997: 142)

Internet service providers (ISPs)

These technologies, particularly the development of PICS, are welcomed by the ISPs as they alleviate, to some extent, their responsibilities for monitoring the content of the Net. The police in the UK have sent a clear message to ISPs: to self-regulate or face tougher policing. They have, for example, warned ISPs to close down certain newsgroups (such as 'alt.sex.' groups) which carry illegal or harmful material, including child pornography, or face the possibility of prosecution. ISPs are reluctant, however, to close down highly profitable pornographic sites. As Jauch (1997) points out, the problem is that ISPs are both providers of access to computer pornography while making profit from such material.

In a test case in Bavaria this year, Felix Somm, the former head of a major ISP, Compuserve, was prosecuted for 'knowingly' disseminating child, animal and violent pornography on the Internet. Compuserve's initial response was to close access to more than 280 news sites, which led to accusations of censorship of the Net. The company subsequently restored access to all but five of the sites (Trayner 1998). ISPs argue that they are as responsible for what is made available on the Web as telephone companies are for conversations. Nevertheless, Somm was convicted on 13 counts of publishing illegal pornographic material (Waldman 1998), a clear message to ISPs that the Internet can and will be policed and is subject to regulation by government.

The Internet Watch Foundation (IWF)
In the UK, the Safety Net proposals in 1996 led to the setting up of the Internet Watch Foundation (IWF). One of the aims of the IWF is to improve the reputation of the Internet. The IWF offers a public hotline for reporting offensive material. In the first four months of operation over 200 reports were received, the majority of which were on child pornography (Kerr 1998). They are developing a rating system, partly in response to complaints by parents that existing screening and filtering software is too complicated to be effective.

While the IWF is to be welcomed as a step in the right direction, particularly in its role of policing and regulating child pornography, its brief does not extend to adult pornography and violence against women.

Conclusion

It can be argued that new technologies and forms of self-regulation are being used by powerful groups to justify a degree of inactivity in the regulation of computer pornography. The police in the UK are taking the problem seriously, but are hampered in controlling the vast amount of pornography on the Net due both to resources and the ineffectiveness of current legislation. They can only police material considered illegal and which falls within the jurisdiction of UK law. Clearly, with regard to computer pornography, new laws are needed that recognize the exploitation and degradation of women, as well as children, in much of the (currently legal) material on the Net. There is a need for legislative changes to facilitate effective policing and regulation of the Internet globally in order to send a clear message to producers and consumers of computer pornography that they will be liable for material which harms or degrades women and children.

It should be remembered that before the advent of feminist campaigns there was little serious recognition within the law of the prevalence of domestic violence and rape. Naming violence against women 'virtual violence' or 'virtual rape' does not make it any less real for those women who have been abused in the production of computer pornography, or who have experienced harassment on-line or off-line as a result of encountering abusive men through the Internet.

It is encouraging to note that women are asserting themselves by developing websites such as WHOA (Women Halting On-line Abuse). WHOA produces a Safe Site List showing 'sites that have adopted and enforced anti-harassment policies'. They also list an Unsafe Site List for 'sites with a history and culture of harassment and abuse. Actions you can take to help fight back!' This is one practical strategy of empowerment for women. Such developments need to be taken forward alongside international campaigns for specific legislation to eradicate harassment and abuse of women on-line, as with other feminist campaigns challenging the international sex industry.

As the Internet develops to become an important means of communication for the millennium, women should not be deterred from its use by men's abusive and violent behaviour. In this, as in all other areas of social life, women will continue to campaign to eradicate gender inequalities and violence against women.

Notes

1 Diane Butterworth and Liz Kelly presented separate papers at the conference 'Policing the Internet: combating pornography and violence on the Internet – a European approach' (London, February 1997).
2 'Flaming' is the term used when someone sends an abusive or intimidating message to another user or group. Women-only groups on the Net are frequently flamed through sexually explicit and abusive postings by men (Spender 1995).
3 Jim Reynolds is Detective Chief Inspector of the Paedophilia Unit, New Scotland Yard.

References

Akdeniz, Y. (1996) 'Computer Pornography' on website http://www.leeds.ac.uk/law/pgs/yaman/ yaman.htm
Brod, H. (1990) Pornography and the alienation of male sexuality, in J.Hearn and D.Morgan (eds) *Men, Masculinities and Social Theory*. London: Unwin Hyman.
Butterworth, D. (1996) Wanking in cyberspace: the development of computer porn, in S.Jackson and S.Scott (eds) *Feminism and Sexuality: a Reader*. Edinburgh: Edinburgh University Press.
Charlesworth, A. (1996) Never having to say sorry. Multimedia Features Section, *The Times Higher*, 10 May.
Consumers Association (1997) *Which? Report on the Internet.* July.

Dewe Matthews, T. (1998) The great British sex scandal, *Guardian Review Section*, 10 July: 6–7.

Dworkin, A. (1992) *Pornography: Men Possessing Women*. London: The Women's Press.

Edwards, S. (1997) A safe haven for hardest core. *Law Review*, 4 ENT.LR: 137–42.

Fowler, R. (1997) http://meet me.www.kill me: death by appointment on the Internet, *Mail on Sunday Review*, 9 February.

Gillespie, T. (1994) Under pressure: rape crisis centres, multi-agency work and strategies for survival, in C. Lupton and T. Gillespie (eds) *Working with Violence*. Basingstoke: Macmillan.

Gillespie, T. (1996) Rape crisis centres and male rape: a face of the backlash, in M. Hester, L. Kelly and J. Radford (eds) *Women, Violence and Male Power: Feminist Activism, Research and Practice*. Buckingham: Open University Press.

Harding, A. (1997) Setting the policy. Paper presented to the Association of London Government Conference, Policing the Internet: Combating Pornography and Violence on the Internet – a European Approach, London, 14–15 February.

Hargrave, S. (1996) Safety net for children arrives, *The Sunday Times*, 19 May: 13.

Hatcher, C. G. (1997) Internet Cyberstalking and Online Harassment, on website http://www.cyberangels.org

Hughes, D. (1996a) Sex tours via the internet. *Agenda: Empowering Women for Gender Equity*, 28: 71–6.

Hughes, D. (1996b) Pimping on the Internet. Paper presented to the Violence, Abuse and Women's Citizenship International Conference, Brighton, 14 November.

Hughes, D. (1997) Protecting the dignity of women. Paper presented to the Association of London Government Conference, Policing the Internet: Combating Pornography and Violence on the Internet – a European Approach, London, 14–15 February.

Itzin, C. (ed.) (1993) *Pornography: Women, Violence and Civil Liberties*. Oxford: Oxford University Press.

Jauch, M. (1997) Cooperation from the police and the legal system. Paper presented to the Association of London Government Conference, Policing the Internet: Combating Pornography and Violence on the Internet – a European Approach, London, 14–15 February.

Jauch, M. (1998) Policing the Internet, *NCH Action for Children Report, Children on the Internet: Opportunities and Hazards*. London: National Children's Home.

Kelly, L. and Butterworth, D. (1997) Women's Perspectives. Paper presented to the Association of London Government Conference, Policing the Internet: Combating Pornography and Violence on the Internet – a European Approach, London, 14–15 February.

Kerr, D. (1998) The UK's hotline service, *NCH Action for Children Report Children on the Internet: Opportunities and Hazards*. London: National Children's Home.

Krum, S. (1996) On a new campaign trail, *Guardian*, 4 June.

Krum, S. (1997) Who's afraid of the big bad Web? *Guardian*, 7 January.

Lillington, K. (1998) Surfing for sex, *Guardian Online*, 14 May.

Mann, D. and Sutton, M. (1998) Netcrime: more change in the organisation of thieving. *British Journal of Criminology*, 38 (2) spring: 201–29.

Michals, D. (1997) Cyber-rape: how virtual is it? in *Ms. Magazine*, March/April: 68–72.

Millar, S. (1997) Anger over net porn magazine, *Guardian*, 8 April.

Reynolds, J. (1997) Enforcing the policies. Paper presented to the Association of London Government Conference, Policing the Internet: Combating Pornography and Violence on the Internet – a European Approach, London, 14–15 February.

Senjen, R. and Guthrey, J. (1996) *The Internet for Women*. Melbourne: Spinifex Press.

Spender, D. (1995) *Nattering on the Net: Women, Power and Cyberspace*. Melbourne: Spinifex Press.

Sussman, V. (1997) Adult sites are the driving force behind many Web innovations, *USA Today*, 20 August.

Traynor, I. (1998) Pornography test case for Internet providers, *Guardian*, 13 May: 14.

Waldman, S. (1998) Internet stockings, *Guardian*, 8 June: 8.

5 Prostitution, pornography and telephone boxes

Ruth Swirsky and Celia Jenkins

It is a curious fact that only in certain areas of the UK, namely London, Brighton and more recently in Manchester, is prostitution being advertised by placing cards in telephone boxes. They are tucked into cracks or attached to the glass with Blu-tack so that they almost cover the interior surfaces. Anyone making a phone call is bombarded by the pornographic display of cards with images of commercialized sex, and for those not interested in contacting prostitutes or in the images themselves, the cards can be a source of acute discomfort and offence.

Over 100,000 cards are being placed each week in approximately 500 telephone boxes in central London. These cards are a major source of embarrassment to British Telecom (BT) because it cannot get rid of them permanently, and it receives complaints about them from the public and local residents. The cost of removing the cards on a daily basis is expensive and they are perceived as undermining BT's family-friendly public image. In 1993 the University of Westminster was commissioned by BT and Westminster City Council, with the support of the Metropolitan Police, to find a solution to the problem. We became involved in the research because as feminists we wanted to try to influence its direction and outcomes, as the research could have an impact on women – both those involved in prostitution and those using phone boxes.

Through our analysis of the cards, which have become increasingly explicit and pornographic we saw (literally) a link between prostitution and pornography. As the research progressed, we began to question whether it was the easy access of men to prostitution via the cards or the public display of pornography on the cards in the telephone boxes which concerned us the most. This led us to explore some resultant tensions in the relationship between prostitution and pornography arising from the use of pornographic images to market prostitution, as well as the prospect of acting them out in the prostitution encounter. This analysis employs a theoretical framework that broadly defines both prostitution and pornography as exploitation of women. Prostitution is the exploitation of women through their being paid for access to their bodies and for the sexual services they perform on (with/ for) men, while pornography is an exploitative practice entailing sexualized representations based on the subordination of women and their sexual availability to men.

A widely held view is that the production of pornography derives from and depends on prostitution; both constitute violence against women and are premised on the objectification and commodification of women as sex (Wynter 1988; O'Hara 1991; Giobbe 1993). However, Barry (1995: 57) extends our understanding of the contemporary connections between pornography and prostitution:

> Prostitution is the enacted version of pornography, where the graphic representation of the subordination of women comes to life. The normalization of prostitution is the pornographic deployment of that subordination into private lives and personal relationships.

She theorizes the exploitation of women across the spectrum of the sex industry and through an analysis of the 'prostitution of sexuality' identifies its impact on all women.

This chapter makes these links between prostitution, pornography and the construction of women's sexuality by examining the function of pornography for prostitution in the public domain of telephone boxes. Our examination of the cards routinely and daily displayed in London's public telephone boxes first establishes that they are indeed pornographic. The phone box serves as a nexus in which cards advertising prostitution function as pornography for some men. Second, we will argue that their location contributes to the normalization of both pornography and prostitution as part of urban social life. They objectify, commodify and dehumanize women, thereby normalizing the sexual violence, which many cards also explicitly promote. Third, we examine the impact of the cards on those who use these phone boxes, and the complexity of public perceptions of prostitution and pornography in relation to the cards. Finally, we evaluate the function of pornography for prostitution.

The research context

At this stage it may be helpful to explain the context of our research. There are a number of different locations described by Jarvinen (1993) as 'prostitution milieux' in which prostitution takes place, each having different activities, relationships and risks associated with them, some held in common with others, some unique (Phoenix 1995). Most of the current research on prostitution focuses on street prostitution, whereas in our research the cards in the BT phone boxes relate to prostitution in flats. One of the features indicated by Phoenix (1995) as differentiating avenues of prostitution is the mode of client contact. Women in prostitution[1] who are based in flats have to find ways of enabling clients to contact them. The phone box is an ideal space to advertise because the cards are easily seen by passers-by, require no prior knowledge about London or where to contact prostitutes, and potential clients can call immediately within the relative privacy of the phone box. Moreover, this unauthorized advertising is not illegal. Now that they are privately owned, telephone boxes are not protected from unauthorized advertising by public by-laws, which make it illegal in other public utilities. Thus BT cannot legally stop the cards being placed in their phone boxes.[2]

Those commissioning the research had a strategic mission to reach a solution which would remove the cards from the phone boxes, without overtly appearing to force these prostitutes onto the streets through cutting off their main means of advertising. At the same time BT was adamantly opposed to any solution which might be construed as condoning prostitution. The terms of reference were established by those commissioning the research: BT and Westminster City Council with support from the Metropolitan Police. In particular, we were to identify the extent of unauthorized advertising, and the viewpoints of the different interest groups involved (namely, the agencies commissioning the research, the women involved in prostitution who advertise through telephone boxes, residents' groups and members of the public) in order to identify the issues and possible solutions. Our research had to confront the difficulties of doing feminist research when the terms of reference were not framed by feminist understandings. Our ways of seeing the issue were indeed very different from those commissioning the research.[3] Also, our views were not shared by other members of the university research team, which consisted mainly of men representing diverse disciplines such as marketing, geography, criminology and sociology. Most of them held liberal views about prostitution as acceptable, whereas we were opposed to the institution of prostitution and disturbed by the pornographic content of some cards. However, many of them dropped out of the project, which gave us more internal influence.

Because the research was commissioned, we were limited in terms of the questions we could ask and how we could ask them. We stretched the boundaries of the terms of reference as far as possible to ask wider questions about prostitution and pornography. Thus we interviewed women involved in prostitution who were working from flats and advertising in phone boxes and surveyed members of the public about the cards, attempting to ascertain their perceptions of pornography in the process.

Prostitution, pornography and the cards

Advertising in telephone boxes was once legitimate, with a designated and controlled advertising space. It was mostly taxi companies who used this form of advertising, although some of the women we interviewed could remember being allowed to advertise, using euphemisms such as 'massage'

Figure 5.1 Phone box[4]

or 'french lessons'. More extensive and unauthorized advertising of sexual services began with stickers with names and telephone numbers, but the women were prosecuted for criminal damage and so they switched to simple hand-written cards. They then progressed to printed cards, which have become bigger and bolder and more professionally produced as changes in technology have made their production cheaper. The content of the cards has also become more explicit about the services offered, and increasingly they include illustrations or photographs depicting the services offered in sophisticated pictorial and symbolic forms (Figure 5.1).

Some of the women in prostitution who advertise using cards are themselves producing pornography which invites men to act out these fantasies with them. These pornographic images contain the explicit message that they refer not just to fantasy but to an accessible reality. Thus the distance between pornography and prostitution is foreshortened through the use of the pornographic image to advertise prostitution. Prostitution's symbolic presence in this public space confronts and positions men and women in different ways. The cards set up all women as sexualized commodities while potentially turning all men into consumers. The cards constitute a display of pornography imposed upon unwilling members of the public, comparable perhaps to the 'top-shelf' magazines in newsagents, but far more intrusive within such a confined space. Moreover, these images are located not within magazines or videos purchased for the purpose of consuming pornography, but within a public telephone box. The intention here is to focus on the implications of the use of pornography both as a marketing strategy to sell sex and in providing scripts to be enacted in prostitution encounters.

It is clear from our analysis of cards that many of them constitute pornographic representations of women according to the definition by Dworkin
and MacKinnon (MacKinnon 1994). They drafted the US civil rights ordinance
in the early 1980s which offers an inclusive definition of pornography as an
exploitative practice based on sex which subordinates and differentially harms
women. Visually the cards represent women scantily dressed or naked in
poses that suggest seduction, but they also range pictorially through scenes
of submission, domination and punishment, bondage, uniforms and trans-
vestism to fetish services of boots and rubber. Some of the textual messages
are coded in ways that are fairly obvious, but others are more opaque to the
uninitiated. While many women and children are confronted with pornography not through choice, this may be a particularly unexpected location
in which to be faced with it and especially upsetting within such a confined,
as well as public, space.

The cards appearing in telephone boxes were categorized for the purposes
of our research in terms of services offered; those advertising domination/
submission (of either the client or prostitute) account for about one-third of
services advertised in the period 1993–94. Such cards may be quite clever in
their use of text and image, for example, 'Ouch! – Slap Happy' are the only
words to accompany a graphic picture of a woman receiving a beating from
a client armed with a strap. The text and graphics doubly emphasize the
submission on sale and suggest that during the prostitution encounter the
woman will enjoy the violence. The depiction of violence against women
has become increasingly explicit on some cards; one which resulted in the
only successful prosecution for obscenity, used a black and white photo-
graph of a woman being caned, with globules of red blood on her buttocks.
Cards promise the acting out of pornographic fantasies of domination or
submission, and prostitution is there just a phone call away to deliver the
fantasy. Women in prostitution are thus producing cards which rely on
pornography as a marketing strategy, thereby reinforcing the idea that it
is acceptable to act out the pornographic fantasies and that the women
will enjoy the experience. In fact, Liz Kelly (1990: 36) in her critique of
pornography stresses that 'the acceptability of pornography and its central
message reinforces and reasserts the myths about rape and sexual assault
that feminists have sought to expose'.

Some cards deploy racist stereotypes through the use of racial differentiation to promote myths of exotic, predominantly black sexuality. For example,
they advertise a 'black mistress' or 'oriental model' which exoticizes the
prostitute and the potential experience, thereby sexualizing racism through
these representations (Kelly 1990: 32). As Davidson argues, racist, sexist
fantasies 'can be briefly enacted with a prostitute, enabling some white men
to simultaneously express and transgress their own "racisms" . . . without
fear of any real intimacy' (1996: 189). Prostitution may enable men to
explore their racist fantasies by selecting women from different ethnic groups
– but only if the woman is willing to sell her services to him. A converse
expression of racism was evident from one white woman we interviewed

who didn't want black clients, and indicated her preference on one of her cards by offering services to 'nice English gentlemen'.

Male clients and their use of the cards

Jarvinen (1993) points out that it is rare for men's behaviour to be subject to scrutiny. Researching clients presents real difficulties, though some studies (mainly of street prostitutes) have included male clients with various degrees of success in relation to both the quality of empirical evidence and the quality of the analytical insights. MacLeod (1982) interviewed some of the regular clients of the street prostitutes she studied, while a more journalistic account can be found in Boyle (1994). Davidson's (1995) research on British male sex tourists covered a broader range of prostitution milieux, and revealed fascinating evidence of their contradictory and self-deluding attitudes towards prostitutes in Thailand and Britain. Høigård and Finstad, in their analysis of street prostitution, offer illuminating data about men's motivation for using prostitutes to act out sexual fantasies of male power through the objectification and subordination of women, explaining how 'the customer uses normatively illegitimate means to obtain this goal: instead of women's voluntary subordination, he resorts to money's tyranny' (1992:105). McKeganey and Barnard, also researching street prostitution, comment that clients felt that because they had paid for sex they were in control of the encounter, many perceiving 'the prostitute as no more than the sex that she sold' (1996: 53).

A project undertaken by Elizabeth Plumridge and her colleagues (1997), in cooperation with New Zealand Prostitutes' Collective, provides additional insights into men's self-serving interpretations of how they benefit from prostitution. These men posit such encounters as emotional relationships while at the same time asserting that all obligations associated with relationships are discharged by payment. The ability to engage in this mental juggling which enables men to construct such a fantasy onto an economic transaction is dependent on the power inequalities of hierarchic heterosexuality. Payment apparently absolves them from responsibility for the emotional damage to women wrought by prostitution.

It is important to consider the cards in the phone boxes from the perspective of the men who use them to contact prostitutes. It is clear that significant numbers of men use the cards and phone boxes to contact prostitutes – if this were not the case then the women would not find it an effective means of advertising. The advantage of the use of the phone box for prospective clients to make a call to a prostitute is that the activity is discreet. Julia O'Connell Davidson (1995) speculates that while thousands of men use the services of prostitutes, many feel profoundly uncomfortable being identified as the sort of men who use them. The privacy of the phone box possibly delays the assumption of this identity by allowing men to enter the role of prostitute's client in gradual stages.

Our research found that men are also using the cards as pornography to provide them with some form of gratification. This was evident when we asked the women who advertised via the telephone boxes to estimate the ratio of telephone calls to prostitution encounters. They claim that only around 1 in 50 of these calls results in a visit from a client. As most of the 'maids' give similar introductory spiels over the phone, the low take-up of services cannot be accounted for simply by clients' choice. It would seem that at least some men are obtaining some measure of satisfaction simply from the cards themselves and the act of phoning one of the numbers. It may be coincidental that the escalation in the number and explicitness of cards in the last few years has paralleled the development and growth of telephone sex. Interestingly, those working in this segment of the commercialized sex industry describe themselves as 'verbal prostitutes' (Hopkins and Burke 1995). It would seem that making a call to a prostitute while viewing cards and the prospect of illicit sex that they portray provides men with a frisson of excitement. While the 'maid' does no more than list the qualities of her employer, the services offered and the prices, it does nonetheless appear to provide a literally cheap thrill (in comparison with the sex chat lines), offering as it does a taste of commercialized sex in a public and therefore symbolically dangerous location for only 10p.

In discussing the areas where street prostitutes work, Høigård and Finstad argue that, 'the district becomes a symbolic arena where the men can obtain confirmation that women exist for men. They stand displayed and available' (1992: 96) – as they do on the cards. It would seem then that the cards that the prostitutes use for advertising their services (along with a call to the number on the card) may also serve a similar function to kerb-crawling, which is common in areas where street prostitutes work. Men drive round and round, watching, staring and sometimes pulling in to the kerb and masturbating (Edwards 1993: 102). Thus the cards may provide a form of voyeurism by proxy.

Cards as a cultural phenomenon

In the course of the research we became increasingly aware that the cards are also viewed as cultural artefacts, neutralizing judgement of their content, even celebrating it. It seems that many men are collecting the prostitutes' cards and that they have become marketable as a cultural artefact (Bennett 1992). Moreover, there is evidence that this practice of collecting cards is not restricted to adult men, but boys have been spotted removing cards from telephone boxes which are then swapped in school playgrounds (Bracchip 1992). This was picked up by the *Sun*, describing it as a 'sick new craze' when 10-year-olds switch from collecting bubble gum wrappers to porn (*Sun* 1992). The collecting of prostitutes' cards was partially endorsed by a member of the government during a debate in 1994 when Lady Olga Maitland moved an amendment to the Criminal Justice and Public Order

Bill to make it an offence to advertise without permission in a telephone box. The Home Office Minister David McLean advised her 'to continue collecting cards and keep them in an album as they will probably be on the *Antiques Roadshow* as rare, valuable, collectors' items in 40 years' time' (*Hansard* 1994).

In 1993, Patrick Jewell, an art student, published a book, *Vice Art*, based on his collection of prostitutes' cards over the previous two years. It is printed on yellow paper, reminiscent of the *Yellow Pages* directory, and is classified according to the types of services advertised.[5] His aim was to produce a contemporary social record that examines the cards as an art form drawing upon both pop and classical art to advertise sexual services. At around the same time, Tom Cook, an artist, exhibited in collage form cards advertising sexual services together with themes from the print media (for example, 'If it isn't hurting it isn't working' was a political slogan of the Conservative Party and the theme of one collage using cards advertising domination/submission). The implication of describing pornographic images as cultural artefacts and collectibles is to legitimate increased public exposure to pornography in the name of art. Andrea Dworkin (1981) strongly challenges this trend, describing it as the 'lie' of pornography masquerading as art. Kelly criticizes the way that 'pornography has managed to create a form of legitimacy: it has become a staple in much of the popular press and commands its own cable TV channels' (1990: 32).

Lacey contends that 'pornography is a regime of representation through which we see the world' (1993: 104), and constant exposure to it can affect the way other cultural forms such as advertising are perceived. Whereas advertisements in the media may contain explicit and sometimes blatantly pornographic images not dissimilar to some of the cards advertising sexual services, the latter convey the promise of acting out the representations of sexual activities contained in them. The cards are seen not only by the potential clients but by anyone making a telephone call in a public phone box.

Naming the problem: prostitution or pornography?

As part of our research we investigated whether those using the phone boxes perceive the cards as pornographic or simply as advertisements for sexual services. A survey of 135 payphone users and passers-by was conducted between November 1993 and March 1994. It should be borne in mind that this survey represents the views of payphone users, not necessarily of the public in general. Nearly three-quarters of the people surveyed were under 30, which may in fact reflect the age structure of those using payphones, but is likely to affect the outcomes significantly. We are well aware of the limitations of survey questionnaires, particularly given the context in which the survey was undertaken. Nonetheless, it does provide some sense of the direction of feeling of those who use public telephones in which these cards are a prominent feature.

From the survey evidence it seems that the majority of people in the central London and Brighton areas do perceive the cards as a problem. The questions were designed to make respondents consider the implications of the cards' presence. It became increasingly apparent that the more people thought about the issue, the more they identified it as a problem. Initially, when asked about their attitudes towards the cards, similar numbers of respondents objected to seeing the cards in telephone boxes as those who said they did not. However, by the end of the questionnaire the number of respondents who thought that some or all of the cards should be banned from the phone boxes had risen significantly to 90 per cent.

Almost two-thirds of the women but less than half of the men found the content of the cards offensive. The reasons for this demonstrated an even more significant gender variation. While all respondents ranked the possible effect on children first, more women did so than men. The most striking gender difference however, was in relation to the perception that these cards reinforced negative attitudes towards women. While under a third of men gave this as a reason for finding the cards offensive, nearly two-thirds of women did so. It could be argued that the women who do object to the cards are implicitly acknowledging the objectification of women 'as sex' (Kappeler 1992) which contributes to their subordination. This accords with Lacey's (1993: 104) argument that:

> the profusion of the pornography regime of representation inevitably affects the social constitution of femininity – affects the ways in which women can be represented and can represent ourselves across all social practices – and hence directly and adversely, albeit intangibly affects the status of women.

There was also a significant gender difference among those who initially said that they did not object to the cards. The main reason given by men was they found the cards entertaining (49 per cent), while only 1 in 10 of the women gave this as a reason. Just over half the women said they found them harmless. Such reasoning belongs to liberal discourses about pornography as a matter of personal taste, which is belied by research evidence of the harm caused to women and children by both the production and the consumption of pornography (Kelly 1988; Russell 1993). In relation to the cards, it is the issue of consumption that is at stake, an issue recognized by many of those using the phone boxes.

While in one sense the survey data could be used to demonstrate that women tend to perceive the cards as pornographic and tend to object to them on those grounds, they could also be interpreted differently. Itzin and Sweet (1993) analysed data derived from three surveys on women's attitudes to pornography and found a far higher proportion objecting to pornography and a far lower proportion deeming it to be 'OK' or 'fun' than we did. This difference might be explained by methodological differences or differences in the degree and severity of pornographic content between their research and ours. However, it is possible that the difference arises from constant

Figure 5.2   Petals

exposure to the cards by frequent users of public phone boxes, which may serve to normalize the images and desensitize the viewers.

All respondents were shown five different cards ranging from a simple name and number to those using images, both photographic or line drawings, and lists of services which varied in comprehensiveness. Only a tiny proportion (less than 10 per cent) found the simplest cards offensive or thought they should be banned. Cards that used images, whether photographs or line drawings, which were suggestive of or portrayed sexual acts were clearly considered offensive. Indeed, a card with a photographic image of a woman (Figure 5.2) which was not significantly different from many images used in magazine advertising, though by the nature of the card clearly linked with the sale of sexual services, was perceived as more offensive (by 57 per cent of respondents) than a card (Figure 5.3) with no images but an explicit and complete list of sexual services, including some that might be considered somewhat bizarre (45 per cent of respondents).

The card which the overwhelming majority (92 per cent) ranked as most offensive utilized a line drawing suggestive of anal sex and included an invitation to 'Spank Me! Cane Me! Do what you want to me!'.

A very large majority (90 per cent) of respondents thought either all cards should be banned (53 per cent), or some cards should be banned (37 per cent) from the phone boxes. In other words, over one-third did not object to prostitutes advertising in phone boxes but did object to pornographic cards. The apparent paradox in responses towards advertising by women in prostitution might be explained in the following terms. While the majority accept the idea that prostitutes might need to advertise their services, they clearly do not want the advertising to take this form which forces any payphone user to have to confront pornographic images advertising sex for sale. Allowing these cards to continue to be displayed in public places is a signal to women of the values of a society which allows them to be represented and perceived in this way.

In effect, the cards reinforce the objectification of women's bodies both as

Figure 5.3 Pick your pleasure

sex and as a commodity, serving as a statement of wider social values in relation to women's sexuality. Høigård and Finstad argued that in order to become a prostitute it was necessary to incorporate a particular female self-image, and from our research it is possible that the cards invite and help to reinforce this image. The cards serve the additional function of advertising a route into prostitution for young women as well as sexualizing them. Høigård and Finstad discuss an autobiographical account by a prostitute, Ida Halvorsen, who comments that 'It was drummed into us over and over that a woman's body was her most important asset' (Høigård and Finstad 1992: 18). Ida describes how she eventually incorporated that image of women into her view of herself. Høigård and Finstad argue that this process represented an essential and necessary self-transformation a woman undergoes before she begins to prostitute herself (1992: 18). That image of a woman's body as potential capital is readily accessible to young women in telephone boxes in central London and Brighton.

Research outcomes and solutions

There has been extensive feminist debate about both prostitution and pornography, at the heart of which are opposed understandings of choice and exploitation. The presence of cards advertising prostitution in telephone boxes reinforces prostitution as a legitimate form of work. In this prostitution milieu, women market their bodies and advertise services thereby allowing their clients to choose between them as sexual commodities. The pornographic content of some cards serves both to market prostitution encounters and provide potential scripts for them. From the perspective of prostitution and pornography as exploitation, the presence of cards increases public access to prostitution to men and women who might not otherwise have become involved. The pornographic cards invite readings of violent and degrading sexual activities as pleasurable for, and to be enacted with women. Although unauthorized and discouraged by BT for other reasons, the presence of the cards in telephone boxes serves to normalize pornography and desensitize public perceptions through constant exposure to the pornographic images.

In proposing solutions to BT's problem, we were keen to find ways of regulating the pornographic content of the cards. Inevitably this would involve compromise solutions as BT could not stop women from continuing to produce and place whatever cards they liked, unless they contravened the obscene publications legislation.[6] Our proposal was that BT should provide an authorized space within the phone boxes, which would be restricted in terms of content, to put an end to the pornographic elements. In return, the cards would remain in the phone boxes thereby reducing the costs of printing and distributing the cards. In our interviews with women who were placing advertisements in the telephone boxes, we met with a mixed response. Some, like us, were disturbed by the explicit and pornographic content of cards and were willing to regulate their own cards and enter a compromise settlement with BT. Others were adamant that the present system suited them and they were unwilling to compromise with BT. As it transpired, BT and Westminster City Council also had no intention of accepting any compromise solutions with the women. In the event, our recommendations for a range of possible compromise solutions were unacceptable to our sponsors and so they suppressed our final report by refusing to publish it or allow us to talk to the media.

Our concern to remove the pornographic cards represented only a partial solution for us. Although we did not recommend any measures to remove all cards from telephone boxes, we were reluctant to endorse prostitution through continued advertising. At the same time, we recognized that for the women involved in prostitution, operating from flats is preferable to street prostitution and depends upon being able to advertise effectively. Also, this method of advertising was unlikely to be stopped. We therefore sought a pragmatic solution, which would meet their needs to advertise while engaged in prostitution but controlling the pornographic content of the cards. The dilemma we faced needs to be addressed through a politics which opposes prostitution while recognizing the needs of women involved in prostitution. One way in which we dealt with this issue was to join a group, Women Against Prostitution of Women (WAPOW), that campaigns against prostitution and seeks wider solutions, such as strategies to enable women to exit from prostitution and better employment and childcare prospects so that women are not driven by economic pressures into prostitution.

Conclusion

The link between pornography and prostitution that we explore in this chapter reverses and expands the more usual connections which conceive the institution of prostitution as the foundation for pornography. Instead, we reflect upon the function of pornography for prostitution. In assessing the evidence for harm of pornographic images displayed on some of the cards advertising sexual services found in telephone boxes, we have argued that such representations of pornography do constitute sexual violence. This is not to shy away from the important issue of the pornography industry involving the abuse of women in its production (Kelly 1990; O'Hara 1991), but to recognize that the representations are nonetheless still an aspect of that abuse, feeding into and stimulating the demand for it. Cameron and Frazer (1992: 381) argue that feminists must challenge pornography because:

> In the sphere of sexuality, pornography is a significant source of ideas and narratives. It transmits to those who use it – primarily men but also women – notions of transcendence and sexual mastery as intrinsic to sexual pleasure.

Given that the primary aim of our research was defined by terms of reference specified by those commissioning the research, our conclusions here are tentative. The presence of the cards in telephone boxes contributes to the normalization of prostitution in urban life and lends an unwelcome legitimacy to pornography, with continuous exposure to such images reinforcing their cultural acceptability, the commodification of women's sexuality and of sexual violence. The impact of this normalization process was evident from our research, which suggests that some of those who use public telephone boxes in affected areas are becoming inured to the images. Initially they stated that they did not object to the cards, but on reflection considered the content of the cards to be offensive. What may be happening is that the ability to reflect critically on the pornographic images contained within some of the cards is being eroded by constant exposure.

The very location of the cards in telephone boxes means that they are available to men who may not normally purchase other forms of pornography. It is cause for concern that pornographic images are used to market prostitution where the cards become an invitation to translate fantasies into an accessible reality during the prostitution encounter. Like advertising, pornography deals expressly in the manufacture of fantasy. Jane Caputi (1992) argues that such fantasies and daydreams represent rehearsals for future activity, and hence represent part of the thinking upon which behaviour is based. Like advertising, these pornographic images with their endlessly reiterated clichés provide images to be incorporated into men's daydreams, scripts to be enacted (Caputi 1992: 216). Indeed, Høigård and Finstad found that some of the clients they interviewed stated explicitly that 'trying out some of the ideas they got from pornography is what prostitution is all about' (1992: 93). Thus the pornographic cards provide exemplars for prostitution encounters as well as invitations to men to purchase the sexual services on offer.

Notes

1 As far as possible, we have tried to maintain a distinction between the institution of prostitution and the women involved in it.
2 Various laws, particularly those aiming at littering offences, have been used in attempts to stop the carding of phone boxes. None have so far proved successful.
3 The difficulties of conducting commissioned research according to feminist objectives in a context where neither the terms of reference nor the rest of the research team were feminist, is discussed more fully in Jenkins *et al.* (1997).
4 The telephone numbers displayed on these cards and in Figures 5.2 and 5.3 date from 1993 and are no longer current.
5 It was once possible to advertise sexual services in the *Yellow Pages* telephone directory but this has been discontinued. However, in Australia, fairly explicit advertisements are placed in the *Yellow Pages*.
6 A police officer we interviewed from the Clubs and Vice Squad remarked that it was almost impossible to bring a successful prosecution under this legislation. He had been involved in a case recently brought to trial in which a prosecution for obscenity was made in relation to a video of anal fist-fucking. The jury acquitted.

References

Barry, K. (1995) *The Prostitution of Sexuality*. New York: New York University Press.
Bennett, C. (1992) Finders and keepers, *Guardian*, 28 May.
Boyle, S. (1994) *Working Girls and Their Men*. London: Smith Gryphon.
Bracchip, P. (1992) Dial-a-sex cards are used for swaps in schools, *Brighton Evening Argos*, 15 October.
Cameron, D. and Frazer, E. (1992) On the question of pornography and sexual violence: moving beyond cause and effect, in C. Itzin (ed.) *Pornography: Women, Violence and Civil Liberties*. Oxford: Oxford University Press.
Caputi, J. (1992) Advertising femicide: lethal violence against women in pornography and gorenography, in J. Radford and D. Russell (eds) *Femicide: The Politics of Woman Killing*. Buckingham: Open University Press.
Davidson, J.O. (1995) British sex tourists in Thailand, in M. Maynard and J. Purvis (eds) *(Hetero)sexual politics*. London: Taylor & Francis.
Davidson, J.O. (1996) Prostitution and the contours of control, in J. Weeks and J. Holland (eds) *Sexual Cultures: Communication, Values and Intimacy*. London: Macmillan.
Dworkin, A. (1981) *Pornography: Men Possessing Women*. London: Women's Press.
Edwards, S. (1993) Selling the body, keeping the soul: sexuality, power, the theories and realities of prostitution, in S. Scott and D. Morgan (eds) *Body Matters*. London: Falmer Press.
Giobbe, E. (1993) Women hurt in systems of prostitution engaged in revolt. *Trouble and Strife*, 26: 22–7.
Hansard (1994) Standing Committee B (1993–4) (Criminal Justice and Public Order Bill), 8th March 1994, c.1292. London: HMSO.

Hopkins, K. and Burke, R. (1995) Women working within the ancillary sex industry: an ethnographic study of live telephone sex calls. Paper presented at the British Sociological Association Annual Conference, Leicester, 10 April.

Høigård, C. and Finstad, L. (1992) *Backstreets: Prostitution, Money and Love*. Cambridge: Polity.

Itzin, C. and Sweet, C. (1993) Women's experience of pornography: UK magazine survey evidence, in C. Itzin (ed.) *Pornography: Women, Violence and Civil Liberties*. Oxford: Oxford University Press.

Jarvinen, M. (1993) *Of Vice and Women: Shades of Prostitution*. Oslo: Scandinavian University Press.

Jenkins, C., O'Neill, M. and Swirsky, R. (1997) Can commissioned research be feminist and can conflicting interests be served? in M. Ang-Lygate, C. Corrin and M. Henry (eds) *Desperately Seeking Sisterhood: Still Challenging and Building*. London: Taylor and Francis.

Jewell, P. (1993) *Vice Art*. London.

Kappeler, S. (1992) Pornography: the representation of power, in C. Itzin (ed.) *Pornography: Women, Violence and Civil Liberties*. Oxford: Oxford University Press.

Kelly, L. (1988) *Surviving Sexual Violence*. Cambridge: Polity.

Kelly, L. (1990) Abuse in the making. *Trouble and Strife*, 19: 32–7.

Lacey, N. (1993) Theory into practice? Pornography and the public/private dichotomy. *Journal of Law and Society*, 20(1): 93–113.

McKeganey, N. and Barnard, R. (1996) *Sex Work on the Streets*. Buckingham: Open University Press.

MacKinnon, C. (1994) *Only Words*. London: HarperCollins.

MacLeod, E. (1982) *Women Working: Prostitution Now*. London: Croom Helm.

O'Hara, M. (1991) Making feminist law? *Trouble and Strife*, 21: 33–9.

Phoenix, J. (1995) Prostitution: problematising the definition, in M. Maynard and J. Purvis (eds) *(Hetero)sexual Politics*. London: Taylor & Francis.

Plumridge, E., Chetrrynd, J., Reed, A. and Gifford, S. (1997) Discourses of emotionality in commercial sex: the missing client voice. *Feminism and Psychology*, 7(2): 165–81.

Russell, D. (1993) *Against Pornography: The Evidence of Harm*. Berkeley, CA: Russell Publications.

Sun (1992) Kids' vice cards craze, 17 September.

Wynter, S. (1988) Whisper: women hurt in systems of prostitution engaged in revolt, in F. Delacoste and P. Alexander (eds) *Sex Work: Writings by Women in the Sex Industry*. London: Virago.

6 Damaged children to throwaway women: from care to prostitution

Melissa Friedberg

This research project was prompted by a passing comment made by a friend working in an anti-pornography organization. She mentioned the number of calls they received from women involved in pornography and prostitution who had been in care, and thought that exploring this area would be a useful piece of research which might interest me. It did, and I decided to concentrate on prostitution (see Swirsky and Jenkins, Chapter 5, this volume for a discussion of the links between pornography and prostitution). It combined my activism in violence against women campaigns and services, and work-based involvement in social services provision and training.

The project focused on exploring the connections between young women's involvement in prostitution and their having been in care. Their experiences as vulnerable girls in the care system were looked at, as well as what it was about the 'care' environment – an environment that was meant to be safer, more protected, more able to 'care' for them and provide them with more options and choices than their family homes – which led to their involvement in prostitution. Though previous research has already noted the number of care leavers involved in prostitution (Høigård and Finstad 1992; O'Neill 1994), I wanted to explore this area further by concentrating on care leavers and looking at ways of improving the care system, while recognizing that it is not the only factor leading to some young women engaging in prostitution.

This chapter focuses on three aspects of this project: methodological issues, difficulties and contradictions encountered in doing this research; the women's experiences of care; and suggestions for addressing some of the policy and practice limitations of the care system.

Methodology

This research was undertaken in 1995–6 in a large city in the UK. I interviewed 25 women aged between 16 and 35. Other than three, they all had

been in care and involved in prostitution. Out of the three, two were prostituting but had not been in care and one had been in care but was not
prostituting. Nineteen women were white, three were black and three were
black of mixed parentage. They came into care at different points in their
childhood, from babies to age 15. The vast majority started prostituting
while in care and were working as street prostitutes (see Swirsky and Jenkins,
Chapter 5, this volume, for a discussion of terminology). For most of the
women it was the first time anyone had asked them about their life stories
in such a focused and detailed way; they were surprised that I was interested. Some of the women were keen for their stories to be told to help
other girls and young women in the care system to bring about change.

Gaining access to women in prostitution and the prostitution milieu proved
to be exceedingly arduous (see Høigård and Finstad 1992 for further discussion). I spent many frustrating months contacting a wide range of agencies,
projects and individuals across the UK before my letters and phone calls paid
off. I found women prepared to be interviewed through a drop-in centre
which ran a weekly support group for street prostitutes. This was the only
project contacted that asked the women if they were willing to speak to me.
Because of the workers' perceived sensitivity of the subject matter and their
tenuous relationship with women in prostitution and/or care leavers, many
did not want to risk jeopardizing their relationship by passing on my re-
quest. This shed light on the women's immediate environment and was
particularly enlightening in relation to the services they were or had been
using. I query the organizational ethos and protectiveness of not giving the
women the opportunity to decide for themselves, and the attitudes workers
have in relation to users' abilities, vulnerability and self-determination.

The problems of access did not stop once I had 'arrived'. Finding women
to interview was a continuous, laborious process. The most effective approaches were participating in group sessions, hanging out on the streets,
and being introduced to other women by women I had already interviewed.
They told them what I was doing, what the interview was like and encouraged them to talk to me. They also approached women they knew by sight
and asked them if they had been in care.

It still proved difficult to get women to spend their working time talking
to me. It was suggested that I pay for the interviews as this would compens-
ate the women for their time, meet their immediate need to earn money,
and matched the women's view that everything is done for something. By
paying I would acknowledge that time spent with me cut into their valuable
earning time. It was also a less exploitative arrangement in relation to a
group who are and have consistently been exploited.

I managed to secure a grant to pay £10 per interview. Word quickly
spread that I was paying for interviews which helped enormously, though
by this stage I had already been around for a while, which was also helpful.
Even with the offer of payment, however, gaining interviews was still a
protracted process. Some of the women were surprised, though pleased at
being paid, and said that they would have done the interview anyway.

Sandy stated that at least she did not have to get her hands dirty for this money.[1]

Joining the women's drop-in sessions facilitated a level of rapport with both the women and the workers. It also helped to spread the word that I was interviewing women who had been in care. The most successful mode of contact, however, was hanging out on and around the same streets, rain or shine, hot or cold. This resulted in my being visible and a familiar face. It also meant that I was not located in a comfortable and distant office, which in any case would not have been productive. The women accepted and became accustomed to my being there. This approach also helped my familiarization with the prostitution environment.

Initially I found hanging out on the streets uncomfortable and awkward. Waiting around trying to find women to interview was an uneasy activity. This decreased as I got to know some of the women and the locality, to the point where I could easily slip into being 'on the street'. It was tedious when few women were around, but exciting and worthwhile when I was able to interview someone. I also spent time chatting to women I had previously met through this research, which was enjoyable. It was good to have someone to talk to rather than walking around by myself in endless circles.

Because I was hanging out on the streets talking to the women, some who did not know me assumed I was prostituting. One offered me advice about how to get punters. Some expressed concern for my safety and gave me advice on how to take care of myself. In fact I did not feel unsafe. Being in the city centre there were always people around and places I could go into if I wanted a break and to get off the streets. Luckily, and in contrast to O'Neill's (1996) experience, I did not encounter any frightening incidents while doing this research.

To the amusement of the women, some of the men assumed that I was 'doing business'. Hanging out in a locality where street prostitutes were working was clearly seen as a sign of my availability, as it would be for any woman. This raises wider issues of men's sexualization of women and assumptions about women's availability to sexually service men.

An interesting part of the process was the parallels between my looking for women to interview and their looking for punters. I hung out on steps and street corners, and followed their route, on their patch. As they did, I also popped in and out of the drop-in centre to get a break from the tedium of the streets and recoup my energy. As they kept going back onto the streets to earn more money, I kept going back to do more interviews. As they set goals for the amount of money they needed to earn before calling it quits, I calculated how many interviews I wanted to do before calling it quits. On the occasions I did consecutive interviews with little break in-between, I felt like I was on a conveyor belt. It made me think of the conveyor belt the women were on, doing one punter after the other. The similarities rested with the monotony of hanging out, in the attempt to accomplish very different aims involving different 'transactions'. I did not have to subject myself to the sexual abuse and harm the women did to earn money.

The interviews took place in a variety of venues, from offices to the street. It was not possible to plan them or make appointments. Once a woman agreed to be interviewed it needed to take place immediately. Most of the interviews lasted approximately 30 minutes as it was not possible to get the women to stay in one place for much longer. The women were often curious as to why I wanted to interview them. The majority stated that nobody had ever asked them these kinds of questions. They were surprised that somebody was interested in them, their lives, their experiences and what they thought.

I chose to do non-standardized interviews as the most appropriate and least oppressive way of getting the women's stories. This enabled them to lead the interview, and emphasize and concentrate on what they saw as the most important issues. I had issues I wanted to cover and a few starter questions. I did not use a written interview schedule as I thought that this might be experienced as off-putting and formal, interrupting the natural flow of conversation, and because of their history of an abundance of formal interviews in care and in negotiating access to services, for example, housing.

After introducing myself and the aims of the interview, the women led its direction and focus. At times they started by discussing what was most pertinent for them at that moment, after which I reintroduced a discussion about their experiences of care. For example, Alice was very angry at having been ripped off by a punter the previous night. She began the interview by describing what had happened and her anger at how she had been treated. Mary spent most of the interview talking about her mother, trying to make sense of her mother's treatment of her. It was important not to interrupt silences and give the women a chance to think. As I got to know the women better I was able to point out some of the contradictions in their stories without being threatening. For example, Karen talked about her family being a happy one, and later went on to say that her father had sexually abused her. I commented that this did not really sound like happy families.

On occasion I was asked for my opinion about something that had occurred in the woman's life. At times I felt that these questions were asked to test me out, to see whose side I was on (see Horn 1995 for further discussion). I did not overtly express opinions in terms of who I thought was right or wrong in the particular situation, but made it clear that I was sympathetic to how the women felt about what had happened. Taking sides would not have made me more trustworthy, but would have revealed a lack of understanding of the women's complex and contradictory relationship to care workers and being in care. It would have blocked their exploration of their experiences and understanding. These questions were also asked because the women were trying to make sense of their experiences. Some used the interviews to reflect on and make sense of their lives (Kelly 1988). Even though some used the interview for reflection I do not think this lasted very long. Their existence involves cutting off emotionally to survive; thinking about what has and is going on for them is too difficult and painful. Also this sole interview was only a brief interlude in their lives.

The women often questioned me to see if I had understood what they said, to ensure that I had. Other than the simple fact of wanting to be heard, we were also communicating across dissimilar cultures and lifestyles. It is difficult to gauge the dynamics of being interviewed by someone perceived as belonging to mainstream society (Høigård and Finstad 1992), and how this might have affected communication, understanding and the content of the interviews. Spending time in the drop-in centre and on the streets was useful in giving me a level of insight and understanding of the women's world which I would not have gained from interviews. Not going into interviews cold helped overcome some of the communication barriers. A simple example is just picking up unfamiliar terminology.

Some of the women thanked me for the interview, stating that talking to me had been good and interesting. Being listened to and having themselves and their experiences validated was significant; on the whole a rare occurrence for them.

While participating in the interview the women had to engage with me to a degree. To enable them to return to the streets they needed to disengage. I spent time after the interviews with the tape turned off chatting about whatever they wanted to talk about to facilitate time and space for disengagement. Some discussed what they wanted to do with their lives, which involved getting out of prostitution. It often involved helping others with similar experiences, as they felt that their experiences provided them with first-hand knowledge and understanding.

Because the interviews raised many difficult and painful feelings it was important that the women had somewhere to go for follow-up support, if they so desired. This was available with the group. After her interview, Carol went and talked to the group about some of the areas she had raised.

As the research progressed I discussed some of my preliminary analyses with the project workers to keep them up-to-date and to get feedback. I also managed to discuss some ideas with one of the women I had interviewed. This was useful in enabling me to check out and refine my ideas. I sent copies of conference papers I presented for the workers' comments and to circulate amongst the women. These papers were also distributed to other workers in the building who had contact with the women. The feedback I got was that the workers found these papers useful. Feedback from the women was limited. The one woman who commented found the paper represented a true picture, but felt that I should have included more material.

It was both impossible and painful to see the women in the situation they were in without identifying with their sexualization, abuse and lack of opportunities (Høigård and Finstad 1992). I had to stop thinking about what they had to do to earn money, and just concentrate on my interviews and interaction with them. I returned to see the women a few months after I completed the research as a way of tying it up, and directly informing them what was happening with it. Unfortunately not many women were on the streets at the time. I still think about them and wonder how they are doing.

As I went along, I attempted to devise a usable blend of ethno/feminist methodology which worked with street prostitutes and their chaotic lifestyle (see Skeggs 1994, for further discussion of feminist ethnography). This approach allowed for necessary flexibility and locating myself in the women's environment. It enabled me to acquire a wealth of material and encourage the women's active participation in the telling of their stories (Stanley and Wise 1993; Maynard and Purvis 1994), with the aim of bringing about change (Kelly *et al.* 1994; O'Neill 1996).

Care

All the women spent the majority of their time in care in group homes, though a few spent some time in foster care. The findings therefore focus on group care. They went into care as a result of physical, sexual and/or emotional abuse; neglect; the inability of their families to adequately care for them; and because of their running away from home. Some found a security in care; Sandy said that care was good because she slept in the same bed every night and was fed three meals a day.

The women raised a wide range of areas in relation to their experiences of care. Though there were differences among them, there was a remarkable consensus of experience and opinion, even though they had been in care at different times, for different lengths of time, in different homes and in different parts of the country. The overriding similarity was their sense of loss and not feeling cared for. The term 'care' is in itself a misrepresentation of their experiences. Interestingly, most thought that the system had improved since they had been in care, whether they had left recently or a number of years ago.

The main issues the women raised were the lack of attention, supervision and support, not having anyone to talk to, too many rules, too strict a regime, and having no one who cared about them. They expressed feeling unloved:

> It was funny being in care, like they fed you, watered you.
>
> (Mary)

> There's no morals. I mean there's no care, there's no love or anything in there, is there?
>
> (Jean)

They also talked about feeling lost, having low self-esteem, and having no sense of self and individuality:

> One thing about the home, it takes away your sense of who you are. Sometimes I feel a bit lost. And I've never sought it [counselling] either. But I keep cracking up though. Because there is a part of me that's sort of missing. It's like doing a jigsaw puzzle with missing pieces, no matter how hard you search you can't find it. Then I think maybe if I went to counselling I probably wouldn't like myself. And at the moment I can just cope with myself. I don't feel bad all the time.
>
> (Diane)

They received little positive encouragement or support which boosted the development of their self-esteem, identity and sense of self. This left them feeling insecure and unsure. This was further compounded for the black and mixed race women; they mentioned the lack of acknowledgement of their colour and culture and their isolation:

> The only kids in the area that were black were kids from [care] homes.
>
> (Diane)

Joan, who is of mixed parentage, talked about her attempts to bleach her skin.

Many of the women reported that they frequently engaged in 'difficult' behaviour and activities, the reasons behind which were often not explored by workers. Constraints on staff time and the structure of the homes usually did not allow for this. It was more a matter of controlling and containing behaviour to enable the home to function with as little disruption as possible. Absconding is a good example of this. In many cases the women reported a history of persistently running away from home – a pattern that was repeated in care. The reasons for the continuation of this pattern of behaviour and their absconding from care was often not discussed. Instead the women found that upon their return they were punished.

While for the most part they did not feel cared for or protected, they overwhelmingly felt sheltered from and unskilled in relation to life outside the homes. They were unaware of the rules and codes of conduct of the outside world and ill-equipped to manage. A few mentioned that they did not know you had to pay for things when you went into a shop. Most did not know how to look for a job. When one of the workers at the drop-in was browsing through the job adverts in the newspaper the women there could not understand why she was doing this. The only example of alternative 'employment' some of the women came up with was shoplifting. They did not have any experience of progressively negotiating their independence, control over their lives and developing the ability to manage in wider society, as can occur with children in family homes.

On the whole, care had not provided the women with stability, security, a sense of self, a sense of belonging, or the ability to make their way in the world. It in fact contributed to their marginalized social positions and problems in coping. They talked about their difficulty in forming friendships as adults, leaving them isolated and alone:

> I got close to no one. It took me a good few, two years or something before I can get close to anyone.
>
> (Marion)

The women spoke of learning about prostitution while in care. The care context provided a route for the girls' entry into prostitution, and access for adults to vulnerable girls who were easy to exploit. Most often they were introduced into prostitution by other girls who they saw earning money and able to buy things. In some instances the girls introduced other girls to adults who were pimping them and to the men who were using them:

It's [care] like prison, you go into prison, and you come out an armed
robber with shotguns and that. It's the same sort of set up. But whereas
in prison you have a time for release.

(Mary)

Most of the women felt that the staff were aware of their prostituting.
They stated that it was obvious and difficult to miss. For example, they had
money, were able to buy things and were seen hanging out on the streets.
Staff either ignored it or punished them by sending them to secure units.
They felt that few measures were taken to challenge either their prostituting
or drug use. They were angry about this and felt that something could have
been done to prevent the way they had ended up. On the other hand, their
responses to attempts by staff to control and challenge their behaviour were
to ignore and resist these attempts.

One of the main contradictions experienced by the women, and one of
the most difficult to address, were their feelings that because staff were
being paid to care for them care could not be real:

Doing what they were paid to do innit?

(Carol)

Because they were paid carers, staff were seen as just doing what they did to
earn money. Staff were not there because they loved, cared for and wanted
to be with the girls. Simultaneously the girls also created barriers and excuses
not to get close to people as survival and self-protection strategies. On the
other hand, some did form positive, caring relationships with individual
members of staff. When they felt they were being listened to they said that
things were different for them:

One, I did talk to her and I did open out to her. And I told her about me
being abused. It helped me, I mean to get it off me chest.

(Karen)

When talking about workers they felt really cared about them, the women's
whole demeanour changed. They were animated, relaxed, often smiled and
recalled 'good times'.

Some did not want too much caring because they could not cope with this
attention. Their pre-care experiences were frequently about getting on with
life and fending for themselves, making it difficult for them to learn to trust
and depend on someone. When workers wanted to help them and talk to
them the women often did not want to know; they did not want to talk to
anyone. They talked about not being able to accept help. Many said that
they now realize things were done to help them, but they could not see it at
the time.

For some of the women, even if they experienced care positively, they
were not with their families and wanted to be with them whatever the
circumstances. Anything else was second best; nobody else could care for
and about them in that way. Although some felt that it was better for them

to be away from home, it was clear that nuclear family ideology negatively affected them; they felt stigmatized and different from other children and the 'norm'. Some did not want other children to know that they were in care. Governmental (of whichever political persuasion) emphasis on the two-parent, heterosexual family as the most acceptable and appropriate place to raise children is very damaging, particularly so for those whose familial circumstances necessitate their removal from home, as was the case for these women. This gives these children confusing messages which are hard for them to make sense of, and their adaptation to being in care, in itself difficult, even more so.

The women talked about wanting to leave care, then feeling shocked when they finally did leave. They were suddenly on their own and living by themselves after being surrounded by so many others. Many felt like they had been dumped without anybody taking responsibility for them. They expressed feeling lost and abandoned:

> Oh no, out the door, that was it.
>
> (Mary)

This isolation and lack of anybody to turn to left them vulnerable and alone in the world.

This research confirmed previous documentation of aftercare experiences in terms of the preponderance of breakdowns in communication, lack of continuity of care, lack of coordination between agencies, high rates of unemployment, shortage of money, and the high percentage of care leavers who are homeless (Page and Clark 1977; Stein and Carey 1986; *Childfacts* 1992; Mackinnon 1992; Fletcher 1993; Woolf 1994; Strathdee and Johnson 1994; Action on Aftercare Consortium 1996).

Ways forward: improving care

Though the reasons for the women's involvement in prostitution do not solely lie in the care system, there are areas of policy and practice that can be addressed, as there is continuity in their progression from care to prostitution.

The need for emotional caring, support, being listened to and valued, having somebody to talk to, stability, clear boundaries, and a consistent, formal education while in care have all been raised elsewhere, as has the lack of continuity of carers in the young person's life (Page and Clark 1977; Stein and Carey 1986; Parker *et al.* 1991; Garnett 1992; Fletcher 1993; Stein 1993; Kahan 1994; Lees 1994; Berridge and Brodie 1998). Approaches are needed in which care can be experienced as caring.

When the women talked about what would have made care better they mentioned having someone to talk to, someone who listened to them, getting support and the homes not being too strict. By the women's own admission they were difficult children, but they were also damaged children. Emotional caring, being valued, getting more attention, having someone who is proud of them, clear boundaries, stability and consistency of carers are all needed. This needs to occur alongside having somebody who will stick with them even when they are 'bad' – naughty, acting out and not obeying the rules; getting help in dealing with and discussing their pre-care experiences and obtaining educational qualifications. Workers they felt cared were ones who paid attention to them, were interested in them, talked to them, spent time with them, and made them feel that they were special, not just one of many. Individual workers clearly can and do make a difference, but consistency and continuity of carers is necessary.

In terms of the future more work is needed to help the children talk about how they feel and establish significant relationships, even when they say that they do not want to talk and are rejecting. All the women mentioned that having had someone to talk to would have improved care. Helping them deal with their pre-care experiences is vital in terms of enabling them to work through their past and move on; take some control over their lives; and develop positive identities, sense of themselves and self-esteem. This again requires ongoing and consistent support, and the ability to engage with difficult children.

Their pattern of running away from home and absconding from care needs to be broken. Girls and young women are particularly vulnerable when they are on the streets. This was the time many began prostituting. While in care they need help in developing safer strategies to deal with situations they find uncomfortable and/or difficult.

Ongoing support and having someone to turn to, depend and rely on is also needed once they leave care, as is the case for many young people when leaving their family homes. Providing this support entails recognizing and addressing the fact that many children in care have not formed significant relationships with staff, foster carers or other children because they have frequently been moved and are unable to form relationships. Many of the women just absconded and made their own way.

The gradual development of independence, knowledge of, and the ability to manage in society needs to be built into their entire time in care. It cannot wait until they are about to leave care, as in the work of leaving-care projects, which are often too little too late.

O'Neill (1994) discusses the emotional neediness of care leavers. The emotional deprivation the women experience is key, since as a result they are vulnerable and easy to exploit. They are looking and are often desperate for love, care, and for somebody to take care of them. It is important that care enables the women to develop a sense of belonging/inclusion, security, stability, control over their lives, a positive sense of self and identity, and that they have options and opportunities. Things 'happen' to these young people and they do not know or understand why. They feel that they have no rights, no future and no control over what happens in their lives. Linked to this is a sense of powerlessness, lack of job opportunities, and messages they are given about their sexuality. This makes going into prostitution an obvious step.

Conclusion

Over the years there have been numerous reports highlighting the inadequacies of the care system and making suggestions for changes (Wagner 1988; Utting 1991, 1997; Howe 1992; Warner 1992). As Utting (1991) has pointed out, the changes required are widespread and substantial. For example, improving care is not just a matter of having better trained staff; the culture and attitudes towards care need transforming.[2] Changes at a local level that are necessary and would make a difference need to occur within a wider context of the fundamental metamorphosis of the culture, ethos, aims and attitudes towards the care system. The low status of care is related to it historically being viewed as women's work which comes 'naturally' (Utting 1991). This implies that it does not require training or skills and is thus not valued. If workers and the work are valued then perhaps so will the children, which would be a positive starting point.

The present Labour government has recently published reports which again highlight the inadequacies and limitations of the care system and put forward suggestions for changes. These include strategic approaches to children's services in setting targets, for example, in relation to educational attainment and the number of times a child in care can be moved; financial rewards for authorities that meet these targets; the need for local authorities to act as 'corporate parents' with a range of departments – for example, social services, housing, leisure, education – taking collective responsibility for children in care; and increased funding for social services (Department of Health 1998; House of Commons Health Committee 1998; Social Services Inspectorate 1998; Social Services Inspectorate/Audit Commission 1998). These reports are more specific than previous ones, though not without criticism, for example, in relation to how targets were set and the strategies for meeting them (Inman 1998; Valios 1998). Nonetheless, there is some demonstration of the political will to actually implement changes. Hopefully they will materialize. In order to bring about the widespread changes needed in the 'care' system, however, they need to take place in conjunction with changes in the ethos as highlighted above.

It is difficult to eradicate the stigma attached to being in care. Høigård and Finstad (1992) found that the women they interviewed had had extensive experience of institutionalization ranging from orphanages, reform schools, psychiatric institutions and prisons. They state that these women were already rejected by normal society before they prostituted. If girls in care felt that they were not viewed as second-class citizens outside of society, and that being in care was not their fault, they might stand a better chance.

The women consistently queried how 'care' could really be care if someone was paid. It is not possible to get past the fact that this is paid employment, though, as pointed out, some of the women were still able to form positive relationships with some staff. What is interesting and requires further exploration is that it is an obvious contractual relationship involving a financial transaction that is repeated, reinforcing their experience and views that all human interaction involves some sort of compensation (everything is done for something). As workers were paid to 'care' for them, so the women are being paid to 'service' punters.

Recognition and acknowledgement of the occurrence of prostitution in care is needed throughout the system, with guidelines and support in place to enable workers to counter it effectively. Although the women felt that they had been sheltered in terms of their limited ability to manage outside of the homes, they certainly had access to learning about one survival strategy. Preventing the women from becoming involved in prostitution is key. Once they are prostituting it is very difficult to get out and turn around their entire lives.

Taking forward the research

In line with my wish, shared by some of the women, for this research to promote change, I have incorporated it into both activist and academic arenas; the latter in presenting my findings at conferences and incorporating this material into my teaching; the former in becoming involved in setting up a national anti-prostitution network, Women Against the Prostitution of Women (WAPOW). This organization opposes prostitution as an institution that sexually exploits women and children, while supporting women in prostitution through extending support services, creating options and developing exit strategies. The long-term aim is to end prostitution.

Acknowledgements

Thanks to Anne for suggesting this research, to Frances for transcribing the tapes, to the Project workers for their help and support, and, most of all, to the women who took part.

Notes

1 All names are pseudonyms.
2 The need for well trained staff who are able to work with difficult and damaged children has consistently been noted.

References

Action on Aftercare Consortium (1996) *Too Much Too Young: The Failure of Social Policy in Meeting the Needs of Care Leavers*. Ilford: Barnardo's.
Berridge, D. and Brodie, I. (1998) *Children's Homes Revisited*. London: Jessica Langley.
Childfacts: Young People Leaving Care (1992) London: National Children's Bureau.

Department of Health (1998) *Quality Protects*. London: Department of Health.

Finch, J. (1984) 'It's great to have someone to talk to': the ethics and politics of interviewing women, in C. Bell and H. Roberts (eds) *Social Researching: Politics, Problems, Practice*. London: RKP.

Fletcher, B. (1993) *Not Just a Name: The Views of Young People in Foster and Residential Care*. London: National Consumer Council.

Garnett, L. (1992) *Leaving Care and After*. London: National Children's Bureau.

Høigård, C. and Finstad, L. (1992) *Backstreets: Prostitution, Money and Love*. Cambridge: Polity.

Horn, R. (1995) Reflexivity in placement: women interviewing women. *Feminism and Psychology*, February, 5(1):94–8.

House of Commons Health Committee (1998) *Children Looked After by Local Authorities*. London: Stationery Office.

Howe, J. (1992) *The Quality of Care*, report of the residential staffs' inquiry chaired by Lady Howe. Luton: Local Government Management Board.

Inman, K. (1998) Thou shalt meet thy new targets. *Community Care*, 15–21 October: 8–9.

Kahan, B. (1994) *Growing up in Groups*. London: HMSO.

Kelly, L. (1988) *Surviving Sexual Violence*. Cambridge: Polity.

Kelly, L., Burton, S. and Regan, L. (1994) Researching women's lives or studying women's oppression? Reflections on what constitutes feminist research, in M. Maynard and J. Purvis (eds) *Researching Women's Lives from a Feminist Perspective*. London: Taylor & Francis.

Lees, B. (ed.) (1994) *Time to Listen: The Experiences of Young People in Foster and Residential Care*. London: Childline.

Mackinnon, I. (1992) Parliament and politics: More help urged for young leaving care, *Independent*, 24 September: 5.

Maynard, M. and Purvis, J. (1994) Doing feminist research, in M. Maynard and J. Purvis (eds) *Researching Women's Lives from a Feminist Perspective*. London: Taylor & Francis.

O'Neill, M. (1994) Prostitution and the state: towards a feminist practice, in C. Lupton and T. Gillespie (eds) *Working with Violence*. Basingstoke: Macmillan.

O'Neill, M. (1996) Researching prostitution and violence: towards a feminist praxis, in M. Hester, L. Kelly and J. Radford (eds) *Women, Violence and Male Power: Feminist Activism, Research and Practice*. Buckingham: Open University Press.

Page, R. and Clark, G.A. (eds) (1977) *Who Cares? Young People in Care Speak Out*. London: Children's Bureau.

Parker, R., Ward, H., Jackson, S., Aldgate, J. and Wedge, P. (eds) (1991) *Looking After Children: Assessing Outcomes in Childcare*. London: HMSO.

Skeggs, B. (1994) Situating the production of feminist ethnography, in M. Maynard and J. Purvis (eds) *Researching Women's Lives from a Feminist Perspective*. London: Taylor & Francis.

Social Services Inspectorate (1998) *Someone Else's Children*. London: SSI.

Social Services Inspectorate/Audit Commission (1998) *Getting the Best from Social Services*. London: Department of Health.

Stanley, L. and Wise, S. (1993) *Breaking Out Again*. London: Routledge.

Stein, M. (1993) The abuses and uses of residential child care, in H. Ferguson, R. Gilligan and R. Torode (eds) *Surviving Childhood Adversity: Issues for Policy and Practice*. Dublin: Social Studies Press, Trinity College.

Stein, M. and Carey, K. (1986) *Leaving Care*. Oxford: Basil Blackwell.

Strathdee, R. and Johnson, M. (1994) *Out of Care and on the Streets: Young People – Care Leavers and Homelessness.* London: Centrepoint.

Utting, W. (1991) *Children in the Public Care: A Review of Residential Child Care.* London: HMSO.

Utting, W. (1997) *People Like Us: The Report of the Review of the Safeguards for Children Living Away From Home.* London: Stationery Office.

Valios, N. (1998) Special Report. *Community Care,* 24–30 September: 2–3.

Wagner, G. (1988) *Residential Care: A Positive Choice.* London: HMSO.

Warner, N. (1992) *Choosing with Care: The Report of the Committee of Inquiry into the Selection, Development and Management of Staff in Children's Homes.* London: HMSO.

Woolf, M. (1994) Youngsters kept off the streets, *Independent,* 12 September: 4.

7 Sexual violence and the school curriculum

Lynne Harne

This chapter discusses some of the issues and strategies involved in under-taking preventative education on sexual violence in secondary schools, and looks at the need for changes in educational policy to support this work. It is based on findings from a small scale qualitative research project undertaken with teachers in seven secondary schools in the south-east of England, and information provided by coordinators of some preventative projects in dif-ferent areas of the country. The research aimed to explore the difficulties and constraints for teachers in undertaking this kind of education and to suggest ways forward.[1]

The term preventative education is used here in its broadest sense to include what is known as primary prevention, that is, education that aims to challenge the socially constructed 'inevitability' of sexually violent, objectify-ing and exploitative gendered relationships. It goes beyond educational approaches, which only look at ways that abuse can be 'avoided' or victims can seek support once it has taken place, by aiming to stop male violence occurring in the first place.[2]

The Zero Tolerance Public Education Campaigns, which were funded by a number of local authorities in Scotland and England in the mid-1990s, are examples of feminist-initiated primary prevention. These have aimed to challenge the acceptability of male sexual violence and placed the respons-ibility for it firmly on men, through a series of publicly displayed posters addressing domestic violence, rape and the sexual abuse of children (Foley 1993). More recently, posters have been produced specifically aimed at young people (Zero Tolerance Trust 1998).

School preventative education is of necessity far-reaching, needing to address aspects of the informal as well as the formal curriculum. It entails critically examining the influence of the school environment and policies and practices on pupil and teacher behaviours, equal opportunities and child protection in order to stop sexual violence taking place in schools, in addition to providing education programmes on the unacceptability of sexual violence more generally.

The context

Within second wave feminism, it has long been recognized that male sexual violence needed to be addressed in the education system. During the late 1970s and 1980s feminists developed an understanding that schools are sites where gendered power relationships and their interconnections with other forms of institutionalized power such as racism and classism are reproduced and reinforced. While the 1970s saw early feminist attempts to change what was then known as 'sex-role' stereotyping in the school curriculum (Sharpe 1976), during the 1980s they were beginning to challenge the 'sexual under-world of schooling', as part of the overall movement to confront sexism within the education system (Wood 1984; Arnot 1994).

Strategies included developing school policies to tackle sexual harassment in the increasing numbers of mixed-sex schools, and initiating education, which included looking at ways of empowering girls to resist different forms of sexual violence (O'Hara 1988; Jones and Mahoney 1989). Within personal and social education these involved challenging normative constructions of male sexuality, undertaking anti-sexist work with boys, as well as providing more positive approaches to sexuality for girls (Askew and Ross 1988; Holly 1989). These approaches were beginning to go beyond the traditional 'plumbing and prevention' approach of much sex education (Lenskyj 1990) which limited itself to education on the 'reproductive organs', and held girls largely responsible for male sexual behaviour and the prevention of pregnancy and sexually transmitted diseases.

The impact of government policy

However, during the 1980s the emergent agenda of sexual politics in education was increasingly viewed as undermining traditional heteropatriarchal family values by the Moral Right. It was used by the Thatcher government to argue for central government control of the content of school education in general and tighter control of the provision of sex education specifically. In the context of sex education, a series of government measures placed responsibility with governing bodies for its content and whether it was taught at all. It was also determined that it should be taught within a family values framework, and Section 28 of the Local Government Act 1988 restricted local authorities from 'promoting homosexuality' in education. Although this Act did not place restrictions directly on schools, part of its impact has been to make many teachers uncertain and fearful of taking a broader approach to the teaching of sexuality and sexual relationships.

Further government measures such as the introduction of the National Curriculum, placed the whole of the personal, social and health education curriculum (PSHE) outside of this framework. It was addressed only in non-statutory guidance on cross-curricular themes, such as 'citizenship and family life' and 'health education'. Consequently these subjects became the poor relations of the national curriculum in terms of funding, teacher training and their ideological importance within schools (Thomson and Scott 1992). The government, for example, withdrew funding to local authorities for advisory support and training in this area.

During the early 1990s this minimalist approach was modified as a consequence of pragmatic public health concerns around teenage pregnancies and sexually transmitted diseases, including HIV. The 1993 Sex Education Act made sex education compulsory for secondary schools.[3] It has, however, remained outside the national curriculum so that its lowly status has continued and parents have the right to withdraw their children. Apart from the required teaching on HIV/AIDS and other sexually transmitted diseases, its content remains the responsibility of governing bodies and the statutory 'family values' framework still applies (Department for Education 1994b). This has given individual schools a certain freedom to determine the content of sex education, but has also enabled more conservative schools to limit its content to the medicalized 'plumbing and prevention' approach referred to earlier (Thomson 1995). This is despite the fact that extensive research with young people has shown that what they most want to know more about and discuss in relation to sex education is what the New Right agenda defined as 'controversial issues', such as sexual abuse and lesbian and gay sexuality (see Ingham 1997).

Separate developments around the 'public crisis' of child sexual abuse in the late 1980s resulted in the government requiring schools to produce 'child protection policies' (Department of Education 1988). However, government guidance placed more emphasis on developing 'technical procedures' whereby teachers could identify and report abuse, rather than education to prevent it (Mahoney 1989). Schools were required to display helpline numbers, such as Child Line, although there was no obligation to inform pupils of their rights in this area.

Guidance on child protection policies has suggested that in considering sex education school governors 'will need to consider whether it should include education on sexual abuse' (Department of Education and Employment 1995: 39–41). There is no statutory compulsion to do so, however, and the guidance stresses that it should not 'upset normal, stable relationships between adults and children', in what appears to be an oblique way of stating that it must not destabilize heterosexual family life.

In general, the approach to education on sexual abuse within non-statutory government guidance has been to confine it to primary school education within the topic of 'personal safety', at Key Stage 1 (ages 5–7) and to separate it from any education about sexual relationships (NCC 1990a, 1990b cited in Sex Education Forum 1994a: 14–15).

As a consequence of these policies, formal 'prevention' programmes provided mainly for primary school children have largely centred around degendered and desexualized 'stranger danger' and 'good touches/bad touches' approaches (Scott *et al.* 1998). These have avoided the use of sexual language or giving children information about sexual behaviour, while conveying the misleading message that they are most at risk from strangers rather than from adult men and boys they know (Kelly *et al.* 1991, see also Kelly and Humphries, Chapter 2, this volume). These approaches often fail to recognize power in relation to abuse, and place responsibility on children to avoid abuse through the promotion of assertiveness techniques (e.g. Evans 1995). As such, they can place impossible requirements on children to avoid or stop abuse, particularly where the abuser is in a position of trust or authority or connected with their own families.

Evaluations of similar programmes used in New Zealand and Australia in the 1980s have shown them to be singularly ineffective in enabling young children to identify or name sexual abuse because they are not given the language or understanding that would enable them to do so (Briggs and Hawkins 1994). There are also contradictions in the aim of protecting children as 'sexually innocent' while failing to address the social realities. For instance, they may fail to challenge popular cultural representations which form the background to children's daily lives. Such representations simultaneously condone sexually violent masculine behaviour and the sexualization and objectification of girls from a very young age (Kitzinger 1988; Connelly 1995; Scott *et al.* 1998). Research has shown that boys, for example, gain most of their 'sex education' from the use of and access to pornography (Measor *et al.* 1996; see also Gillespie, Chapter 4, this volume).

The degendering and desexualization strategies of the New Right in the formal curriculum have also been reflected in their approach to school policies generally and to the informal curriculum. For example, 1980s discourses of gender inequality have been redefined more narrowly by limiting their meaning to that of equal access to the national curriculum and equality in exam and test results. This has enabled issues such as sexual harassment to disappear off the equal opportunities agenda in some schools. Further, while government guidance on pupil behaviour requires schools to have policies on racial harassment and bullying and to record incidents, it is left up to schools to decide whether or not they have specific policies on sexual harassment (Department for Education 1994a). This guidance offers no definition of sexual harassment so that schools may be unclear as to its actual meaning.

These UK education policies are in marked contrast to preventative policies and school programmes developed in the Antipodes and Canada since the late 1980s.[4] A central feature of the latter has been to recognize male sexual and physical violence as an abuse of power and an institutionalized form of social control of women and children. Furthermore, there is a recognition that school programmes need to address primary prevention as illustrated by the aims of an Australian state supported programme:

This resource aims to prevent family and community violence as well as violence in schools. The responsibility for violence clearly lies with those who perpetrate it. Since the majority of these are boys and men this resource includes the examination of gender constructions and the values and attitudes that lead to violent behaviour. [It] also aims to raise awareness of the way social structures institutionalise violence by the control and abuse of power.

(Forsey 1994: 10)

On the positive side, renewed opportunities for the development of preventative education have resulted from the UK's signing of the Beijing Platform of Action at the Fourth World Conference on Women in 1995. This international governmental agreement states that woman abuse constitutes a violation of women and girls' human rights and freedoms, and recognized the need for preventative and awareness education in schools. This led to the government acknowledging that schools could address domestic violence through national curriculum subjects and PSHE (Department of Employment 1996). The ratifying by the government of the United Nations Convention on the Rights of the Child (1989) and Council of Europe initiatives also gave some recognition of children's need for 'access to information on non-exploitative sexuality' (Kelly *et al.* 1995: 8). As a consequence, preventative resources on sexual violence developed in the UK may utilize the non-statutory curriculum guidance on the theme of citizenship and family life where the study of human rights and their violation is suggested as a basis and justification for this work (see Morley 1997).[5]

A workshop on school education at the International Conference on Violence, Abuse and Women's Citizenship in Brighton in November 1996 illustrated that there were a number of diverse preventative initiatives in both primary and secondary education taking place around the country, and that there exists a renewed impetus for feminists to be central in its development.

The research

This research, conducted in 1996–7, involved in-depth interviews with teachers who were mainly coordinators for PSHE, many of whom also had responsibility for their schools' equal opportunities and child protection policies.[6] While the teachers participating in the study were found largely through contacts via students and colleagues, efforts were made to represent a range of different types of secondary schools, and from different localities including rural areas, which are often neglected in this type of educational research. Representation ultimately included teachers from inner-city, surburban and semi-rural schools, and involved a single-sex girls school, one mixed-sex grammar school and a number of mixed-sex comprehensive schools. All the schools included pupils from a range of ethnicities, but as might be expected the inner-city schools had a higher number of black and Asian pupils.

Teachers were asked about school policies and practices and the content of the PSHE curriculum, and many also supplied written policy statements. Since familiarity with the meaning of the term sexual violence could not be assumed, their approaches to teaching about sexuality and relationships were explored, as well as the way they addressed issues of gender and power. Questions were put about whether they felt able to address specific forms of sexual violence from sexual harassment and sexual abuse to domestic violence, coercive sex, date rape, pornography and prostitution. Since a number of schools had curriculum programmes on bullying, these were also explored to see if teachers felt able to address gendered violence within this context. Other significant aspects included teachers' experiences of difficulties and constraints and any support and training received.

Issues around confidentiality were particularly important for some teachers who were initially cautious of talking openly about the constraints. In discussing the findings, details about particular schools have therefore been omitted to ensure anonymity. All the teachers interviewed were extremely pressurized in terms of time but gave up free periods and lunch hours in order to take part. In many cases the interviews took the form of conversations where information was exchanged; all teachers were keen to know more about existing research and resources, and many felt that the interviews themselves had raised their own awarenesss and understanding of sexual violence and its place in sex education.

Information from coordinators of local education authority (LEA) preventative projects was mainly sought through letters and phone calls, owing to the limited funding for the project, although an interview with one coordinator took place in London.

Structural constraints on teachers

While the schools participating in this research can in no way be considered representative of all secondary schools, even with a small number of cases, there were significant commonalities and considerable differences in teachers' understandings and school practices. All felt that what they could do was limited by structural and institutional factors such as constraints on school budgets where the PSHE curriculum invariably lost out. Examples of this included a teacher who felt that since she was not being paid for taking on the extra responsibility of being the child protection coordinator she was not going to do more than the minimum required by the Ofsted inspection criteria. In another school where the coordinator had received funding to set up a specific project with a group of girls, financial circumstances limited the project to one year despite its obvious success.

Teachers in general felt they were constrained by government policies, inspection criteria and non-statutory guidance, although their understandings and interpretations of these varied considerably. A few feared the disapproval of their governing bodies if they addressed certain aspects of sexual violence, such as pornography.

All complained of lack of time to properly develop the PSHE curriculum, and lack of support and training both in the schools and from the LEAs. A number pointed out that initial teacher training provided virtually nothing on sex education or child protection.

Sexual harassment – a disappearing act

In discussing sexual harassment, I use the term to mean sexually violent behaviour which takes place in public and institutional contexts and is undertaken mainly by boys and men. In school settings it can be defined as a range or continuum of behaviours that are designed to objectify, humiliate, intimidate and control girls and women. These range from verbal jokes or comments about their bodies, sexuality, or sexual reputations, to staring, leering or showing pornography, to actual physical touching and behaviour which amounts to sexual assault (Herbert 1989; Lees 1993; Larkin 1994; Burton et al. 1998).[7]

There has been considerable previous research that has highlighted the extent and nature of the sexual harassment of girls and women teachers in co-educational and boys' schools since the late 1970s (Kelly 1992). Significantly, Walkerdine (1981) found that boys as young as 4 had learnt to use verbal sexual harassment to challenge the authority of women teachers and to humiliate and degrade girls. This behaviour was accepted and explained by teachers within a discourse of the 'natural' development of boys and viewed merely as a 'normal' 'game'. Connelly's more recent ethnographic research in an inner-city primary school indicated that the verbal and physical sexual harassment of girls played an important part in the construction of masculine and racialized identities in 4 to 6-year-old boys. He observed the frequent pinning down and sexual abuse of individual girls by groups of boys within the school playground, and found that they described their relationships with girls 'overwhelmingly' in terms of 'power, violence and domination' (Connelly 1995: 185–6). Other ethnographic research in secondary schools has highlighted the specific contexts and locations around which the sexual harassment of girls takes place in co-educational settings, including that of the sex education context itself (Prendergast 1995; Measor et al. 1996). Measor et al. found that girls were demanding separate sex education classes as a result of the constant sexual harassment by boys. But they also found that such demands were resisted by teachers because the presence of girls was viewed as a restraining influence on the boys' behaviour.

More recent survey and focus group research undertaken for the Zero Tolerance Trust on young people's attitudes towards sexual harassment has indicated that behaviour such as 'grabbing girls' breasts' and 'pushing them to watch pornography' were regarded as commonly acceptable behaviour by boys and viewed as 'just a laugh'. It also suggested that while girls might be uncomfortable with this, 'they were inhibited from protesting through the fear of being labelled a prude or oversensitive' (Burton *et al.* 1998: 2). Furthermore, Larkin's research on girls' experiences in Canadian high schools indicated that one of the main reasons girls 'tolerated' the sexually harassing behaviour of boys was that it was given no recognition by school officials and was 'seldom if ever discussed in school' (Larkin 1994: 266).

Despite the extent of research in this area, my investigation indicated something of a 'backlash' in many of the schools' approaches. Only two schools had written school policies that addressed sexual harassment and only one took it seriously in its practice.

A number of teachers seemed to be confused about its meaning and understood it as gender stereotyping in relation to 'non-traditional' subjects and careers. For these teachers, the naming and identification of sexual harassment as a form of intimidating behaviour appeared to have disappeared, or, if it was recognized at all, it was only in its most extreme form of sexual assault. This confusion seemed to be reflected in a variety of different discourses within the schools' practices. On the one hand, there was an unwillingness to acknowledge the gendered and sexualized nature of threatening behaviours by male pupils and sometimes male teachers. These teachers in the study considered that all 'offensive behaviours' were dealt with by the schools' anti-bullying policies, and individual pupils could make complaints about sexual harassment under these policies if they chose; but in practice this did not happen.

One teacher, in discussing her school's failure to address sexual harrassment in the hidden curriculum recounted how a girl who had been sexually assaulted by a group of boys on the school premises had told her father, who then reported it to the school, but this pupil had clearly not felt able to report it herself. Even when the incident was reported, there was a reluctance by some of the school governors to acknowledge that it had happened, or that action needed to be taken against the perpetrators. As a result of this incident, the school did accept that there was a need for closer monitoring of the school playground on the grounds of 'personal safety', but it did not lead to the development of a specific sexual harassment policy. However, teachers at this school did raise issues of 'respect' towards girls in PSHE classes and stressed that where boys tried to force physical contact on girls this constituted assault. Significantly, this example illustrates the difficulties for teachers in attempting to address aspects of sexual harassment in the formal curriculum when it is not supported by whole school policies and practices.

At the other extreme, in a school which on paper had a fairly good policy, there appeared to be a general postfeminist perception, particularily amongst the male teachers, that women and girls 'enjoyed' being sexually harassed. It was recounted that the female teacher who had been instrumental in developing the policy was regarded as 'an extremist' who did not have general staff support. In this school the teacher interviewed, reported that she and a number of other women teachers had raised concerns about constant verbal sexual harassment by boys towards female staff in the classroom and the collusion of male teachers in this behaviour. On occasion, boys had also used physical threats of violence towards women teachers. However, the school's senior management had chosen to regard this as a problem of 'classroom management', perceiving women teachers as not having the skills to control lessons.

In this school, as a result of the practice of streaming pupils in some subjects, girls were often in a considerable minority in the lower streamed classes, a situation that made them more vulnerable to abuse. As a consequence, these girls were often afraid to participate in lessons in case they became further targeted. This teacher also recounted incidents where girls might resist by turning the tables on boys, particularily where they were in the majority in the classroom or were in a position to pick on 'weaker' boys. However, she also reported a conversation with two Year 8 girls who expressed the view that they had to learn to put up with sexual harassment from boys because in the end they were expected to marry them.

Most of the schools viewed equal opportunities as meaning addressing the 'underachievement' of boys. This contrasted sharply with the one school that did take sexual harassment seriously and took action both against boys who carried it out and offering support for girls. It was in this context that a project had been set up within the formal PSHE curriculum for a volunteer group of mainly Asian girls who were the particular targets of verbal sexual harassment from Asian boys, who were in the majority in this school. The initial aim of the project was to empower the girls to resist such harassment on the school premises and the streets, when teachers were not present to intervene. However, it soon expanded to include other forms of sexual violence that the girls had to deal with at home, such as sexual and physical abuse from brothers and male relatives, domestic violence and their expectations of future relationships with men. Lunchtime sessions were established where the girls were able to discuss their experiences and locate their fears of sexual violence within a context of gendered power relationships between men and women, and to look at ways that this might be challenged. They were also able to discuss positive constructions and practices of female sexuality, including masturbation and female sexual pleasure (topics that are infrequently raised in standard sex education lessons), in contrast to their expectations of coercive sex. While the project included 'assertiveness training' and 'peer education' on sexual health, one of the teachers involved reported that the most successful aspect was the lunchtime discussions.[8] These enabled the young women to name and re-evaluate their experiences of sexual violence, and develop a sense of solidarity and resistance in being able to challenge them. One of the significant outcomes of this project was that all the girls involved elected to stay on at school and gain further qualifications, rather than leave and enter early marriages. By aiming to deal with sexual harassment this school had made a difference to their lives.

Personal relationships: sexual abuse and coercive sex – 'too sensitive an issue'

The initiative above was one of the few examples of an approach that was able to develop the connections between public and private forms of sexual violence and gendered constructions of sexuality. In the majority of the schools, topics such as sexual abuse were regarded by teachers as 'too sensitive' to be raised in the classroom. This statement appeared to mask teachers' own fears and uncertainties of how to discuss such 'private' issues as well as concerns about pupil confidentiality. There also appeared to be a lack of understanding of the causes of sexual abuse, whereby individualistic and pathological explanations were paramount, as well as a failure to make connections between different kinds of sexually abusive relationships.

In these schools, sexual abuse seemed to be defined only as adult child abuse, and abusive sexual relationships between peers would go unrecognized. These teachers were unfamiliar with the extensive research undertaken in relation to AIDS education which shows that young women's experiences of (hetero)sexual relationships with their peers frequently range from pressurized to forced sex, and over which they feel they have no control or expectations of enjoyment (Holland *et al.* 1990, 1991). An additional problematic factor was that many felt that sex education must be taught in mixed-sex groups in order to meet their equal opportunities obligations on equal access to the curriculum.

The benefits of single-sex groupings, particularly in enabling girls to discuss sexual violence and other topics connected to gendered constructions of female sexuality, has been evidenced in a number of research projects on sex education, as well as in this research (Epstein and Johnson 1998). It was not surprising that with the exception of the school discussed above, it was only in the all-girls school that these areas were able to be addressed. This school took an approach using issues raised in the letters pages of young women's popular cultural magazines such as *Sugar* as a basis for discussion, which has shown to be relatively successful in sex education approaches.

What about the boys?

Acknowledging that girls benefit from single-sex groupings raises the question of how education for boys can be addressed. Debates about the content and approaches to sex education for boys, and whether it is possible to challenge their sexually violent behaviour within formal programmes in schools are highly contested between feminists, teachers and within mainstream educational discourses in this country (Epstein and Johnson 1998).

Some sex education experts have suggested that boys are blamed too much already within preventative discourses on sex education and argue for a needs based approach (Sex Education Forum 1994b). However, if taken up uncritically, addressing boys' 'needs' can end up merely reinforcing normative and naturalistic beliefs about male sexuality that justify sexual violence. Such discourses have been used to justify the exploitation and harm of women and girls in pornography and prostitution on the basis that males have strong biological sex drives or desires which must be fulfilled. Boys can also use beliefs that their sexuality is uncontrollable to force sex on girls in personal relationships (Burton *et al.* 1998; Scott *et al.* 1998).

However, there are also indications that some boys at least welcome education that challenges peer group pressure to have sexual intercourse with girls and discusses less oppressive ways of relating (Lees 1993; Davidson 1995; Burton *et al.* 1998). A further problem that has been raised in relation to some of the research mentioned is that the sex education context itself may encourage boys to compete in demonstrating their 'macho stud' status (Measor *et al.* 1996). Related to this are questions as to who should undertake preventative education with boys. On the one hand, if undertaken by women it can serve as a further opportunity for sexual harassment. On the other, education undertaken by men may entail a 'matey' collusion and merely reinforce sexually violent attitudes in boys (Epstein and Johnson 1998). The latter concern has also been raised in relation to preventative education for adult men on perpetrator programmes, and one solution has been to use joint female and male teams (Burton *et al.* 1998).

Davidson (1995) has argued that the only way to break through boys' negative attitudes towards sex education and to take a more positive approach, is to have single-sex teaching for boys which critically questions normative constructions of masculinity and looks at the limitations of the role models and choices offered. Within such an approach, constructions of male sexuality and male sexual violence can be challenged, including violence between boys.

There are also long-running feminist debates related to anti-sexist work in education generally. These are concerned with the use of scarce resources, and whether these are more effectively used in work with girls in empowering them to resist sexual violence, rather than in attempting preventative work with boys. This was a key concern in the school that had run the girls' project on sexual harassment, and subsequently lost its funding to a specific project for boys. Feminists have pointed out that the current focus on 'boys' needs' in relation to educational policy can be both used to discriminate against the employment of women teachers who, it is argued, do not provide 'appropriate role models', and challenge the gains made in anti-sexist work in schools (Cameron 1998).

Strategies for preventative education

Teaching and learning approaches

While these debates raise difficult questions they are not insurmountable, as has been shown by successfully run prevention programmes both in the UK and elsewhere. What they do highlight is that the way that such education is approached is important.

One example of a successfully piloted project in this country, which has drawn on programmes from Australia and Canada and combines education for both boys and girls, is the *Respect* pack (Morley 1997).[9] Developed as part of a local authority multi-agency approach to addressing sexual violence, it takes a human rights values position, and as such is able to draw on discourses of children's as well as women's rights. It has also deliberately drawn on more neutral and individualistic concepts that have been used in mainstream 'relationships' and 'anti-bullying' education such as respect for others, with which young people and teachers are already familiar. It then utilizes these concepts to move into developing an understanding of the unacceptability of different forms of gendered violence and to discuss these as abuses of power. A significant feature is that it does not avoid sexualized violence. It places discussions of sexual abuse, forced sex, rape and pornography in the context of gendered stereotypes and discussions around sexuality while encouraging young people to think about positive alternatives to sexually violent and exploitative relationships where equality is a principal value. Feedback from boys on the pilot programme highlighted the need to make connections between boys' and men's violence towards women and girls and violence between boys, not only in relation to bullying, but also racist violence and homophobic abuse. The pilot successfully used single-sex activities. These enabled in-depth discussion for girls to explore ways of being strong, while for boys it combined exploration of why boys enjoy being violent, and encouraged consideration of alternative ways of opposing violence.

A key feature of this project is its focus on primary prevention, and its clear message that survivors are in no way to blame for being abused. One of the ways it does this is by challenging the common myths that women and girls 'ask for', 'deserve' or 'provoke' rape or assault. Another is to give young people the language and concepts with which to name sexually violent behaviour. At the beginning of the pilot programme pupils were given a questionnaire designed to explore their beliefs about sexual violence based on similar research (Edinburgh Women's Unit 1992). This indicated that sexual violence was regarded as acceptable in certain circumstances, for example, rape was seen as acceptable where the woman had 'led the man on', and for domestic violence where the woman had been unfaithful.

As far as teachers anxieties about how to undertake this kind of education are concerned, the programme adopts participative and 'distancing' learning methods with which many teachers will already be familiar. These include using stories about other young people's experiences and role-plays around hypothetical situations that encourage empathy. Building on discussions with local teachers, it also gives clear guidance about how to deal with disclosures of abuse and how to handle issues of confidentiality. These were issues that were raised by teachers in this research and are also of key concern to pupils (Burton *et al.* 1998). In addition to providing information on where young people who have been abused can seek help, it explores ways for them to provide support for friends who may talk to them about their experiences of abuse.

One significant aspect the pilot indicated was that pupils are not necessarily aware of schools' policies on child protection – an ironic situation since these policies are supposedly there for their benefit. It therefore encourages pupils to make suggestions about how schools' policies and practices can be improved to provide support to pupils as well as prevent sexually harassing behaviour within the school.

Other projects have taken similar teaching and learning approaches, with some using pair work between girls and boys to break down peer group pressure (see for example Elfyn 1996), and some inviting presentations from local women's support and survivor groups such as Women's Aid or Rape Crisis.

The majority of preventative projects however do appear to focus on one specific aspect, such as domestic violence. This is not surprising given that it has had a longer history in terms of the public policy agenda, and it may be regarded as a more acceptable topic to raise in schools, often because it is viewed as only incorporating physical as opposed to sexualized violence. Certainly some of the teachers expressed more enthusiasm for resources on domestic violence than for aspects such as sexual abuse. This may reflect their fears and uncertainties about addressing such issues as well as a lack of understanding that domestic violence can involve forced sex and rape, and is also linked to the sexual abuse of children (Hester and Pearson 1998). More recently, prostitution has become a focus for some LEA supported preventative education, particularily where it has been identified as a key means of the sexual abuse of girls in specific localities.[10]

Policy

This section relates to the issue of how schools can be persuaded to take up preventative education (if the need is not identified internally), and how it can be supported and integrated throughout the curriculum and in school policies. This is a hugely problematic area in itself which can only be briefly discussed.

Local policies

One aspect this research has shown is that teachers with responsibility for PSHE and policies such as child protection, are often in a relatively powerless position within schools. One project coordinator stated that it was therefore important to go to the top and convince headteachers of the need for preventative education. She described her own success in doing this at a conference for local heads in relation to convincing them for the need of preventative education around prostitution. This strategy is also important in enabling it to be integrated throughout the curriculum and in school policies, as without the senior management's support this is unlikely to happen.

Coordinators of local projects also spoke of the problem of short-termism in providing support and training to schools. The usual practice was to second a teacher, or employ a consultant to develop resources and work with teachers in schools for at the most two or three years. It would then be assumed that teachers would carry on the work and need no further support. This raises the whole question of training for teachers, since evaluation research has shown that many will not use preventative education programmes, or will only use them partially, if they are contrary to their own understandings and beliefs about sexual violence (Johnson 1994).[11] One aspect this investigation highlighted is that teachers lacked knowledge and understanding of the prevalence and causes of sexual violence, and were also unfamiliar with much of the educational research in this area.

National policy

Many of these questions relate to issues of national educational policy, financial resources and initial teacher training. While the present Labour government has given indications that it recognizes that preventative education needs to take place in schools, other messages suggest that no additional financial resources will be available. Its recognition is also limited to the need for education on domestic violence, rather than on sexual violence more broadly (Home Office 1998). However, recent survey evidence suggests that while there has been a small shift in young people's beliefs around physical violence towards women, it is the acceptability of sexualized violence amongst boys particularly in relation to 'sexual harassment' and 'forced sex' in personal relationships that remains a key problem (Burton and Kitzinger 1998). Current genderless and desexualized anti-bullying policies are clearly not adequate to deal with this kind of abuse, and as a consequence, there are much needed changes required to national policies.

In line with UK government recognition that sexual violence against women and girls constitutes a violation of their human rights, at a minimum national policies should require schools to take action on sexual harassment and support them with sufficient information, guidance and training. The government has indicated that it intends to strengthen legislation to deal with sexual harassment in the workplace (*Guardian*, 5 November 1998). It would be ironic in this context if it continued to ignore that which takes place in schools themselves.

Although this research has focused on secondary schools, it is evident that preventative education on gendered sexual violence that challenges 'normative' gender constructions for both boys and girls needs to begin in the early years with nursery education and continue throughout the school years.

Acknowledgements

Thanks to co-researcher Celia Jenkins and all the teachers and coordinators who participated in this research.

Notes

1 The research was funded by the School for Policy Studies at the University of Westminster and took place with my colleague Celia Jenkins. It arose out of my own background as a former teacher and researcher on gender and sex education in the early 1980s and more recently in working in the area of education policy.
2 Education is only one strategy that needs to take place in conjunction with others (see Skinner, Chapter 3, this volume).
3 The Education Act 1996 S.351 provided for the statutory basis for PSHE as a whole, but continued to leave it largely up to schools themselves to determine its content through non-statutory guidance.
4 *Standing Strong* (Wangarei Rape Crisis and Bagnall 1990) was an early example of a preventative programme that addressed the sexual abuse and harassment of girls in New Zealand, but was supported for use in schools by the state of Victoria, Australia. Since then Victoria has developed preventative resources for use across different subject areas (Forsey 1994).
5 It is now proposed to make citizenship education compulsory at secondary level (Qualifications and Curriculum Authority 1999).
6 Although it is recognized that education on sexual violence needs to take place across the mainstream curriculum, the personal and social curriculum is an obvious starting point.
7 There are debates about definitions of sexual harassment and whether it should include all misogynist behaviour towards women or be limited to behaviour that has a specifically sexualized content (Wise and Stanley 1987; Herbert 1989). Other debates have been raised in relation to boys who may experience what Epstein has called 'sexist harassment'. Epstein suggests that sexual harassment needs to be renamed sexist harassment to include boys' experiences (Epstein 1996). One of the problems with this is that it can be used to ignore sexualized violence against girls and women – something that was indicated in this research.
8 Peer education involves the use of other pupils as educators. However its content is usually determined by adults.
9 This information was gained mainly through an interview with Rachel Morley, who is the coordinator and author of the *Respect* pack. This can be obtained from Rachel Morley, Community Psychology, Child and Adolescent Services, St Leonards Hospital, Nuttall Street, London, N1 5LZ.
10 For example, the 'Streets and Lanes Project', Barnardo's, Bradford.
11 Information to support this statement was also provided by the coordinator of a preventative programme elsewhere.

References

Arnot, M. (1994) British feminist educational politics and state regulation of gender, in M. Arnot and K. Weiler (eds) *Feminism and Social Justice: International Perspectives.* London: Routledge.
Askew, S. and Ross, C. (1988) *Boys Don't Cry: Boys and Sexism in Education.* Milton Keynes: Open University Press.
Briggs, F. and Hawkins, J. (1994) Choosing between child protection programmes. *Child Abuse Review,* 3: 272–81.
Burton, S. and Kitzinger, J. (with L. Kelly and L. Regan) (1998) *Young People's Attitudes Towards Sexual Violence, Sex and Relationships: A Survey and Focus Group Study.* Edinburgh: Zero Tolerance Charitable Trust.

Burton, S., Regan, L. and Kelly, L. (1998) *Supporting Women and Challenging Men: Lessons from the Domestic Violence Intervention Project.* Bristol: Policy Press.

Cameron, D. (1998) Could do better, *Trouble and Strife* 38: 46–53.

Connelly, P. (1995) Boys will be boys? racism, sexuality and the construction of masculine identities amongst infant boys, in J. Holland, B. Blair and S. Sheldon (eds) *Debates and Issues in Feminist Research and Pedagogy.* Clevedon: Multi-lingual Matters and The Open University.

Davidson, N. (1995) Someone should do something about the boys: sex education with boys and young men, in D.E. Massey (ed.) *Sex Education Source Book: Current Issues and Debates.* London: Family Planning Association.

Department of Education (1988) *Working Together for the Protection of Children from Abuse: Procedures within the Education Service,* Circular 4/88. London: DoE.

Department for Education (1994a) *Education Act, 1993: Sex Education in Schools,* Circular 5/94. London: DfE.

Department for Education (1994b) *Pupil Behaviour and Discipline,* Circular 8/94.

Department of Education and Employment (1995) *Protecting Children from Abuse: The Role of the Education Service,* Circular 10/95. London: DfEE.

Department of Employment (1996) *United Nations Fourth World Conference on Women, Beijing 1995, Report of the United Kingdom of Great Britain and Northern Ireland.* London: DoE.

Edinburgh District Council Women's Unit (1992) *Adolescents' Knowledge about and Attitudes to Domestic Violence, Report to the Edinburgh District Council Women's Committee.* Edinburgh: Edinburgh District Council Women's Unit.

Elfyn, M. (1996) *Hands Off.* Wales: Save the Children Fund/Welsh Women's Aid.

Epstein, D. (1996) Keeping them in their place: hetero/sexist harassment, gender and the enforcement of heterosexuality, in L. Adkins and J. Holland (eds) *Sex, Sensibility and the Gendered Body.* Basingstoke: Macmillan.

Epstein, D. and Johnson, R. (1998) *Schooling Sexualities.* Buckingham: Open University Press.

Evans, G. (1995) A place in the curriculum for child protection. *Health Education,* 5: 14–19.

Foley, R. (1993) Zero tolerance. *Trouble and Strife,* 27: 16–20.

Forsey, C. (1994) *Hands Off: The Anti-Violence Guide to Developing Positive Relationships.* Victoria: West Education Centre Inc.

Herbert, C. (1989) *Talking of Silence: The Sexual Harassment of School Girls.* London: Falmer Press.

Hester, M. and Pearson, C. (1998) *From Periphery to Centre: Domestic Violence in Work with Abused Children.* Bristol: Policy Press.

Holland, J., Ramazanoglu, C. and Scott, S. (1990) *Sex Risk and Danger: AIDS Education Policy and Young Women's Sexuality.* London: Tufnell Press.

Holland, J., Ramazanoglu, C., Scott, S., Sharpe, S. and Thomson, R. (1991) *Pressure, Resistance, Empowerment: Young Women and the Negotiation of Safe Sex.* London: Tufnell Press.

Holly, L. (ed.) (1989) *Girls and Sexuality.* Milton Keynes: Open University Press.

Home Office (1998) *Supporting Families. A Consultation Document.* London: The Stationery Office.

Ingham, R. (1997) *The Development of an Integrated Model of Sexual Conduct Amongst Young People,* End of Award Report. London: Economic and Social Research Council.

Johnson, B. (1994) Teachers' role in the primary prevention of child abuse. *Child Abuse Review,* 3: 259–71.

Jones, C. and Mahoney, P. (eds) (1989) *Learning Our Lines: Sexuality and the Social Control of Education.* London: Women's Press.

Kelly, L. (1992) Not in front of the children: responding to right-wing agendas on sexuality and education, in M. Arnot and L. Barton (eds) *Voicing Concerns: Sociological Perspectives on Contemporary Education Reforms*. Oxford: Triangle.

Kelly, L., Regan, L. and Burton, S. (1991) *An Exploratory Study of Sexual Abuse in a Sample of 16–21 Year Olds*. University of North London: Child Abuse Study Unit.

Kelly, L., Wingfield, R., Burton, S. and Regan, L. (1995) *Splintered Lives: Sexual Exploitation of Children in the Context of Children's Rights and Child Protection*. Ilford: Barnardos.

Kitzinger, J. (1988) Defining innocence: ideologies of childhood. *Feminist Review*, 28: 77–87.

Larkin, J. (1994) Walking through walls: the sexual harassment of high school girls. *Gender and Education*, 6(3): 263–80.

Lees, S. (1993) *Sugar and Spice: Sexuality and Adolescent Girls*. London: Penguin.

Lenskyj, H. (1990) Beyond plumbing and prevention: feminist approaches to sex education. *Gender and Education*, 2: 217–30.

Mahoney, P. (1989) Who pays the price? Sexual abuse and education. *Gender and Education*, 1(1): 87–91.

Measor, L., Tiffin, C. and Fry, K. (1996) Gender and sex education: a study of adolescent responses. *Gender and Education*, 8(3): 275–88.

Morley, R. (1997) *Respect – A Primary Prevention, Schools-based Approach to Challenging Violence and Abuse in Relationships. Progress Report 17/04/97*. Hackney: Community Psychology, Child and Adolescent Services.

O'Hara, M. (1988) Developing a feminist school policy on child sexual abuse. *Feminist Review*, 28: 158–62.

Prendergast, S. (1995) *With gender on my mind: menstruation and embodiment in adolescence*, in J. Holland, B. Blair and S. Sheldon (eds) *Debates and Issues in Feminist Research and Pedagogy*. Clevedon: Multi-lingual Matters and Open University Press.

Qualifications and Curriculum Authority (1999) *The review of the National Curriculum in England. The secretary of state's proposals*. London: Qualifications and Curriculum Authority.

Scott, S., Jackson, S. and Backett-Milburn, K. (1998) Swings and roundabouts: risk anxiety and the everyday worlds of children. *Sociology*, 32(4): 689–705.

Sex Education Forum (1994a) *Developing and Reviewing a School Sex Education Policy. A Positive Strategy*. London: National Children's Bureau.

Sex Education Forum (1994b) *Men, Boys and Fatherhood: The Role of Sex Education*, Forum Factsheet 4. London: National Children's Bureau.

Sharpe, S. (1976) *'Just Like a Girl': How Girls Learn to be Women*. Harmondsworth: Penguin.

Thomson, R. and Scott, S. (1992) *An Enquiry into Sex Education*. Report of a survey into local authority support and monitoring of school sex education, Sex Education Forum. London: National Children's Bureau.

Walkerdine, V. (1981) Sex, power and pedagogy; republished in V. Walkerdine (1990) *School Girl Fictions*. London: Verso.

Wangarie Rape Crisis and C. Bagnall (1990) *Standing Strong. My Body Belongs to Me – What to do About Sexual Violation*. Victoria: Ministry of Education.

Wise, S. and Stanley, L. (1987) *Georgie Porgy: Sexual Harassment in Everyday Life*. London: Pandora Press.

Wood, J. (1984) Groping towards sexism: boys' sex talk, in A. McRobbie and M. Nava (eds) *Gender and Generation*. Basingstoke: Macmillan.

Zero Tolerance Charitable Trust (1998) *The Respect Campaign. Campaign Briefing*. Edinburgh: Zero Tolerance.

8 Shifting the margins: black feminist perspectives on discourses of mothers in child sexual abuse

Claudia Bernard

Introduction

Within dominant discourses of intrafamilial child sexual abuse the 'collusive mother' remains the most frequent accusation made against mothers. Embedded gender-biased assumptions about mothers are among the most difficult and challenging aspects of thinking about sexual abuse in families. Feminists have been at the forefront of critiquing mother-blaming theories, and are transforming the conceptualization of mothers in child sexual abuse discourse. By centrally addressing gender as a locus of power relations, feminists have been careful to draw a sharp distinction between abusing and non-abusing parents in their analyses of child sexual abuse in the home. Therefore, an important starting point is how we understand the role of mothers, as they are the non-abusing parent in the majority of cases, and children are largely dependent on them for support and protection in the aftermath of abuse.

This chapter explores and develops the construction of black mothers of African and Caribbean descent in discourses of child sexual abuse to illuminate some central concerns. Drawing on black feminist insights, I focus on an exploration of the intersectionality of race and gender oppression in framing black mothers' responses to the sexual abuse of their children. Data generated from a qualitative study highlights different ways in which black mothers' reactions are compounded by the intersection of race and gender. The chapter concludes with some reflections on understanding black mothers' help-seeking strategies, and considers the implications for assessing the safety needs of black children.

Representations of mothers in child sexual abuse: challenging the 'collusive mother' myth

A review of the literature on child sexual abuse shows significant gender differences in the way mothers and fathers are represented in child protection discourse and practice (Corby 1996; Mittler 1997; Trotter 1997; Parton 1998). These perspectives have pointed to the way arguments about mothers' complicity in their children's abuse moves the responsibility for the abuse away from men and attributes blame to women as mothers (Hooper 1992; Johnson 1992). This mother-blame discourse contrasts with the large amount of research which shows that fathers, stepfathers, male relatives and other men are overwhelmingly the perpetrators of child sexual abuse (O'Hagan 1997; Pringle 1998). Nonetheless, a tendency remains in research and practice to pay more attention to mothers' supposed 'failure to protect', rather than focusing on men's abusive behaviour in the aftermath of child sexual abuse (Farmer and Owen 1998; Hooper and Humphreys 1998). Though legally both parents may have responsibility for the safety and protection of children, it is women as mothers who are routinely scrutinized and who most encounter the negative attention of child protection agencies; they are assumed to have primary responsibility for their children's well-being (Milner 1993).

Feminist analyses have called attention to the complex processes involved for mothers in the aftermath of intrafamilial child sexual abuse. They have long recognized that emotional and social processes are critical in shaping mothers' responses (Hooper 1992; Jacobs 1994; Green 1996). What has been highlighted most succinctly is that with the disclosure of sexual abuse the cognitive, emotional and relational world of mothers is shattered (Hooper 1992; Johnson 1992; Dempster 1993).

In addition, feminists have stressed that issues of power and gender relations in families are critical to an understanding of their impact on mothers' psychological, emotional and behavioural responses (Nelson 1982; MacLeod and Saraga 1988; Hooper 1992; Johnson 1992; Print and Dey 1992; Dempster 1993). Green (1996), exploring the construction of mothers in incest cases, points out that mothers' responses will be determined by the extent of unequal power relations within the family, and are augmented by the emotional, social and financial stresses that they face.

Practitioners' first-hand accounts suggest some mothers may have no knowledge of the abuse, others may not have picked up the 'clues' surrounding abuse, while others may know about it but are fearful of seeking help (Hildebrand 1989). Particularly where the abuser is the woman's husband or partner, learning of the abuse can elicit a powerful grief response in mothers, involving shock, numbness, denial, fear, anxiety, guilt, anger or depression (Hooper 1992; Green 1996). Moreover, as Farmer and Owen (1998) found, some mothers may not be able to protect their children when their male partners are violent. In their study of 44 children whose names had been placed on the child protection register, they found that in two-fifths of cases where children were being sexually abused the mother was also experiencing domestic violence. Similarly, Hester and Pearson (1998), in their study of the links between child abuse and domestic violence, found that domestic violence occurred in more than half of the 37 cases where children had been identified as being sexually abused by a father or father figure.

However, a careful reading of the feminist literature reveals a paucity of work addressing the specificity of black mothers' experiences. A criticism that could be levelled against much feminist work is that it has typically focused on the experiences of white mothers, from which generalizations are made to all mothers. Black mothers' exclusion and marginalization from debates means the particular problems they face have not been fully explored. There may be strong parallels and similarities between all mothers, but the very different conditions of women's lives operate to shape their experiences. Significantly, race will not only influence attitudes towards black mothers, but will also profoundly frame how black mothers perceive their choices and help-seeking actions in the aftermath of the abuse of their children.

Child sexual abuse in black families

A discussion of black mothers' reactions to the abuse of their children must be located within broader debates about child sexual abuse in black families. A careful examination of a number of important and controversial key issues should be undertaken. Little attention has been paid to the specific issue of sexual abuse in black families. Accurate data on its incidence is not easy to come by. This poses a major problem in measuring the true scale of childhood sexual abuse in black communities (Wilson 1993; Jackson 1996; Mtezuka 1996). A good deal of sexual abuse is not reported to official agencies such as the police or social services departments and thus does not appear on official registers (Wilson 1993; Bernard 1998).

One of the major problems associated with reporting sexual abuse in black families is that there can be a great deal of fear and mistrust of statutory agencies, which are perceived as powerful and white dominated institutions (Mtezuka 1996). Moreover, sexual abuse is not discussed openly for fear of exposing the black community to coercive intervention by statutory agencies (Wilson 1993; Jackson 1996). The threatening nature of a topic like child sexual abuse may make some people hesitant to seek outside help. For example, telling about the abuse may not be safe for children. From a very early age black children experience racism, and cushioning the effects of racism are usually undertaken within the family network. Here black children are particularly dependent for support on networks of family and this may make disclosure especially difficult. If a black child is abused within their family, it becomes especially traumatic and can be almost impossible for the child to disclose to outsiders what is happening to them. In addition, they may feel they are betraying their families. As hooks (1989: 2) has so cogently argued: 'so many black people have been raised to believe that there is just so much that you should not talk about, not in private and not in public'. The reporting of sexual abuse in black communities generates fear of reprisals and could incur marginalization or even exclusion from families and communities (Bernard 1997). Furthermore, black people may feel alienated from law enforcement (Mama 1993; Mtezuka 1996). It is accepted by large numbers in the black community that there will be little justice in the criminal justice system and as a result black people are less confident that their concerns will be taken seriously when they are victims of crimes (Mama 1993).

Also black men's involvement in sexual abuse towards their own children may open up painful and difficult issues for black women. For many, an area of concern is that negative and distorted messages about black men are conveyed through the media and other social institutions (Mercer and Julien 1988). Dominant representations of black men portray them as feckless, absent fathers. Additionally, black male sexuality is represented as wanton and bestial. To some degree, the negative stereotypes of black men act to shape the way they are responded to, and may reinforce the general racism directed against them in their dealings with welfare agencies (Bryan et al. 1985; Arshad 1996). Moreover, it is suggested that as the state plays a significant role in the demonization of black men, for black women to raise the issue of their violence and abusive behaviour in public is to invite a racist backlash (Wilson 1993; Mama 1995; Mtzeuka 1996). To name the reality means confronting difficult questions that evoke strong feelings within black communities, and moreover bring the possibility of a racist interpretation (Wilson 1993). Given this set of circumstances, perhaps not surprisingly, there is reluctance to engage publicly with the issue of childhood sexual abuse in black communities and a general resistance to change.

The complex ways race intersects with gender have been addressed most interestingly by black feminists to consider how black women occupy a range of multiple and contradictory positions that have implications for their relationship to welfare agencies (Carby 1982; Mama 1996). Black feminists interrogate race from a standpoint that examines the intersection of gender, race and class to highlight the multifarious roles of women as mothers and as members of their families and communities. Most significantly, analyses from black feminist thinkers have illuminated the need to examine the gendered experiences of black mothers within the private sphere of their families as well as their relationships to the public sphere to consider how these will profoundly influence their help-seeking behaviour.

An analysis of the intersecting effects of gender and race in black women's lives shows that gender and power relations are embodied in black families in complex ways, and identify the contradictions that are posed for black women and children in giving a voice to their experiences of violence and maltreatment (Mama 1989). Black feminists' analyses usefully direct us towards an understanding of how the family is both a source of black women's affirmation and a source of their oppression (Carby 1982). This contradictory position makes it a site of resistance in struggles against state and police racism and deaths in custody, for example. Yet it is also a site of oppression, and poses dilemmas and challenges for black women in the aftermath of child sexual abuse and other forms of male violence in the home. Significantly, an exploration of gender relations in black families and communities emphasizes some of the contradictions for black women in their families, which have implications for their help-seeking behaviour in the aftermath of violence and abuse. Perhaps most importantly, the reality of male violence to black women and children in the family sits uneasily with the notion of the family as being a site of affirmation and resistance for black women.

Wilson (1993) proffers a black feminist analysis of the silence surrounding child sexual abuse in black families. She emphasizes the importance of race and gender to illuminate pervasive factors such as feelings of loyalty, shame, and fear of a racist backlash that create a climate of silence around the subject of childhood sexual abuse in black families. As a consequence, the subject is surrounded by a wall of silence because of black women's alliances with black men and general feelings of responsibility to the black community. She suggests that the simultaneity of oppressions operate to contribute to secret-keeping about child sexual abuse in black families, and asks at whose expense are we denying that sexual abuse occurs in black families? As Villarosa (1994: 520) points out, 'Silence only fuels the problem and leaves survivors feeling lost, confused, guilty and painfully alone'. Similarly, Kelly (1996: 34) remarks that, 'Silence has been a major weapon in men's arsenal which has prevented women and children from talking about their experiences of sexual violence'. If we are not to lose sight of the rights of black children to be protected from sexual abuse, it is imperative that we interrogate the issues at play and find ways to explore the dynamics, thus breaking the silence surrounding the abuse of black children. Such an unravelling of the issues is important and indeed necessary if we are to identify and understand the complexities of child sexual abuse on black families.

Lived experiences

In the rest of this chapter I will draw on data generated from in-depth interviews with 30 self-selected black mothers of African and Caribbean origin. The research focused on the views of mothers whose children were sexually abused by someone in the family, or someone known to them. Participation in the study was voluntary and the respondents were recruited through social services departments, voluntary agencies, community groups and publicity material distributed in health centres. The research is centrally concerned with the way race and gender intersects to influence black mothers' help-seeking strategies, and seeks to explore what factors influenced their help-seeking and protective strategies on discovery of the abuse of their children. Only some of the mothers had reported the abuse to child protection agencies. All the children had been abused by someone related to or acquainted with them, for example, father, stepfather, relative, family friend, teacher, or other trusted adult. To be eligible for the study, mothers had to have acknowledged that the sexual abuse had occurred, and discovery of the abuse had to have taken place at least six months before the interview. The research sought to explore a range of questions. This included asking what meanings mothers attached to their children's well-being and safety needs in the aftermath of child sexual abuse, and what had influenced their decision-making on discovery of the abuse.[1] A primary aim was to undertake research that would candidly bring the experiences of black mothers into full view and generate knowledge about the particular impact of sexual abuse on black families.

Divided loyalties

Faced with the devastating impact of abuse, a number of mothers in the study reported having to balance their own needs with the needs of their children in the context of divided loyalties. When sexual abuse takes place within the home it brings family members to crisis point, presenting them with a challenge to re-evaluate their relationship with each other. For mothers, coping with the reality of their children's abuse can mean reconstructing their perceptions of self and identity, and can create blocks to acting decisively. For example, some mothers reported that the devastating effects of the violation of their children left them suffering from confusing emotions of disbelief, shame, guilt, sadness and anger. For some, the anger, stigma, and shame they felt led to intense feelings of self-blame and doubt and they became mired in uncertainty. In their struggles to deal with their own feelings about the abuse some mothers displaced their anger on themselves, as can happen when people are too traumatized to speak about painful experiences.

Additionally, a number of mothers expressed anger at themselves for not picking up sooner that something was wrong. Such instances are highlighted in other research. As Green (1996) notes, some mothers may consciously or unconsciously hold personal anger at the child for disclosing or not disclosing the abuse. Furthermore, a number of mothers expressed ambivalent feelings towards their partners as well as their children, and such ambivalence often jeopardized their relationship with their children. For instance, a number of mothers noted strains in their relationships with their children due to conflicting emotions. Research suggests that some children may believe that their mothers are already aware of the abuse and direct their anger on to them because of feelings of betrayal (Jacobs 1994). According to Jacobs, children may harbour anger towards their mother out of an idealization of mothers as omnipotent. Additionally, at stake are not just women's relationships with their children, but also their relationships with their wider kinship support networks. Thus the conflicting loyalty experienced by mothers gave rise to a set of powerful feelings that created a tension for them which significantly influenced their capacity to assert their agency on their own behalf.

It could be argued that most of these points are true for all mothers. Nevertheless, it has to be recognized that black mothers often have to make difficult choices in the context of divided loyalties. Accordingly, as Hill Collins (1998) notes, within some black families, there is an unwritten rule that black women will support black men no matter what has happened. Correspondingly, hooks (1995) offers a poignant critique of the pressures on black women and points out that efforts on the part of black women to assert agency over their own lives are perceived as attacks on black manhood and acts of betrayal. Extended family members may experience black mothers seeking outside help as betrayers.

Paradoxically, there is a pressure on black mothers to present themselves as strong and ever-coping. Villarosa (1994) discusses the way black women internalize notions of the 'strong' black woman. She notes that this internalization can be a hindrance to acknowledging pain and vulnerabilities that may significantly constrain women in seeking help to deal with emotional hurts, particularly on issues that are shameful to reveal. This situation has implications for black children, as ultimately their safety and long-term emotional needs may be compromised.

Bringing their feelings out into the open will reveal that black mothers may experience a range of conflicting loyalties. Most notably, the uncertainty generated by conflicting loyalties can powerfully immobilize mothers, and act to obstruct their abilities to adequately support and protect their children just when strength is most needed to act decisively. Many of the women in the study struggled with inherent contradictions of loyalty and anger and suffered periods of confusion.

A 40-year-old Caribbean mother of a 6-year-old girl who was abused by her stepfather explained:

> The whole process is very tiring, it's very time and life consuming. It can alter your self-esteem . . . your directions in life. I was extremely confused – feeling angry, feeling inadequate, feeling stupid.

For some black mothers a lack of alternatives, or the belief that they have no choice to shape and determine what is best for their children may be central in their minds. Black women's uncertainty and ambivalence requires a safe and supportive space to explore the inherent complexities and to make sense of and communicate their own experiences. Thus, the way gender and race oppression intersect to create a context where black mothers experience conflict needs to be understood by child welfare professionals.

Help-seeking: challenges for black mothers

Other factors underlying mothers' responses may be their concerns about routes open to them to access help. On the discovery of abuse, a number of mothers when seeking support and justice for their children, faced the complicated task of having to negotiate a path through what can often be hostile territories from a position of social powerlessness. This set of circumstances intensifies black mothers' problems, and seeking help becomes fraught with difficulties. Unquestionably, they have to weigh up not only how to seek help, but must also be selective about whom they approach, because they may be afraid of further stigmatization and concerned not to betray their families. Foremost in the minds of many mothers is that they may experience a negative result as a consequence of accessing formal help. What is also at stake here for mothers is the consequence of involving agencies such as the police, which could result in marginalization or exclusion from their communities (Bernard 1997). For example, although some mothers reported feeling betrayed and angry on discovery of the abuse, they still wished to protect their partners from perceived punitive intervention, and were thus reluctant to seek the support of professional helpers or law enforcement agencies.

Black mothers struggle with inherent contradictions in conflict of loyalties to their male partners, their families and communities. These important factors will significantly influence how they make choices for themselves and their children. Social belonging in their families and communities is of utmost importance to many black women in a society where race is a significant marker for experience. Their possibilities of seeking outside help may be further diminished by feelings of shame. It is within this context of divided loyalties that black mothers have to make sense of their children's abuse while also dealing with their own feelings of loss and betrayal. Black mothers may thus find it more difficult to resist the pressure not to involve outside agencies, as the consequences for women involving social services or the police could be exclusion or marginalization from their wider families and communities.

These are the reflections of one mother whose 12-year-old daughter was abused by a male relative:

> Talking about an experience which was black on black with white professionals was very difficult to do. I kept thinking they must be thinking this is typical of black families. It felt that as if something like that is happening in your family is maybe a justification for how the white society sees you in the first place.

Another example that speaks of how the experience will be perceived by white professionals is provided by a 42-year-old mother whose child was abused by her partner:

> There was a pressure – not only from white society, but within your own society, like a lot of covering up. The pressure is there to cover up.

In considering these mothers' responses, an understanding of the way secrecy and silence fuelled by shame can lead some mothers to not bring the abuse to the attention of child protection services is needed.

As has been indicated, the reality for black mothers is very contradictory. This contradictory position puts pressure on them to exalt the virtues of the family as harmonious and conflict free, while at the same time forcing them to rely on their own resources to help their children come to terms with their experiences. Paradoxically, mothers must continue to struggle with emphasizing the strengths of their families while also confronting such problems as sexual abuse within them (Wilson 1993). It could be argued that the more marginalized the group, the more likely they will wish to protect their image (Ritchie 1996). However, for black women being put into the position of having to extol the virtues of the family disguises the incongruencies inherent in their families. An exploration of the varying layers of oppression can offer insights into the factors that act as a barrier for black mothers to respond in the best interest of their children and themselves. Furthermore, an exploration of these factors might help untangle the reasons why some black mothers may not involve statutory agencies. Perhaps most importantly, this may not simply be down to complicity with abusers, but may have something to do with the contradictory dimensions of black women's experiences in their families.

Key findings from this research suggest that in their quest to protect their children from child sexual abuse, mothers can often find that the expected support from the helping professionals cannot always be relied on. A number of mothers reported a slowness by professionals in responding to their concerns and an unwillingness to intervene. These women stated that they felt they were not deemed worthy of serious attention by professionals. Most notably, all the mothers perceived that the child protection services would take a blaming attitude towards them. Professionals routinely question the validity of mothers' stories and mothers often feel judged and blamed as a result. These mothers feared being judged as bad mothers, and some indeed blamed themselves for not protecting their children. The perception is as important as the reality for black mothers. It could be argued that the intrusive nature of child protection work engenders powerlessness in mothers. For some, the effects of the investigative process were disempowering and disenabling.

A number of mothers reported that once the initial child protection investigation was over, they were left with little or no family support services or therapeutic input to help deal with the aftermath of their children's abuse. It is fundamentally those mothers who felt disempowered by the investigative processes who reported not feeling helped by statutory agencies' involvement.

However, some mothers were satisfied with the help from professionals. A 38-year-old mother whose daughter was abused by a close family friend offers some thoughts on the help she received from her social worker:

The female social worker that they allocated to me gave me strength, talking me through the issues. She made me realize it wasn't my fault, I had no control over it happening. That helped a lot for me to put some things into perspective.

What appeared to make a difference for this mother was the efforts of the practitioner not to prejudge her, and to be clear with her about the child protection processes that would come into operation. She also valued efforts to involve her as much as was possible in the decision-making processes and to be clear with her about expectations.

In contrast, a number of mothers had not involved child protection services. My data suggested this seemed more likely to happen where the abuser was the woman's husband or male partner, or someone else close to the family. For example, one mother explained her reasons for not involving social services when her 9-year-old daughter was abused by her partner (not the child's father):

> In the days after I found out, I thought I was going nutty. You know, I really felt like I was from Mars or something. At that stage, I didn't think I could go to any professionals or they would lock me up. And yet my decision not to go to the professionals was also influenced in part by discussions with my daughter as well. I didn't want to put her through any more stress, and to be honest I was fearful of what may happen to my daughter.

Some mothers expressed feelings of deep mistrust of professionals, and invariably feared that their children would be removed from them. These mothers relied on families and friends to deal with the aftermath of the abuse. For some, with the help of supportive family members, they were able to confront the abuser.

One of the main reasons these mothers gave for not approaching social services departments was perceived racism and discrimination within the institutional structures of statutory agencies. Some mothers may indeed see themselves as protecting their children by not subjecting them to what they perceive to be coercive intervention from statutory agencies. These factors will significantly influence black mothers' decisions about using professional helping services or law enforcement agencies as a means of dealing with the aftermath of child sexual abuse. In considering these issues, agencies need to be aware of and committed to wanting to understand the way their practices impact on black mothers, and how this will create mistrust. Such awareness is the first step towards developing policies and tools of assessment that are sensitive to the predicaments of black mothers and their families. Agencies that want to improve their practice must be willing to develop policies that foster work with black mothers, that helps them feel supported to help their children in the recovery process.

Some mothers reported that drawing on the help of supportive family members was a means to mitigate some of the effects of isolation. Others, however, attempted to hide the abuse from family and friends, because of feelings of fear and shame. As a 35-year-old Caribbean mother whose 8-year-old daughter was abused by her stepfather described her position:

> Had I realized that at the time I would have been bright enough to phone my mother and get her support. But I didn't. I didn't tell her.

She doesn't know. My daughter's father doesn't know either. That's something about me I realize now, but I didn't then.

Balancing needs

Practitioners have to strike a difficult balance between the protection of black children and the rights of their parents. The main challenge for practitioners is to be able to weigh up the risks to children, while at the same time working in an enabling and empowering way with their mothers and other significant carers. In assessing parenting, practitioners need to understand that there are key processes for mothers – their relationship with the child's abuser (if the abuser is the mother's partner) and the grieving process for mothers – as sources of additional stress factors. Practitioners will need to explore the inherent tensions and dilemmas to identify when a mother's needs and children's needs may be enmeshed. Certainly, if there is a conflict between a child's needs and the mother's needs, then ultimately, the child's needs must be the paramount concern.

A key concern here is whether mothers' fears of approaching statutory services may unintentionally leave some black children exposed to further harm. It must be borne in mind that while some mothers' family networks and support systems may offer protection to children, others may not. As indicated, some mothers may have split allegiances that may make it difficult for them to access outside help. Some families may inadvertently collude with abusers and perpetuate the silence, denial and secrecy that normally surrounds child sexual abuse. There will clearly be a tension here between the needs of mothers, their extended families and their children. I suggest that there are major complexities surrounding some mothers' reluctance to involve child protection services. However, while strongly warning against pathologizing mothers' behaviour as collusive, I would urge that we must not lose sight of black children's safety needs, since it is important to remember that children are the least powerful members in families (Mittler 1997).

It is possible that some mothers' distresses can easily overshadow the emotional needs of their children. Certainly, mothers need to attend to their own feelings, and to come to terms with what has occurred. There is also the danger, however, that a mother struggling with confused emotions and ambivalent feelings towards her partner may turn her anger on her child, whether consciously or unconsciously. We need to find ways to understand these reactions without adopting a blaming and punitive approach, which would not be helpful for mothers or their children.

In balancing needs, it is important to ascertain the mother's conceptualization of her child's safety and emotional needs. Understanding their own assessments of risk is a critical starting point for making judgements about their ability to protect their children from further harm. What point of references mothers begin from in interpreting and making sense of their children's experience will be framed by their emotional, cognitive and social well-being. Professionals therefore need to create a climate where mothers feel they are being heard throughout the child protection investigation process.

Given these types of dilemmas for black mothers, what criteria will be used to judge their actions? Practitioners have to make evaluative judgements regarding whether a mother has the capacity to empathize with her child and protect him or her from further abuse. Principally, those struggling to comprehend the nuances of black mothers' experiences will have to examine mothers' behaviour to understand what reactions may stem from coping strategies developed for survival in a racist society, and explore whether some of that behaviour may at times endanger their children. For example, if a mother has not discussed the matter with anyone, how can she be assured that the child is not exposed to further harm?

For practitioners attempting to work from an anti-racist and anti-oppressive standpoint, conflicts of interest between the child and mother may be especially hard to discern. Farmer and Owen (1996) found that black families were particularly disadvantaged in relation to service provision by not being provided with an appropriate worker who understood their needs. To assess present and future risks to children, professionals must be satisfied that mothers have their children's best interests and safety at heart, but also have an avid interest in the factors that can present obstacles to women's parenting. To address both sets of needs, professional helpers are required to think about how they create a space for black mothers to give voice to experiences from their own perspectives, while also being open to the conflict of needs that can exist between mothers and children in the aftermath of child sexual abuse.

At this point, we must consider that while white practitioners need to engage with issues of race in their practice with black mothers, black practitioners are faced with a different set of challenges involving race. Although black practitioners may be more likely to adopt an anti-racist approach in work with mothers, there may be barriers for them to translate this commitment into practice because of their occupational situatedness (Lewis 1996); that is, they may not have decision-making powers due to their subordinate status in their organizations. Moreover, some may centre exclusively on race and ignore the impact of gendered power relations in mediating black mothers' experiences in their families, resulting in an oppressive practice towards black mothers. Therefore, the differing issues involved for black and white practitioners need to be explored for developing anti-oppressive practice with black mothers.

Professional helpers are charged with helping black mothers create a different frame of reference to help them understand their own needs but at the same time enable them to make changes that meet their children's needs. Recounting their own stories can bring mothers' meanings to their children's experiences, thus enhancing their capacities to help their children in the recovery process. In assessing standards of acceptable parenting, social work practitioners need to look for the strengths and adaptive mechanisms of black mothers. Starting from a strengths approach acknowledges those characteristics that enable black mothers to overcome obstacles in the context of racism. However, at the same time practitioners must be aware of the factors that act as barriers, preventing some mothers from effectively advancing their children's welfare. To be able to start from a strengths perspective, practitioners will need to be sensitive to the subtleties of gender and race oppression in the reality of black women's everyday lives, and be aware of the consequences for the way choices are perceived. Policies and procedures that facilitate the assessment of parenting are crucial, particularly where non-abusing mothers are seen as allies in the safety planning for their children. This would not only help to reduce the tendency to blame mothers, but would also enable them to participate fully in any child protection investigation.

To what extent would those mothers who chose not to involve social services or the police because of their fears, be seen as colluding with abusers and endangering their children? This point is pertinent because ultimately, assumptions and ideas practitioners draw upon to underpin their professional judgements about mothers' actions may be informed by cultural and racial stereotypes of black men, women, and families.

An accurate assessment of mothers' protective strategies may require an increased surveillance of their parenting skills, a situation that may in itself be oppressive. As Channer and Parton (1988: 105) so cogently argue, 'Protecting the interests of black children may well involve the intensive supervision of their parents'. We certainly need to consider how adopting such an approach exposes black women's mothering to an oppressive scrutiny. As anxiety about risk grows, professionals will continue to focus heavily on mothers, which may have a direct negative impact on the outcomes for their children. As O'Hagan and Dillenburger (1995) and Pringle (1995) note, the avoidance of working directly with men in child protection reinforces mother-blame and promotes an oppressive practice towards women. Pringle suggests that social workers fearful of confronting abusive fathers may find it *'easier and safer to deflect attention on to allegedly "colluding" mothers'* (1995: 45).

We must therefore confront embedded gendered assumptions about the role of men and women in the family without losing sight of deep-rooted ideas about race. It is necessary to think through the implications of engaging with men in child protection work for the safety of women and children. If we fail to examine gendered power relationships in black families, we run the risk of exposing women and children to further harm by the way we involve men in the work.

Developing a framework for understanding black mothers' responses

In light of the points raised above, I offer some reflection on a number of issues. First, the complexities of black mothers' multiple social locations need to be explored to understand the ambiguities and uncertainties they face in seeking professional help. Black mothers' gendered and racial locations influence how they come to understand what has happened to their children and how they perceive their choices and options. In particular, paying attention to the broader context in which black women's experiences are embedded is of importance for grasping how they perceive their choices. Practitioners who fail to do so run the risk of undermining or undervaluing the protective strategies of black mothers and leaving black children exposed to harm.

Another important factor is the extent to which the negative portrayal of black families consciously and unconsciously influences statutory agencies' responses to child sexual abuse in black families. Black mothers will have manifold experiences of their family life and different renditions of those experiences. The power relations embodied in black families require a much more complex exploration to bring into focus the ways black mothers are caught between their own expectations and the expectations of families and partners that they be loyal. It could be argued that this factor alone would exert a powerful influence on black mothers to be resistant to involving statutory agencies on discovery of abuse. While we need to understand the wider context of the black male experience in Britain, we need to find ways to do so without excusing black men's violence against the women and children in their lives, thus propagating the silence and resistance to male violence in the home. By centrally addressing gender and race as a locus of power relations, we can begin to delineate between abusing and non-abusing black parents. A reliance on stereotypical ideas can lead to overlooking gender inequalities in black families, and abuse can be explained away on cultural grounds. Practitioners who fail to confront these issues in work with black families are unwittingly colluding with gender inequalities, and may not see how their intervention will replay or reproduce dominant power relationships.

How welfare policies and practice construct black mothers' parenting and incorporate their concerns is an issue for ongoing debate. Definitions of good and bad mothering function to control women in welfare provision. Efforts to respond sensitively to black mothers will be influenced by ideological assumptions of what is a good mother. In a context where black women's experiences are rendered invisible, how black motherhood is constructed and the meaning that mothers bring to their role is of importance. Black mothers' responses may be interpreted in terms of their not conforming to the values of the dominant society.

Moreover, policy initiatives underpinned by the philosophy of 'invisible fathers' serves to reinforce mother-blaming and promotes a negative attention on mothers. How practitioners involve and work with black men who abuse their children is of importance. In her analysis of the differing career paths of fathers and mothers in child protection, Milner (1993) calls attention to the ways stereotypical ideas of black fathers were drawn upon to make assertions about their supposed lack of involvement in the caregiving of their children. Additionally, she comments on the way prevailing assumptions about the 'dangerousness' of black men may implicitly inform practitioners' decisions not to strenuously involve black fathers, and thus reinforce the idea that it is the mother's sole responsibility to protect children.

Conclusion

In conclusion, this chapter has been centrally concerned with identifying the interconnectedness of race and gender for black mothers in framing their responses in the aftermath of sexual abuse of their children. In particular, I have emphasized that one of the best ways to help abused black children is to support and empower their mothers as part of a broader strategy whose ultimate goal is the empowerment of the child. If we are to engage effectively with black mothers, practice must be rooted in an understanding of how matrixes of domination have an impact on black mothers' parenting of their children. To empower black mothers, we need to understand the structural, cultural and emotional factors that can be barriers to effect change. It is by being alert to mothers' perspectives that we can begin to help them to protect and meet their children's safety needs. Professional helpers are in a powerful position to bring about positive change, or conversely to exacerbate black mothers' problems. Recognition of the way deep-seated attitudes and beliefs influence and distort black women's everyday realities, can help us to evaluate their responses. Ultimately, practitioners who ignore such factors run the risk of reinforcing negative views of black mothers and may undermine their contribution to their children's recovery. An understanding of the culturally and racially gendered dimension of black mothers' experiences in their families is necessary to consider the implications for their responses to the sexual abuse of their children. The role of mothers remains central in the recovery of children. As such, work with mothers must be undertaken as part of a broader strategy whose ultimate goal is the protection of children.

Note

1 For a more detailed discussion of the methodological and conceptual issues arising from the research see Bernard (1998).

References

Arshad, R. (1996) Building fragile bridges: educating for change, in K. Cavanagh and V. Cree (eds) *Working With Men: Feminism and Social Work*. London: Routledge.

Bernard, C. (1997) Black mothers' emotional and behavioral responses to the sexual abuse of their children, in G. Kaufman Kantor and J.L. Jasinski (eds) *Out of the Darkness: Contemporary Perspectives of Family Violence*. Thousand Oaks, CA: Sage.

Bernard, C. (1998) Race, gender and class in child sexual abuse research, in M. Lavelette, L. Penketh and C. Jones (eds) *Anti-Racism and Welfare Practice*. Aldershot: Ashgate.

Bryan, B., Dadzie, S. and Scafe, S. (1985) *The Heart of the Race: Black Women's Lives in Britain.* London: Virago.

Carby, H. (1982) White woman listen! black feminism and the boundaries of sister-hood, in The Centre for Contemporary Cultural Studies (eds) *The Empire Strikes Back.* London: Hutchinson.

Channer, Y. and Parton, N. (1988) Racism, cultural relativism and child protection, in Violence Against Children Study Group (eds) *Taking Child Abuse Seriously.* London: Unwin Hyman.

Corby, B. (1996) Risk assessment in child protection work, in H. Kemshall and J. Pritchard (eds) *Good Practice in Risk Assessment and Risk Management.* London: Jessica Kingsley.

Dempster, H. (1993) The aftermath of child sexual abuse; women's perspectives, in L. Waterhouse (ed.) *Child Abuse and Child Abusers.* London: Jessica Kingsley.

Farmer, E. and Owen, M. (1996) Child protection in a multi-racial context. *Policy and Politics,* 24(3): 299–313.

Farmer, E. and Owen, M. (1998) Gender and the child protection process. *British Journal of Social Work,* 28(4): 545–64.

Green, J. (1996) Mothers in 'incest families'. *Violence Against Women,* 2(3): 322–48.

Hester, M. and Pearson, C. (1998) *From Periphery to Centre: Domestic Violence in Work with Abused Children.* Bristol: The Policy Press.

Hildebrand, J. (1989) Groupwork with mothers of sexually abused children, in W. Stainton Rodgers and E. Ash (eds) *Child Abuse and Neglect.* London: Batsford.

Hill Collins, P. (1998) *Fighting Words: Black Women and The Search For Justice.* Minneapolis, MN: University of Minnesota Press.

hooks, b. (1989) *Talking Back: Thinking Feminist – Thinking Black.* London: Sheba.

hooks, b. (1995) *Killing Rage: Ending Racism.* New York: Henry Holt & Co.

Hooper, C.A. (1992) *Mothers Surviving Sexual Abuse.* London: Routledge.

Hooper, C.A. and Humphreys, C. (1998) Women whose children have been sexually abused: reflections on a debate. *British Journal of Social Work,* 28(4): 565–80.

Jackson, V. (1996) *Racism and Child Protection: The Black Experience of Child Sexual Abuse.* London: Cassell.

Jacobs, J.L. (1994) *Victimised Daughters: Incest and the Development of the Female Self.* London: Routledge.

Johnson, J.T. (1992) *Mothers of Incest Survivors: Another Side of the Story.* Indianapolis, IN: Indiana University Press.

Kelly, L. (1996) When does the speaking profit us: reflections on the challenges of developing feminist perspectives on abuse and violence by women, in M. Hester, L. Kelly and J. Radford (eds) *Women, Violence and Male Power.* Buckingham: Open University Press.

Lewis, G. (1996) Situated voices: 'black women's experience' and social work. *Feminist Review,* 53: 24–54.

MacLeod, M. and Saraga, E. (1988) Challenging the orthodoxy: towards a feminist theory and practice. Family secrets: child sexual abuse (special issue). *Feminist Review,* 28: 15–26.

Mama, A. (1989) Violence against black women: gender, race and state responses. *Feminist Review,* 32: 30–49.

Mama, A. (1993) Black women and the police: a place where the law is not upheld, in W. James and C. Harris (eds) *Inside Babylon: The Caribbean Diaspora In Britain.* London: Verso.

Mama, A. (1995) *Beyond The Mask: Race, Gender and Subjectivity.* London: Routledge.

Mama, A. (1996) *The Hidden Struggle: Statutory and Voluntary Sector Responses to Violence Against Black Women in the Home.* London: Whiting & Birch Ltd.

Mercer, K. and Julien, I. (1988) Race, sexual politics and black masculinity: a dossier, in R. Chapman and J. Rutherford (eds) *Male Order: Unwrapping Masculinity.* London: Lawrence & Wishart.

Milner, J. (1993) A disappearing act: the differing career paths of fathers and mothers in child protection investigations. *Critical Social Policy*, 38: 48–63.

Mittler, H. (1997) Core groups: a key focus for child protection training. *Social Work Education*, 16(2): 77–91.

Mtezuka, M. (1996) Issues of race and culture in child abuse, in B. Fawcett, B. Featherstone, J. Hearn and C. Toft (eds) *Violence and Gender Relations: Theories and Interventions.* London: Sage.

Nelson, S. (1982) *Incest: Fact and Myth.* Edinburgh: Stramullion Co-op Ltd.

O'Hagan, K. (1997) The problem of engaging men in child protection work. *British Journal of Social Work*, 27: 25–42.

O'Hagan, K. and Dillenburger, K. (1995) *The Abuse of Women within Child Care Work.* Buckingham: Open University Press.

Parton, N. (1998) Risk, advanced liberalism and child welfare: the need to rediscover uncertainty and ambiguity. *British Journal of Social Work*, 28: 5–27.

Pringle, K. (1995) *Men, Masculinities and Social Welfare.* London: UCL Press Ltd.

Pringle, K. (1998) Current profeminist debates regarding men and social welfare: some national and transnational perspectives. *British Journal of Social Work*, 28(4): 623–33.

Print, B. and Dey, C. (1992) Empowering mothers of sexually abused children – a positive framework, in A. Bannister (ed.) *From Hearing to Healing: Working With the Aftermath of Child Sexual Abuse.* London: Longman.

Ritchie, B.E. (1996) *Compelled to Crime: The Gender Entrapment of Battered Black Women.* New York: Routledge.

Trotter, J. (1997) The failure of social work researchers, teachers and practitioners to acknowledge or engage non-abusing fathers: a preliminary discussion. *Social Work Education*, 16(2): 63–76.

Villarosa, L. (1994) *Body and Soul: The Black Women's Guide to Physical Health and Emotional Well-Being.* New York: Harper Perennial.

Wilson, M. (1993) *Crossing the Boundaries: Black Women and Incest.* London: Virago.

9 Supping with the Devil?: multi-agency initiatives on domestic violence

Ellen Malos

Introduction

Feminists have held complex and varied positions on working with state agencies. During the period of the Conservative government after 1979, with its emphasis on law and order and the curtailment of social expenditure, it was difficult to avoid suspicion of hidden coercive agendas or strategies to shuffle off state responsibilities in areas such as housing, health or social services (Hague and Malos 1993/1998; Radford and Stanko 1996). Feminists have mixed views, broadly sharing an analysis of state institutions as patriarchal and potentially coercive, but recognizing differences within and between state agencies, and seeing the room, or necessity, of working with at least some of them. These 'middle' positions open up possibilities for work with official organizations, as well as huge areas of debate and differences of emphasis, which can give rise to significant disagreements about the best strategies.

Attitudes to multi-agency initiatives on domestic violence raise a number of concerns for feminists relating to questions about the hidden agenda that may lie behind state support for domestic violence initiatives. There are also fears of the adoption of analyses centering on personal 'inadequacies' or individualist solutions such as counselling. Shared misgivings also exist about possible police or social services domination of inter-agency initiatives, a takeover of the issue by statutory services in general, the co-option or marginalization of feminist analyses and feminist or women's front-line organizations, and competition over funding (see Skinner, Chapter 3, this volume) or perpetrator programmes. Related concerns are voiced about the nature of 'criminalization' of domestic assault, or alternatively its 'decriminalization' and deflection into possibly inadequate civil protection orders. Alternatively, decriminalization can operate through deflection to inadequate, non-existent, or possibly uncaring or inappropriate services – such as housing, social or health services, and treatment (outside a penal context) rather than punishment of violent men. A major question is whether the development of inter-agency initiatives involves an inevitable takeover of 'professional' services for women by the state and statutory agencies, leading to a dilution or distortion of explanations of the nature and causes of domestic violence and a redirection of action into 'safe' channels.

In order to look at some of these issues, from 1994 to 1995 a team within the Domestic Violence Research Group at Bristol University carried out a national investigation of multi-agency responses to domestic violence (Hague *et al.* 1996). We set out to: investigate how different responses were developing; assess how far they were centred on improving the safety of women and their children experiencing domestic violence and increasing the support available to them; describe the development of good practice; and identify problems that were beginning to emerge. From this we intended to stimulate discussion on policy, practice and guidance, and facilitate the development of effective inter-agency approaches.

Although the danger of appropriation of services is recognized, and has occurred in some respects in multi-agency domestic violence initiatives (often called forums or action groups), our findings point to more complex and contradictory outcomes. We saw imaginative and innovative work, sometimes overcoming early difficulties about definitions of domestic violence, and arriving at a common understanding that the safety of women and their children must be the central concern. In others this had not happened. In all there were problems related to resources, and some difficulties in defining the nature of the relationships within and between statutory agencies, as well as between voluntary and statutory agencies. In general, our findings favoured a cautious optimism despite strong concerns – particularly at the failure of some forums to move beyond the initial networking phase, or in others a failure to develop a clear working commitment to ensuring the safety of women and their children experiencing domestic violence. Some participants in the more developed forums believed that clear policy direction and commitment at the national level by government ministries to which agencies were linked might be even more crucial to the success of local initiatives than local factors. The overall verdict might be that the situation is a complicated dance consisting of one step forward, half a step back and a great deal of shuffling sideways, but movement is definitely taking place. This chapter describes the major research findings, and draws upon them to suggest an approach to assessing this development.

The historical context: what led to the setting up of multi-agency initiatives on domestic violence?

Changes in attitudes to policing domestic violence, and to the development of multi-agency initiatives and models of good practice have been the culmination of a number of processes. Domestic violence has become more visible and more recognized as an important social issue over the last 25 years (Rose 1978, and see later editions; Hague *et al.* 1996), and has been the subject of explicit government policies, guidance and legislation for a number of years. Examples are the Home Office Circulars of 1985, 1990 and 1995 and the Family Law Act 1996 Part IV, the Protection from Harassment Act 1997 and the Crime and Disorder Act 1998 (see Kelly and Humphries, Chapter 2, this volume).

The process by which this has happened is interesting in itself because domestic violence, like other forms of violence against women, had not been considered to be a current social or political issue. It was brought into the public policy agenda by the growth from the late 1960s of a women's movement basing itself on the premise that the personal is political. The subsequent emergence of Women's Centres led to women, who were experiencing violence from men, including domestic violence, going to women's liberation groups to seek support. This in turn led to the setting up of Women's Aid groups and the development of refuges, which in 1974 gave rise to a nationwide Women's Aid Federation, which later devolved into autonomous federations for England, Northern Ireland, Scotland and Wales. These new organizations engaged with statutory and voluntary agencies locally and nationally, and brought about the recognition of domestic violence as a significant issue by parliament, government ministries and statutory agencies (Rose 1978; Dobash and Dobash 1980, 1992; Hague and Malos 1993/1998).

Second, an inter-agency, or more recently multi-agency approach, came from the coalescence of two different, though ultimately connected developments. One arose from the fact that domestic violence, unlike many other serious social issues, was not the responsibility of any particular statutory agency or government department, but could be the responsibility of many or indeed none. Women's Aid groups were therefore working with a variety of agencies of necessity, and were engaged in a critical appraisal of the nature of the services offered in a range of agencies. In some areas they had initiated inter-agency meetings on these issues, which in some cases later became the core of a multi-agency forum. Equally, when government and statutory agencies began to recognize the issue, an inter-agency or multi-agency approach, such as those developing in a number of other service areas, seemed an appropriate mode, giving further impetus to such developments (Hague *et al.* 1996). Simultaneously, in a slightly different context, community policing involving consultative committees, which had initially developed as a highly contentious concept following the Scarman Report and initially concentrated on inner-city multiracial communities (Patel forthcoming), also seemed relevant to domestic violence.

A third element was a change in attitudes to policing domestic violence. There were various stages in this process which were initially fuelled by growing criticism of police responses to violence against women from a variety of sources (Edwards 1986, 1989; Radford 1987), and given substance by a comprehensive Home Office research review (Smith 1989). Multi-agency coordination, involving statutory agencies, including the police, and voluntary agencies in a domestic violence forum were set up in a number of localities. Such developments were influenced by the increasing international scope of the movement against domestic violence (for example, United Nations 1986, 1993). Some of the best known examples of integrated responses to domestic violence, those in Duluth, Minnesota, USA, and London, Ontario, Canada, had adopted an inter-agency or multi-agency approach (see Pence 1988). Further, multi-agency coordination was recommended by the influential House of Commons Home Affairs Committee Inquiry in 1993.

For a number of people, including civil libertarians and feminist activists, there was concern that so much of the official response was Home Office and police led. Such concern was strengthened because of cuts in direct services such as social services and housing, and pressure on local government and publicly funded voluntary sector organizations to deliver slimmed down, narrowly targeted and financially 'cost effective' services (Hague *et al.* 1996). Although feminist activists and researchers are strongly convinced that domestic violence has to be taken seriously as a crime, and some see civil protection as a second-best option (part of the notorious 'no-criming' tendency in policing practice), few believe that a criminal justice response on its own would be adequate either to provide protection for women and children or diminish domestic violence, even if it were to be carried through in the best manner possible (Morley and Mullender 1994; Grace 1995).

The overall picture from the research study

The research was conducted in two parts: an initial 'mapping' survey by telephone, and a more in-depth study of initiatives in eight areas. In four areas this included interviews with women who had experienced domestic violence, exploring their views on the responses of the different agencies, and knowledge of and attitudes to multi-agency coordination. The telephone survey began with local authority housing departments' homelessness sections in all 365 housing authorities in England, Wales and Northern Ireland, the Scottish regional authorities and women's refuges. We identified more than 150 initiatives in different stages of development during the first year of the study; by the end there were more than 200.

The development of the forums

Most initiatives were set up by groups of agencies working in concert. Although there were exceptions, the initiators were most commonly either Women's Aid groups and local refuges (e.g. Cleveland, North Manchester); the police (e.g. Walsall, West Midlands, Dorset, Lambeth); or local authority units: women's equality, community safety, equal opportunity, citizen's or other specialist units (e.g. Hammersmith and Fulham, Waltham Forest, Sheffield, Islington, some of the Scottish regions, Leeds).

Differences in origin might be expected to influence and relate to differences in structures and ways of working, but we found that this was not necessarily the case. Forums which might be thought to be similar because they were initiated in response to national stimulus by the same statutory agency, for example, the police or probation service, were often very different in approach. One of the important findings, though not unexpected, was the way in which the origins, nature and shape taken by multi-agency initiatives, and the projects to which they gave rise, were influenced by local factors. These included: existing relationships between agencies; existing networks; the pattern of agency participation; the strength or otherwise of women's community group activities (including refuges, Women's Aid groups, groups of black women and women from different minority ethnic communities). Other important differences might arise from the nature of the local community, as well as from national policy and international practice.

The research results suggest that the initiating agency became less important if there was a healthy spread of agency participation, and sufficient time taken to explore the impact of domestic violence and ways of cooperating to ensure women's safety. It was also important that the differences between agencies in terms of their role and power base were taken into account, and means were developed to try to ensure that no one agency took an overly dominating role. The research also offered tentative evidence that a positive factor in this respect is the active involvement of direct women's services, refuges and grass-roots, voluntary agencies. The existence of strong feminist or women's community organizations could be an important factor, as could the presence of feminists within the statutory sector or the more mainstream voluntary agencies.

In many cases there was a lively and sometimes heated debate on explanations of domestic violence and the major orientation of the work of the forum. In the majority of the study areas this resulted in an explicit recognition of the importance of gendered differences of power within relationships and society at large as, at the least, an important ingredient in explaining domestic violence. It also led to the adoption of the understanding that domestic violence was predominantly directed by men against women, and that the main work of the initiatives and the different agencies must centre on this. In one or two of the study areas however, these initial discussions took a very long time, and some issues, in particular that of 'battered men' were returned to again and again. Sometimes this was despite the group having agreed that the clear priority for their work was the coordination and development of services for abused women and children. This problem could be aggravated by sporadic attendance or the addition of new participants after the forum had adopted its aims and terms of reference, and could be extremely frustrating for those who attended forum meetings regularly and wanted to move on from talk to action.

Tables 9.1 and 9.2 give information on agency participation in the forums in the study areas, and from a randomly chosen selection of 50 forums identified in the mapping survey. The evidence indicates that police and refuge services are the agencies most often involved. Probation, social services and housing departments are involved significantly less frequently. Of the statutory agencies, other areas of the justice system, local authority education departments or specialist units, and health services are less commonly represented, although they were very active participants in some areas. Voluntary sector participation was similarly variable. Representation from Victim Support was relatively common. There was a sprinkling of other voluntary groups such as Relate, Citizens Advice Bureaux, and representatives of national children's charities or local community groups, including groups for black or disabled women. These might sometimes play a significant role in individual forums. Local solicitors were active participants in some forums. The picture of participation in the in-depth study areas was very similar to that in a randomly chosen sample of 50 forums identified from the survey, as shown in Table 9.2.

In some cases, one of the important problems faced from the beginning involved tension between statutory agencies and less powerful community women's organizations. Where this occurred there was a danger that the views and interests of Women's Aid, women experiencing domestic violence, women from minority ethnic communities, disabled women and lesbians would be marginalized. There were also problems in ensuring consistency of attendance and a clear commitment from the statutory agencies. Some forums were developing strategies to tackle these problems.

Many forums found it helpful to develop a set of guiding principles, which could involve dealing with philosophical and operational differences between agencies. Resolving such differences without resorting to a 'lowest common denominator' situation while attempting to build trust, was identified as a difficult issue in conducting inter-agency work. Differences of opinion and philosophy about understandings of, and responses to, domestic violence could be a specific difficulty. These differences were often played out through power differences between agencies.

Even where basic agreement on aims and principles had been achieved, the development of inter-agency cooperation demanded careful communication and interpersonal interaction. In addition, interviewees described how members from different agencies sometimes made a decision 'to agree to differ'. In these situations, it was useful if there was clarity between all participants about which subjects were included in such an agreement and which were not. For example, issues of confidentiality could arise where individual women or families were mentioned in discussions about good or bad practice. Another related type of difficulty could arise where agency practice was scrutinized and agency representatives might feel defensive, relay individual opinions expressed back to their agency without agreement, or find themselves accused of disloyalty when they took up criticisms raised in the multi-agency forum.

Table 9.1 Active participation of agencies in domestic violence inter-agency initiatives: agencies most prominent and active in the in-depth study areas

	Cleveland	Derby	Walsall	Sheffield	Greenwich	Dorset	N. Wales	Bristol*** Forum 1	Forum 2
Police	✓	✓	✓	✓	✓	✓	✓	✓	✓
Police DVU	✓	✓	✓	✓	✓	✓	✓	✓	
Probation	✓	✓		✓			✓		
Family court welfare			✓						
Legal/court personnel*	✓	✓		✓	✓			✓	
Local authority special unit**	✓	✓	✓	✓	✓			✓	✓
Local authority social services departments	✓	✓	✓	✓	✓	✓	✓	✓	
Local authority housing departments and housing bodies	✓								
Local authority education department			✓	✓					
Health services	✓		✓			✓		✓	✓
Benefits agency			✓						
Women's aid refuges	✓	✓	✓	✓	✓	✓	✓	✓	✓
Specialist refuges (e.g. for black women and children)				✓	✓			✓	✓
Other refuges									
Victim support	✓	✓	✓	✓		✓		✓	
Children's charities			✓	✓		✓			
Relate	✓					✓	✓		
Community organizations (including women's, disability and black community groups)	✓	✓		✓	✓			✓	✓
Youth projects			✓						
Other voluntary sector projects	✓	✓	✓	✓	✓	✓	✓	✓	
Solicitors in private practice				✓			✓	✓	✓

* Legal/court personnel could include judges, magistrates, magistrate's clerks etc.

** Local authority special units may include community safety, women's equality or other similar units.

*** Forum (1) was in South Bristol.
Forum (2) was in Lawrence Weston in North Bristol.

Table 9.2 Active participation of agencies in domestic violence inter-agency initiatives: 50 randomly chosen domestic violence forums from the mapping study

Agency	Number of forums participated in
Police	43
Refuges	40
Local authority special units (where these existed)	18
Local authority housing departments	27
Local authority social services departments	28
Local authority education departments	6
Probation	26
Legal/court personnel	5
Crown Prosecution Service	5
Solicitors	14
Health services	13
Victim Support	21
Voluntary sector/charities/women's community groups	2

Forums adopted a number of strategies to overcome these problems. These might include initial domestic violence awareness training to assist agencies in increasing their knowledge about domestic violence and starting to build a joint approach, a process which could last a year or more. The use of facilitators for team building training, development of communication skills, and open and honest discussion of differences and difficulties could assist in reducing such problems.

In some areas the domestic violence forum was able to act as an informal service monitor. In Sheffield, senior officers from different agencies had been invited to forum meetings to describe the work of their agency and to respond to comments on their practice. Although such measures cannot entirely overcome the inherent difficulties for feminists and voluntary and statutory agencies with different philosophies and remits, by attempting to work together they could reduce tensions and unproductive disagreements. In some of the forums it was evident that working agreements arrived at were sometimes hard won.

Some forums set up working parties so that planned work could be carried forward while the forum meetings could remain an arena for discussion of issues and agency practice, where necessary. Alternatively, the forum might create a tiered structure with a steering group that met regularly and the larger forum meeting less often. These kinds of developments could be combined with organizing periodic conferences for a wider range of agencies and individuals to open up the issues, inform them of the work of the forum and help develop plans for the future.

Moving beyond networking, developing structures and types of work taken on

Many inter-agency projects are networking groups in which member agencies exchange information and educate each other. Networking of this type has value in itself. The 'talking shop' aspect of inter-agency work could fulfil a useful function if it concentrated on the needs of women and their children experiencing domestic violence, rather than becoming bogged down in repetitive discussions of aims, process and structures. However, some initiatives had lost their momentum due to remaining networking groups. Lack of time and resources often inhibited groups from moving on.

Apart from networking and exchanging information, the main work undertaken by inter-agency initiatives comprised:

- coordinating local services, for example, developing information leaflets or pamphlets, or 'one-stop shops' to reduce a woman's need to contact a variety of agencies before reaching the one she most needs;
- attempting to improve the practice of agencies and service delivery;
- engaging in public education, awareness raising and preventative work;
- developing new services on a multi-agency basis.

Coordinating services and improving service delivery often included formulating and assisting in implementing multi-agency practice guidelines to be used by member agencies. However, a considerable amount of liaison work and building bridges may have to occur before an inter-agency forum reaches a position to influence local policy and practice. The support of higher management and colleagues is essential in this endeavour.

Some interviewees commented that multi-agency work at the local level would only be given proper value when it was the subject of specific guidance from the responsible ministry at the national level. It is to be hoped that the more active stance taken by the current Labour government will lead to clearer guidance for more effective participation by the range of statutory agencies, and of health and education services in particular, to participate more fully and effectively. The requirement under the Crime and Disorder Act 1998 for local and police authorities and others to develop effective strategies for tackling crime should also create an opportunity for developing measures for improving women's safety in which multi-agency forums can be involved (Harwin 1998).

Many domestic violence forums design and provide domestic violence training, sometimes in partnership with Women's Aid, or coordinate its provision by other agencies. Training programmes usually involve a mixture of awareness-raising and training on specific local policies and practice, often delivered on a cascade 'training the trainers' model. Current best practice is that equalities issues and the development of anti-discriminatory practice should be integral parts of all training offered, rather than something that is added on as an extra feature. Some forums were engaged in actively developing equal opportunities practices throughout their work.

Many domestic violence forums produce leaflets, booklets and posters for the public or for women and children experiencing domestic violence. However few involve women who have experienced domestic violence directly either in the work of the forum or public education work. Of course it is likely that a high proportion of the agency representatives may themselves have experienced domestic violence in the past, but it is not sufficient to rely on this to ensure that the views and expertise of abused women are incorporated in the work of the forum. Some forums have been able to draw directly on the experience of abused women by setting up advisory groups or subgroups of women who had experienced domestic violence in order to work on particular issues (Hague and Malos 1996). This could help overcome the problems for women in developing the confidence to participate in a public forum. Such measures are likely to be most effective for women who have experienced violence in the past and have been able to begin to build a new life. Direct participation of women who are currently experiencing domestic violence is likely to be much more difficult. Some forums have initiated Zero Tolerance campaigns, and a number have set up night and other help lines and services. Self-help groups and drop-in sessions for abused women and their children have been established. Additionally, there is a growing trend for multi-agency initiatives to undertake preventative work in schools and youth projects (see Harne, Chapter 7, this volume).

At the time of the research many perpetrators' programmes were being set up throughout the country with the aim of preventing further violence, and some inter-agency projects are involved in this work. These vary greatly in their form and content, with some being viewed as part of the criminal justice system and run by the probation service, and others being run by voluntary agencies. Perpetrators' programmes remain problematic and contentious in a number of ways, and their effectiveness is still being evaluated (Pence 1988; Dobash *et al.* 1996; Burton *et al.* 1998). It remains questionable whether this work should take a high priority while funding for refuges and other services for women is insecure and insufficient.

Problems of multi-agency initiatives: inter-agency work in the wider national context

A number of participants in forums suggested there was a danger that multi-agency coordination could act as 'a way of saving face and looking as though you are doing something', unless there was a supportive policy and practice framework both nationally and at local level.

As well as describing and analysing the nature of multi-agency initiatives, identifying effective practice and suggesting some of the ways in which multi-agency forums may develop, the research also identified some important weaknesses in the way that multi-agency initiatives were perceived at government level.

The explicit policy as set out in the circular, *Inter-agency Co-ordination to Tackle Domestic Violence*, served as a useful starting point (Home Office 1995, section 4:9). Although the approach of the circular is not, of course, feminist, it does state firmly that the majority of domestic violence is directed by men towards women with whom they have, or have had, an intimate relationship; and it does place the emphasis clearly on ensuring the safety of women and children and developing action across the full range of agencies and services.

It is clear from the circular that responsibility for the success of multi-agency approaches to domestic violence does not lie with local agencies alone. In Section 4, the circular states that the Home Office has the lead responsibility to coordinate the response of central government.[1] In addition, the approach of the government is said to be 'based on the premise that domestic violence is a serious crime which must not be tolerated' (Home Office 1995, section 4: 2, p. 9), with a priority given to stopping the violence occurring. However, none of the agency representatives interviewed had access to specific guidance from ministries other than the Home Office.

Since completion of the research the community services division of the Department of Health and the Social Services Inspectorate have been very active in encouraging multi-agency approaches, particularly in relation to children experiencing domestic violence (Ball 1996). In 1997 a circular was issued by the Department of Health for social services departments on the implications of the new power of courts to apply domestic violence protection orders to children under Part IV of the Family Law Act 1996. The Department has also recently funded the publication of a training pack and reader on children and domestic violence produced by the major children's charities, Barnardo's and the National Society for the Prevention of Cruelty to Children (NSPCC), and Women's Aid Federation of England and feminist domestic violence researchers (Barnardo's, NSPCC and the Department of Health, 1998; Hester *et al.* 1998). Similar initiatives from other ministries would be very welcome, along with clearer encouragement to participate in multi-agency initiatives.

A number of agency interviewees referred to a combination of financial and statutory limitations on the ability of agencies to provide effective support for the aims enunciated in the inter-agency circular (Home Office 1995). The major weaknesses of the circular are its emphasis on action by local agencies and lack of reference to resources. This suggests a need for the Women's Unit in the Cabinet Office to review existing laws, and discuss the content of proposed legislation from the viewpoint of its impact on the provision of effective services for safety and support of women experiencing domestic violence. The promised national strategy on domestic violence first promised by the Labour Party while in opposition (Labour Party 1995) remains an urgent priority. While the more active stance of the new government is very welcome, the new strategy has not yet materialized. Although the Women's Unit has carried out consultations about such a new comprehensive strategy this has not yet made its way into policy documents (Women's Unit, Cabinet Office 1998; 1999).

Major weaknesses of the circular and the government approach

Many interviewees were particularly concerned at the lack of secure funding and a national funding strategy for refuges, and the possible consequence of inter-agency services competing with refuges for scarce resources. Such problems were viewed as a severe drawback given the almost entirely local and piecemeal nature of funding for multi-agency initiatives. This was sometimes seen as a matter of central government willing the ends, but not providing the means to carry out effective inter-agency work at a time of retrenchment of expenditure.

Although a few judges, magistrates and magistrates' court clerks are involved in multi-agency work, the general lack of involvement of legal personnel is worrying. Rather than being trained in their own environment, it would be beneficial for the judiciary to receive training with other agencies. This would enable them to develop their understanding of domestic violence outside of a hierarchical legal system in which 'judges know best'. Such joint training could be initiated by a directive from the Lord Chancellor's Department.

An additional weakness is that there are no signs so far that coordination includes scrutiny of legislation and policy for its impact on domestic violence (e.g. Children Act 1989, Child Support Act 1991, Housing Act 1996). As the example of the Children Act 1989 shows, legislation intended to benefit children can lead to problems where there has been domestic violence. Child contact orders have often ignored the issue of domestic violence and have led to renewed violence towards women or children or both. This is due to the presumption under the 1989 Children Act that children need contact with both parents, which tends to take precedent over all other considerations when judges are considering orders (Hester and Radford 1996; Hester *et al.* 1998).

Laws have often been bad, or have been mixed in their impact on women experiencing domestic violence. Immigration law with its 'one year rule' may give women a 'choice' between deportation or living with domestic violence. The Family Law Act 1996 is highly problematic because of the danger that domestic violence will be ignored or discounted in the emphasis on joint mediation meetings during divorce. However, Part IV which embodies most of the withdrawn Family Homes and Domestic Violence Bill offers the hope of more effective civil protection orders for women and their children experiencing domestic violence.

The Protection from Harassment Act 1997 represents a new departure in that it is based on the recognition that violence can arise from a series of acts, some of which may be trivial in themselves, and that it can transcend the boundaries between criminal and civil law (see Kelly and Humphries, Chapter 2, this volume). The task remains to develop an integrated framework of law on domestic violence crossing the civil/criminal divide, incorporating child contact and child protection (Mullender 1996), immigration, and the promotion of 'self-preservation' as a defence option in the context of women who kill violent partners. Such a comprehensive approach is not simple to devise, but lessons from other countries could be drawn upon in the development of a national strategy to eliminate domestic violence.

Conclusion

Despite the possible dangers of dilution and co-option of multi-agency initiatives, the evidence suggests that they represent a valuable arena for debate about the social meaning of domestic violence and the development of services. Despite the difficulties, they do seem to represent possibilities for improved services for women and their children experiencing domestic violence. Much energy and imagination is going into the development of multi-agency work on domestic violence at a local level. It is of course possible that despite their best efforts the forums will ultimately reconfirm existing power structures within the local community and the state. Women's movements and organizations, however, will continue to contest these power structures, attempt to develop their own analyses of the social and political issues facing women in society, and persuade by various means those in powerful positions to take them seriously.

One potential strength lies in the fact that multi-agency initiatives have often initially arisen from the grass-roots movement against domestic violence, violence against women and women's rights generally. The Women's Aid Federations, women's refuges and campaigning groups such as Southall Black Sisters, Rights of Women and Justice for Women have also been important influences. Even if not directly involved in multi-agency forums, they have all had an impact on the context within which multi-agency initiatives have grown up.

Lack of clear definition and lines of responsibility can be problematic, but these can sometimes have important advantages in that they give freedom to experiment with different ways of working, and can lead to an emphasis on empowerment and support rather than 'protection' alone. They leave the way open for the meaningful participation of grass-roots groups, and of women who have experienced domestic violence as participants in the development of policies and services, rather than only as 'users' consulted about delivery.

There is still a long way to go and many possibilities of tokenism, co-option and cut-back of services. Nevertheless, multi-agency initiatives could be of major importance in the future as part of an overall strategy of building awareness about domestic violence and its consequences, in increasing women's safety and in developing and coordinating effective and wide-reaching services. At their best the multi-agency approaches offer an example of a way of working geared to support, empowerment and coordination of services. They can also identify service gaps and inadequacies, help develop good practice in and between agencies directed towards the needs of women and children experiencing domestic violence, and wherever possible involve them in decision making and service development priorities. This can happen alongside developing public awareness, and challenging attitudes on gender and relationships between men and women through work in schools or community awareness campaigns.

Although the research found that there was much innovative and exciting inter-agency work going on at local levels, it is clear that there is a need for strong continuing feminist advocacy and campaigns on violence against women and children at both local and national levels. Ideally these would link campaigning groups such as Justice for Women, Southall Black Sisters and Women's Aid groups and federations, with their dual focus on campaigning and service provision.

Such linked approaches can be a protection against the dangers of multi-agency work on domestic violence becoming a smokescreen to hide inertia, or an erosion or withdrawal of essential services. This would open the way for multi-agency work to build awareness about domestic violence, its consequences and links to other kinds of violence against women, so developing and coordinating effective and far-reaching services, and helping to create a society that no longer condones such violence or minimizes its impact. It may well be, though, that we need to be aware of the old saying that if you sup with the devil you must carry a long spoon.

Acknowledgements

The Joseph Rowntree Foundation supported this research which was carried out in conjunction with Gill Hague and Wendy Dear. The views expressed in this chapter draw heavily on our joint work, but reflects my opinions and not necessarily those of my colleagues or the Foundation.

Note

1 The Home Office chairs official and ministerial intergovernmental groups on domestic violence. The Lord Chancellor's Department, the Law Officer's Department, the Crown Prosecution Service, the Departments of Environment, Health, Social Security, the Department for Education and Employment, the Welsh, Scottish and Northern Ireland Offices and the Treasury all participate in these groups.

References

Ball, M. (1996) *Domestic Violence and Social Care: A Report on Two Conferences Held by the Social Services Inspectorate.* London: Social Services Inspectorate, Department of Health.
Barnardo's, the NSPCC and the Department of Health (1997) *Making an Impact: A Training Pack on Children and Domestic Violence.* London: Barnardo's in association with the Department of Health.

Burton, S., Regan, S. and Kelly, L. (1998) *Supporting Women and Challenging Men: Lessons from the Domestic Violence Intervention Project.* Bristol: Policy Press.

Department of Health Circular (1997) *Part IV of the Family Law Act 1996.* London: Department of Health.

Dobash, R. and Dobash, R. (1980) *Violence against Wives.* Shepton Mallet: Open Books.

Dobash, R. and Dobash, R.E. (1992) *Women, Violence and Social Change.* London: Routledge.

Dobash, R.E., Dobash, R., Cavanagh, K. and Lewis, R. (1996) *Research Evaluation of Programmes for Violent Men.* Edinburgh: Scottish Office Central Research Unit.

Edwards, S. (1986) The real risks of violence behind closed doors. *New Law Journal,* 136(6284): 1191–4.

Edwards, S. (1989) *Policing Domestic Violence.* London: Sage.

Family Law Act 1996, Part IV. London: HMSO.

Grace, S. (1995) *Policing Domestic Violence in the 1990s,* Home Office Research Study No 139. London: HMSO.

Hague, G. and Malos, E. (1993/1998) *Domestic Violence: Action for Change.* Cheltenham: New Clarion Press.

Hague, G. and Malos, E. (1996) *Tackling Domestic Violence: A Guide to Developing Multi-agency Initiatives.* Bristol: The Policy Press.

Hague, G., Malos, E. and Dear, W. (1996) *Multi-agency Work and Domestic Violence: A National Study of Inter-agency Initiatives.* Bristol: The Policy Press.

Harwin, N. (1998) *Briefing Paper: The Implications of the Crime and Disorder Act 1997.* Bristol: Women's Aid Federation of England.

Hester, M., Pearson, C. and Harwin, N. (eds) (1998) *Making an Impact – Children and Domestic Violence: A Reader.* London: Barnardo's in association with the Department of Health.

Hester, M. and Radford, L. (1996) *Domestic Violence and Child Contact Arrangements in England and Denmark.* Bristol: The Policy Press.

Home Office (1985) *Violence Against Women: Treatment of Victims of Rape and Domestic Violence,* Home Office Circular No. 69. London: Home Office.

Home Office (1990) *Domestic Violence,* Home Office Circular No. 60. London: Home Office.

Home Office (1995) *Inter-agency Circular: Inter-agency Co-ordination to Tackle Domestic Violence.* London: Home Office and Welsh Office.

House of Commons (1993) *Home Affairs Committee into Domestic Violence.* London: HMSO.

Housing Act 1996. London: HMSO.

Labour Party (1995) *Peace at Home: A Labour Party Consultation on the Elimination of Domestic Violence and Sexual Violence.* London: The Labour Party.

Morley, B. and Mullender, A. (1994) *Preventing Domestic Violence to Women.* Home Office Crime Prevention Series, Paper No. 48. London: Police Research Group, Home Office.

Mullender, A. (1996) *Rethinking Domestic Violence.* London: Routledge.

Patel, P. (forthcoming) The multi-agency approach to domestic violence: a panacea or obstacle to women's struggles for freedom from violence? in N. Harwin, G. Hague and E. Malos (eds) *The Multi-agency Approach to Domestic Violence: New Opportunities, Old Challenges.* London: Whiting and Birch.

Pence, E. (1988) *Batterers' Programmes: Shifting from Community Collusion to Community Confrontation.* Duluth, MN: Domestic Abuse Intervention Project.

Protection from Harassment Act 1997. London: HMSO.

Radford, J. (1987) Policing male violence, policing women, in J. Hanmer and M. Maynard (eds) *Women, Violence and Social Control*. London: Macmillan.

Radford, J. and Stanko, E. (1996) Violence against women and children: the contradictions of crime control under patriarchy, in M. Hester, L. Kelly and J. Radford (eds) *Women, Violence and Male Power*. Buckingham: Open University Press.

Rose, H. (1978) Women's refuges: creating new forms of welfare? in C. Ungerson (ed.) *Women and Social Policy*. London: Macmillan.

Smith, L. (1989) *Domestic Violence: An Overview of the Literature*, Home Office Research Studies, No. 107. London: HMSO.

United Nations (1986) *Report of the Expert Group Meeting on Violence in the Family*. New York: United Nations Organization.

United Nations (1993) *Declaration on the Elimination of Violence against Women*. New York: United Nations Organization.

Women's Unit, Cabinet Office (1998) *Delivering for Women*. London: The Stationery Office.

Women's Unit, Cabinet Office (1999) *Living without Fear: an integrated approach to tackling violence against women*. London: The Cabinet Office.

10 Caught in contradictions: conducting feminist action orientated research within an evaluated research programme

Emma Williamson

This chapter explores the dilemmas, tensions, contradictions and competing needs generated in undertaking feminist action orientated research within an evaluated PhD programme. The aim of the research was to examine the response of the medical profession to domestic violence, particularly, the interaction between women who experience domestic violence and health care professionals within the context of wider help-seeking activities.

The different needs and power relations of the four constituencies – the university, the voluntary sector agencies, the participants and the research student – can create acute difficulties in feminist research. These problems are further compounded by the fact that not all of these constituencies are unitary ones. The university is a complex institution whose aims include: the production of academic excellence and rigorous research; teaching and training the research student; good scores in degree ratings; and generating income. The problems that can arise relate to the priorities of the university and the ambitions of the researcher for academic success often being championed over other considerations, including the aims of the research and the needs of the locality. The agencies' needs are equally pragmatic and include access to research information to support and progress their work. The participants, like the researcher, are caught within these contradictions, although the researcher is at least empowered by academic training. The powerlessness of the participants is reflected in the rare explorations in methodological discussions of their experience of and contributions to the research process. These various needs and positions create epistemological and empirical contradictions between the aims and objectives of the institution, the agencies likely to benefit from the research and the participants. The researcher is often positioned in the centre of this matrix of competing demands.

In this project, the single feminist research student had several aims: to produce research that makes a difference in women's lives; was of practical use to the voluntary agencies; and to win an academic award that would further her career. Consistent with feminist ethics, it was important to consider the impact of feminist action orientated research on all constituents. Such research must balance the complexities of obtaining knowledge from the participants while simultaneously ensuring that the process is not oppressive or abusive.

The participants in this study consisted of two groups, professionals providing a service and women service users. The research was divided into two stages, the first being interviews with 10 women survivors of domestic violence. These were mostly conducted in the women's homes. Although a limited number of specific questions about their experiences and perceptions of health professionals were asked, the focus of these interviews was largely dictated by the participants, who were given space to discuss their experiences in any way they felt comfortable. By interviewing the women survivors first I was able to ensure that any specific questions they raised were addressed by health care professionals. Thus the research process began with the 'expert' testimonies of women survivors of domestic violence to ensure that their experiences of gendered abuse were not overlooked within the research process.

The 23 second stage interviews were conducted with a wide range of health care professionals, including general practitioners, health visitors, practice nurses, midwives, counsellors and health care managers. The majority of these interviews were conducted at the participants' place of work. It is important to acknowledge that gendered power structures were evident in the medical hierarchy within which the professionals were located. In particular, health visitors and practice nurses (mostly women) frequently focused their professional frustrations towards the general practitioners (mostly men) with whom they worked. On occasion, their discussions of clinical practice mirrored similar relationships to general practitioners as those described by the participating survivors. While this is not addressed in depth, the different ways in which both groups constructed their participation in the research process will be discussed.

Balancing competing needs

The first step in balancing the needs of the various agencies, institutions, and individuals central to this study was acknowledging the contradictions and paradoxes that a feminist action orientated approach to research elicits. The most important personal revelation was recognizing at one point in the research process that the requirements of the academic institution and the personal rewards offered, had become divorced from the research process itself. It was through a realization of the importance of implementing the research within the wider community that I was able to comfortably locate myself and the research participants within the research process.

While academic language facilitates discussion of often complex issues on a theoretical basis, it inevitably excludes from these debates the subjects of research and those who would most benefit (Morgan 1981). This exclusion alienates research participants, in this case women who have experienced domestic violence. It is a salient reminder of Oakley's (1981) point concerning feminist ethics and not using research subjects. While a PhD thesis focuses on the theoretical analysis of 'research data', a report prepared for professionals needs to focus on the more practical, political and professional implications. To be of practical use the research needs to be located within the context, dynamics and politics of local inter-agency initiatives and collaborations. In contrast to the scholastic needs of academia, the needs of the relevant agencies include an accessible presentation of empirical results, analysis and discussion (Kelly *et al.* 1992).

A specific frustration in this project was that its action orientated approach was not recognized in the evaluation. The narrow academic evaluation criteria reinforces stereotypes of academic elitism and maintains distance between 'town and gown' and academic and activist feminism. Meeting this criteria meant excluding much data of importance to the participating agency. As the focus on domestic violence as a health issue constituted an 'original contribution to knowledge', wider issues raised by service users had to be excluded.

Many participants felt that by talking to me about very personal experiences of violence and abuse they would be helping other women in similar situations. Many assumed that my position as a university research student was sufficient assurance that this would happen. Unfortunately, due to the structure and emphasis of the academic evaluation process my position within the university was more likely to prevent my producing useful research. The wider implementation of the research findings was initiated by the individual researcher in cooperation with community agencies, rather than within the process of academic evaluation per se.

Phase one: interviewing women – the pain, the process and the purpose

In attempting to ensure an ethical approach I drew on feminist methodologies using qualitative interviews. The problems inherent in this approach have been acknowledged elsewhere (Kelly *et al.* 1992).

While 'traditional' research takes the perspective that people like talking about themselves because it makes them feel 'important', feminist research has acknowledged that talking about the effects of experiences of violence can be both cathartic and traumatic (Kelly *et al.* 1992), as was the case in this study. Many of the women found talking about domestic violence extremely traumatic. Some visibly broke down. The research process did not make them feel important; it made them realize how angry they were, how used and abused they were or had been and it made them remember.

While at times the research process was traumatic for the participants and the researcher, it also gave the participants space to voice their opinions and experiences of violence, abuse and help-seeking processes. Although this in itself did not provide the women a channel through which to convert their anger into direct action, it gave them a space where their experiences were validated. This process also contributed to a validation of the women's anger, which was specifically manifested in the gendered social and political explanations which the women offered as explanations for the abuse they experienced. These included general comments about male power and its manifestation in individual relationships. For a number of the women this was the first time such explanations had received validation and space for discussion.

The women's responses to the research process, like their responses to male violence generally, were diverse. The following conversation is a quotation from one of the taped interviews:[1]

(Iris became visibly upset)[2] I didn't think this would do this to me.
Do you want me to turn it off?
No it's OK, keep going, I think I need to do this.
It's not a test.
Yeah I know, it's my test. Does that make sense?

While I was conscious that taping a woman in distress and making her so unhappy was not a legitimate part of the interview process, Iris was clear in her reasons for wanting to continue the interview. In attempting to act according to feminist ethics, at points where the participants became upset or agitated I acknowledged their feelings. Depending on the wishes of the participant, I either discussed those feelings or moved the interview onto a more positive aspect of the woman's experience. Without breaching confidentiality, by placing these experiences in the context of the general issues and feelings that had emerged in other interviews, I was able to validate the participants' experiences. This process of discussing the research holistically enabled the women to indirectly empower and support each other, and the role of researcher to become a facilitative one.

It was helpful for me as a researcher, and I believe also for the participants, to focus on the strengths and resources they demonstrated in discussions of their experiences of violence and abuse. As a researcher, a feminist and a survivor, I could not have justified putting women through such a process for the abstract concept of 'original contribution to knowledge'.

I perceived the women survivors' consent as a continuous process. At the initial meetings I made it clear that I would be happier to return or destroy any material such as tapes or transcripts than continue with the research process if they were uncomfortable with it. This might have jeopardized the project as it would have been difficult to conduct further replacement interviews with other women where the same issue would probably arise, but it was a necessary commitment on my part in seriously adhering to the feminist research methodologies I advocated in theory.

In attempting to make the process more collaborative I sent each woman a copy of the transcript of their first interview (Kelly 1988). At the outset I believed this would give back to them the knowledge they had shared with me, as well as ensure they had the opportunity to revise or verify their testimonies. In most, but not all cases, the participants were happy with the transcripts as an accurate representation of their interviews. Follow-up interviews demonstrated their varied and ambivalent responses to receiving the transcript:

> It was a bit upsetting . . . it's because I basically have come to terms with the situation I was in and I was putting it all behind me . . . I'd just, I think got over it . . . probably one of the reasons why I hadn't read it before, I've only recently read it these past last two weeks. I've read bits of it each night, and I must admit that's probably the reason why it took so long is because I found it quite upsetting to read the whole thing, so I read a bit one night and probably leave it for a couple of days and read it again but it was like reliving it really.
> *Would you have felt better if I'd just done the tape and not sent you the stuff?*
> I felt all right, it was like you said, when you see it in black and white and you're reading, like reading a book or something but it's about you, something you've actually gone through yourself . . . it was like I was there again . . . and there was certain things that I . . . I think there was certain things that I thought I'd got over that I hadn't got over.
>
> (Carol)
>
> I found it a very strange experience looking at that. For me straight away when I looked at it, it hit me like a brick in my face, it was just so powerful that I had to put it to one side and I don't think I looked at it for quite a few hours after that. It took me a long time and it was just sat there and I was looking at it and then I'd move away. It was just such a strange experience to see the way I'd spoken. I think y'know about the layers of feelings as well, I mean I don't think I would write it the way that I said it . . . It's an amazing experience that first time, because I've always written it in a way that would be taught at school and describe it but sometimes you just can't find the words, but saying it how it is and looking at it, it was a very strange experience, and I would like to actually try that. I've actually got a Dictaphone myself and many a times I've thought about when I'm in my car or when I'm on my own, just say it, just say it and see what happens, but I don't.
>
> But you know sometimes I look at that transcript and I think, god did I really go through all of that? Because you don't verbalize it, you don't hear yourself talking about it and then you start thinking, wow was it really as much as that?
>
> (Debbie)

Both women talked in a similar way about the impact of reading the transcript. They commented on the strangeness of seeing their words in written form. In retrospect, Carol said she would rather have not received it. Talking about her experience was 'all right', but reading the written version brought them back, which she experienced as further trauma. Carol's reaction made me realize that you cannot adequately warn and prepare people of the possible impact on them of participating in a research project. By also focusing on their strength and resilience, I had hoped that the transcripts would represent positive experiences and recollections.

Evaluating the effectiveness of feminist methods necessitates considering the negative and positive reactions to the research process. It is through this reflexive process that methods can change in light of the constantly expanding body of feminist knowledge. If I were to expand on this current study I would utilize these existing testimonies rather than ask further women to engage in such a process. I feel their testimonies to be sufficiently powerful to inform whatever subsequent research I was to engage in, and that this study adequately examines the medical encounters women survivors of domestic violence experience in relation to wider help seeking. This suggests that the shifting reality of feminist research methodologies refers to both collective and individual experiential knowledge.

Returning the transcripts also highlighted epistemological and methodological issues at the heart of the research process, issues of 'truth' and the reliability of participants' memory (Stanley and Wise 1993). Many women who have faced and lived through the trauma of domestic violence develop coping and survival strategies (Kelly 1988). Rewriting the past to construct one more comfortable to live with may be one of these strategies. This is illustrated in the following quotation where Carol revised the version of events initially recounted:

> It's the part where I was leaving, it's like something out of Mills and Boon . . . I thought to myself that it must have been what I was hoping would have happened. It didn't happen that way. It was when I was at the point when I left and it was saying something about 'he had tears in [his] eyes and I looked back and he was saying, don't go, don't go' . . . he didn't say that, he just said, contact me when you're sorted . . . but not 'don't go, don't go' and that was it . . . and I thought y'know wishful thinking . . . when I was thinking about it . . . I was trying to really strain my mind back to that actual moment when I was going and I felt he was outside the house, but he didn't really make a big thing about it. He just said, well contact me when you're sorted. Because at the end of the day he just thought I was going away for a break, he thought I was going back.
>
> (Carol)

Rather than undermine the reliability of the research, this extract demonstrates how difficult it is to ask participants to recall incidents and events which have been part of a larger history of abuse lasting many years. By acknowledging the unreliability of her first recollection of this event, Carol offered an insight into why she would have wished the event to have proceeded in this way (due to traditional concepts of 'romantic love'), but goes on to explain how and why it is so difficult to remember such events.

Though this raises questions for the research process, I do not believe that this 'unreliability' undermines the research as a whole. The epistemological standpoint of the research project acknowledges that oral history narratives are individual accounts of particular events. The extracts document the cumulative impact of domestic violence as experienced as a day to day reality. The issue of continuity appears significant for the women survivors, and is central to a discussion of professional responses to domestic violence. Where contradictions have arisen and been identified, they are presented as such not to question the accuracy and reliability of the women's accounts, but to contextualize the effects and objectives of the research process. In instances where the participants were able to identify that an incident had not taken place in the way they had previously described, I was able to remove that particular extract from any subsequent research analysis. As the research was conducted on a collaborative basis, the participants were able to comment on and alter their previous statements. In most cases this collaboration resulted in the women feeling comfortable that the interviews adequately represented the complexities of their experiences. It also enabled recognition of how a rewriting of personal history may be part of the survival process. Denial and minimalization of domestic violence has been recognized as one coping strategy (Kelly and Radford 1996); this research has revealed another.

Attempting to establish a collaborative relationship between myself and the participants was the only way to ensure awareness of the process in which we were engaging. The only way I could attempt to establish such a relationship was to be honest about my own experiences, to answer questions about the research and my personal investment and rewards from it, to give advice when requested, and to acknowledge the power dynamics of the research process. Carol, in a conversation about counselling, said she sometimes felt she would like to have counselling, but had felt self-indulgent when she had been referred to counsellors in the past. In this instance I gave Carol the number of the local women's centre who I knew had a feminist counsellor as well as a crèche.

Another dimension of the collaborative process involved maintaining some subsequent contact with the women. For example, after the interviews Carol had been worried about facing her abuser in court in connection with access to the children. I was able to contact her and offer her support by being someone to talk to who knew about her abusive situation but who was not a family member, solicitor or court welfare officer. Maintaining an element of contact, albeit chosen by the participants, was also an enormous support for me as a researcher, as it made me feel valued by the women and reinforced the personal reasons why I was conducting the research.

Introducing principles of collaboration into the research process has often been identified as contradictory, particularly in relation to the analysis and interpretation of interviews (Maynard 1995). The limits to collaboration are defined by the power relations of research and the distribution of power in the research process. In this project, the range of participants constructed complex power relations. The 'professionalism' of the health care workers gave them power and status in interviews in relation to me. In contrast, while I attempted to interact with stage one participants on a personal as well as professional level, my university and researcher status (though marginal within the university hierarchy) led them to accord power to me; and while I attempted to minimize the power dynamics, such power obviously existed (Sapsford and Abbott 1996). For example, this was evident in the fact that I had access to question health care professionals, which they did not. This also demonstrates, however, how power can be used positively in a research context, as I considered myself both researcher and advocate of the women's experiences. My honesty about how I intended to utilize that power was, in most cases, enough to assure the women that I was genuine about representing their experiences in a positive and empowering way.

My work aimed to challenge any further harm on the part of providers of support services, specifically health care professionals. I dealt with the contradictions of power in my relationship with the women by learning from their strengths, while also ensuring that I addressed their concerns, which mainly centred around the following:

1 the distinction made by health care professionals between physical injuries and psychological damage;
2 the medicalization of the women and their 'symptoms', as opposed to a validation of their experiences of domestic violence and the mental and physical impact on them. Attempting to get validation led to some women representing psychological damage in a physical way, for example, attempted suicide and self-harm;
3 the employment of cultural myths and stereotypes about women who experience domestic violence in the health care professionals' explanations of its 'causes'.

Phase two: interviewing the professionals

The second phase of the research involved interviews with health care professionals to ascertain their understanding of, and response to domestic violence, with a view to identifying 'good' and 'bad' practice. They were all informed about the nature of the research, and the fact that I had already conducted interviews with women who had experienced domestic violence.

These interviews were significantly different from those conducted with survivors. Health care professionals were not asked questions that related to their lived experience, rather they were given the opportunity to talk about their professional practice. Second, health care professionals, and general practitioners in particular, limited the amount of time available for interviews. While a limit of one and a half hours was set and adhered to, the women survivors frequently continued to talk about their experiences after the tape player was put away. None of the interviews with health care professionals overran the allotted time by more than 15 minutes. These interviews ranged from 30 minutes to one and a quarter hours, depending on their availability. Due to time restrictions, I was required to structure these interviews more rigidly to ensure that specific issues raised by the women were addressed. The health care professionals were offered full interview transcripts to change and edit any comments they had made, either through a follow-up interview or in a written format. Three chose to receive a written transcript, though none asked to change their transcript or participate in a follow-up interview.

A number of health care professionals, general practitioners in particular, used their professional power to undermine my competency by emphasizing my lack of medical training and questioning my ability to comment on their professional practice. This echoed the experiences of the women as clients. Differences also existed in my relationships with different health care professionals depending on their relative status within the medical hierarchy. General practitioners in particular appeared threatened by the subject of the research. In contrast, health visitors and practice nurses seemed more comfortable discussing this issue, perhaps because of differences in professional discourse and also that they did not have ultimate responsibility for patient care. These professionals, who were all women, also described their relationships with particular doctors in ways that were similar to the accounts of the survivors. In the context of debates within feminist methodology this research has demonstrated that a range of power relations between researcher and participants can coexist. Those with higher status in the medical hierarchy (the doctors) were able to exert more power in the research process in relation to determining the length and content of the interviews. Interestingly, they appeared to be more threatened by a feminist evaluation of services. In contrast, those with least power in the medical hierarchy (the users) attributed more power to the researcher, for example, in assuming her ability to effect change.

A number of key issues arose from these second stage interviews, which confirm the women's experiences and dissatisfaction with their treatment. These included definitions of domestic violence, identification of injuries, and differentiation between physical and non-physical injuries. These points illustrated the ways health care professionals identify non-accidental injuries and options considered appropriate in treating both physical and non-physical injuries. The interviews also identified how their patients' experiences were located within a particular discourse of domestic violence. These included perceptions of women who present with domestic violence-related injuries, the perpetrators of violence and the wider community. A key concern of women survivors related to their medical files. The women reasonably assumed that these would provide evidence of domestic violence often required in court hearings. In fact they did not. The survivors also identified their treatment after para-suicidal activity, threats of being struck off a doctor's list, and the judgemental approach of health care professionals as areas where they wanted responses and explanations from health care professionals. Health care professionals were asked about their relationships with each other as well as with other non-health professionals within an inter-agency context. This was intended to ascertain the knowledge that they possessed about women survivors' wider help-seeking activities.

The following interview extracts identify some of the assertions made in relation to how women who experience domestic violence are sometimes perceived by health care professions:

> I am going to write in the record the facts, not my opinion, which might be I think the silly tart has asked for it, which is not a very constructive thing to say, but there are some women who do actually make themselves overtly attractive to men and wonder why having done this they are victims of unscrupulous men. I have got one or two of those, and you have to say their lifestyle does put them highly at risk and whilst no woman perhaps deserves violence, if she is going to associate with these people she is going to put herself very much more at risk. [. . .] Well I think that you have to assess what the overriding need is. Do they need something to do with their depression? Do they need something to deal with their physical problems? Do they need something? In some cases hormone replacement therapy, because it is actually menopausal symptoms which are provoking the whole situation. Once you settle those down and they then feel more comfortable, then their relationship improves with their husband and the frustration and violence disappears.
>
> (Dr Jones)

> They're often not necessarily the most articulate anyway. That can often be the case if we take it as an overall thing. No you can't say domestic violence only affects social class 4 and 5, it happens in 1 to 5, but perhaps it happens more in 4 and 5, doesn't it?
>
> (Ms Naylor)

The explicitness of these attitudes validated the women's experiences and perceptions. These and other key findings were included in a preliminary report (Williamson 1997). This was subsequently distributed to all the professionals who participated in the research, a number of health care managers, a variety of inter-agency domestic violence forum members, as well as other voluntary and statutory agencies. The preliminary findings were also written up in an academic context (Abbott and Williamson 1998).

What about the agencies?

Action orientated research also assumes contact and collaboration with relevant local organizations, private sector research funders (Swirsky and

Jenkins, Chapter 5 this volume) or voluntary sector agencies. This can prove problematic as many people and agencies are sceptical about the academic researcher, particularly when it is unclear who will benefit. The tension that exists between academic women's studies and grass-roots feminist activism has been well documented (Humm 1991).

In this research I was considering the ways in which the findings could be implemented by the local inter-agency domestic violence group. It was only when I began to take seriously my role as an active participant in that inter-agency process that I felt my work was taken seriously. Other agencies had developed guidelines to help the integration of different agencies within the inter-agency forum, but the university had never done so. In an attempt to identify and prevent some of the problems we had faced, myself and the coordinator of Derby Domestic Violence Action Group (DDVAG), Bimmy Rai, developed guidelines based on our experiences of working together on this research project.[3]

These guidelines first included the need for researchers to consider if and how the research process can itself further victimize those who experience domestic violence, either directly as research participants or indirectly through research focuses which silence women and their experiences. This incorporates the premise that those who experience domestic violence are the 'experts'.

Second, that researchers not only consider their responsibility to the inter-agency project but seriously consider themselves as located within that practice on both a personal and professional basis. At the outset, this includes defining how the research will benefit the wider inter-agency project and/or specific agencies within it. Outlining such responsibilities also ensures that the expectations of researchers and professionals are fulfilled in terms of the dissemination of the research at the end of the project.

The third area of concern relates to the conflicts that can exist between researchers and professionals working at a service provision level. It is necessary for researchers to understand that other agencies might be wary of their objectives (and their position within society) and attempt to appreciate this perspective. One of the ways this can be achieved is by developing adequate personal support for the researcher within the university and elsewhere. Researching domestic violence can be traumatic, and professionals may not have the time or opportunity to offer support. Acknowledging this can help to dissipate some conflicts that can arise where they are ill-prepared to deal with the responses they receive from statutory and voluntary agencies.

The final guideline emphasizes the importance both personally and professionally of considering how research can be justified in relation to sensitive areas, and beyond limited academic requirements and/or rewards.

These guidelines are not revolutionary but they reflect and address the problems a researcher may face in relation to action orientated research. They outline the responsibilities to agencies and individuals working in those agencies for whom the research is intended to be useful. Developing and implementing such guidelines are a flexible alternative to formal contracts with voluntary organizations. A flexible approach is important as the nature of voluntary agencies and their funding is constantly shifting. Setting out objectives in this way may seem like a tiresome task but it reassures partners in a collaborative project that you are serious about the implementation of your work and your commitment (whether voluntary, unofficial or formal) to their organizations and long-term objectives.

These guidelines have been successfully implemented on a number of occasions with both positive and negative outcomes. In relation to my own experience I was able to put the above guidelines into practice by becoming a DDVAG volunteer trainer, implementing the research in the form of a training module to be utilized by DDVAG, and working in close collaboration with numerous inter-agency representatives. All of these aspects of my work emanate from the same research, which will constitute a PhD thesis that has been funded by a university.

Conclusion

The academic requirements I was requested to follow moved my research in a direction that was not conducive to producing feminist action orientated research. The agencies with whom I liaised were suspicious of my motives and methods, and therefore over the course of my research I have in effect written two theses. Despite the many contradictions, which have been examined, the advantages of conducting feminist action orientated research within an evaluated process is that as well as obtaining a PhD, I feel that my research has made a difference outside of academia. I was given the opportunity to work with those involved with the issue of domestic violence at a grass-roots level, which has added to my knowledge of the subject and has also provided me with valuable support and encouragement. Most importantly, through this approach, I have been able to acknowledge the participants of the research, who through reliving the pain of their experiences have really made a difference to the lives of other women who are experiencing violence and abuse.

Acknowledgements

I would like to thank all of the people who participated in this research, in particular the women who had themselves experienced domestic violence. Their courage and strength was a great inspiration to me both personally and professionally. I would also like to thank the editors of this collection as well as other members of the BSA Violence Against Women Study Group, Professor Dr Serpil Salacin and the Adana Women's Group in Turkey, Bimmy Rai from the DDVAG for being a great friend and support. On a personal note I would like to thank Scott McCabe, Lisa Flint and my parents Roy and Gail Williamson. For more information about DDVAG please contact Marjorie Lawes, c/o The Smith Partnership, 25 The Wardwick, Derby, DE1 1HA. Tel: 01332 346084.

Notes

1 My comments are in italics and the women's comments are in plain text.
2 All names of interviewees in this chapter are pseudonyms to ensure confidentiality.
3 These guidelines are held by the coordinator of Derby Domestic Violence Action Group.

References

Abbott, P. and Williamson, E. (1999) Women, health and domestic violence. *Journal of Gender Studies*, 8(1): 83–102.

Humm, M. (1991) Thinking of things in themselves: theory, experience, women's studies, in J. Aaron and S. Walby (eds) *Out of the Margins: Women's Studies in the Nineties*. London: Falmer Press.

Kelly, L. (1988) *Surviving Sexual Violence*. Cambridge: Polity.

Kelly, L., Burton, S. and Regan, L. (1992) Defending the indefensible? quantitative methods and feminist research, in H. Hinds, A. Phoenix and J. Stacey (eds) *Working Out: New Directions for Women's Studies*. London, Falmer Press.

Kelly, L. and Radford, J. (1996) Nothing really happened, in M. Hester, L. Kelly and J. Radford (eds) *Women, Violence and Male Power*. Buckingham: Open University Press.

Maynard, M. (1995) Methods, practice and epistemology: the debate about feminism and research, in M. Maynard and J. Purvis (eds) *Researching Women's Lives from a Feminist Perspective*. London: Taylor & Francis.

Morgan, D. (1981) Men, masculinity and the process of sociological enquiry, in H. Roberts (ed.) *Doing Feminist Research*. London: Routledge.

Oakley, A. (1981) Interviewing women: a contradiction in terms, in H. Roberts (ed.) *Doing Feminist Research*. London: Routledge.

Sapsford, R. and Abbott, P. (1996) Ethics, politics and research, in R. Sapsford and V. Jupp (eds) *Data Collection and Analysis*. London: Sage.

Stanley, L. and Wise, S. (1993) *Breaking Out Again: Feminist Ontology and Epistemology*, 2nd edn. London: Routledge.

Williamson, E. (1997) *Domestic Violence and Health Care Professionals: Results of Quantitative and Qualitative Research*, report prepared for Derby Domestic Violence Action Group, based partly on research by Prof. P. Abbott. Derby: DDVAG.

11 Domestic violence in China

Marianne Hester

Domestic violence against women has been a common social phenomenon found in the present and old society, at home and abroad. It is an important legal subject involving women's personal rights. Domestic violence refers to violent acts which cause injury, torture, ruin and pressure on family members by means of beating, tying up, insult, murder, confinement and sexual maltreatment, etc. The victims are mainly women.

(Chang Xianye 1996: 152)

The past decade has seen increasingly public debate and awareness of violence against women in China. There has been new legislation regarding the 'Protection of Women' (1992), and various attempts at setting up support services and activities aimed at women experiencing violence and abuse within the family, at work and elsewhere. In this chapter I look at some of the issues and developments in China regarding violence against women, focusing on domestic violence in particular.

Background

I am probably one of many women who, with the reactivating of western feminist activity from the late 1960s, looked to China as a place where women were being hailed in the Communist revolution as 'holding up half the sky'.[1] The Chinese pamphlets and posters showing women dressed in androgynous 'Mao suits', as members of the Red Guards and engaged in other non-traditional (for both East and West) work and activities, imparted an optimism and excitement about attempts to overcome gender inequalities.[2] While the details of atrocities during the Cultural Revolution, which eventually reached the West, dampened that enthusiasm, curiosity remained. What we tended not to hear about, however, were the sexual violence and exploitation of women in particular which took place before and during the Cultural Revolution – such as the widespread nature of male violence against women by Red Guards (Evans 1997: 222), and Mao's 'sexual exploits with hundreds of young party women' (Bulbeck 1998: 26).

The starting point for my interest in researching violence against women in China was an invitation to attend a seminar on 'Women and the Law' in Beijing in 1996, organized jointly by the University of Beijing and the British

Council, as part of the follow-up to the Fourth UN Conference on Women, which had been held in Beijing the previous September. In addition to four of us from the UK, the participants were Chinese academics, judges, lawyers, and practitioners from women's support services. My paper at the conference was on domestic violence – men's violence against women within existing relationships and postseparation. An important feature was marital and post-relationship rape. Other papers looked at a range of family law and family policy issues. The Chinese participants were especially interested in discussing violence against women, and the possibility of legislating around rape in marriage (which had by then been recognized in British case law) was a particular concern.[3]

After the seminar I was invited to develop training in conjunction with one of the main organizations providing support for women experiencing violence and abuse – the Beijing Women's Hotline – and to hold discussions with a variety of organizations about violence against women (and domestic violence in particular) on behalf of the British Council's Gender and Development programme. Through the training and these other contacts it has been possible to obtain insights into Chinese experiences and perspectives, and thereby begin to develop an understanding of violence against women in the Chinese context.

This chapter thus draws on the training sessions, conversations and meetings I have had in China since March 1996 (usually via interpreters) with researchers, officials and those involved in support work around violence against women. I have also drawn on material written by Chinese and other authors in English, or other European languages (or translated into these). The chapter has inevitably been written from the outside – I am not Chinese, have not lived in China and do not speak or read the languages (although I am in the process of learning Mandarin).

While I cannot present the material from within the Chinese perspective, it still seems important, despite my limitations, to show how Chinese academics, researchers, other professionals and activists are debating and tackling violence against women. It would be easy from my position to represent Chinese women's experiences of, and actions against, violence and abuse as some intriguing and exotic 'other', or Chinese women as poorer, more powerless and vulnerable than women in western countries (Mohanty 1991). That would be both simplistic and erroneous. Debates and activities around violence against women in China are varied, contextually situated and complex. I hope to provide some insight into these, not least because of the important questions they raise for western feminists working in the area of violence against women.

Making violence against women in China public

Following the 1985 UN Women's Conference in Nairobi, academics and others began to examine the 'maltreatment of women in Chinese families'

(Sun Xiaomei 1997: 1). However, it was particularly in the period leading up to and following the 1995 UN Women's Conference that research and support work regarding women in China became more highly profiled and gained momentum. The 1995 UN conference, and its location in Beijing, created a space where violence against women, whether domestic violence, sexual harassment or rape, could increasingly be made public. As Evans (1997: 182) outlines:

> Unofficial women's groups have pointed out that the international focus on women in 1995 gave them their first opportunity to bring the issue [of sexual violence] into the public arena. Discussions have begun to focus on women's experiences and difficulties in reporting rape that signify a qualitative difference from the more distanced, 'factual' reporting of the mid-1980s.

Women's organizations

It is important to distinguish between the official organizations set up by the Chinese state, and the popular women's organizations whose existence is more precarious. The only 'official' women's group is that set up by the Communist Party, the All China Women's Federation. In recent years a variety of other women's groups, often started by intellectual and professional women, have also developed. These have different degrees of official support. The All China Women's Federation (Women's Federation) was set up in 1949 by the Communist Party with a view to implementing and generating active support for the Party's policies among women (see Croll 1983; Rai 1992). The Women's Federation's agenda has largely been driven or shaped by the Party's policies rather than necessarily prioritizing women's interests. None the less, officials from the Women's Federation are keen to point out that the Federation is deemed to be 'quasi-official' or 'non-governmental' rather than a direct extension of the Communist Party; although clearly resourced by central state funds, it does appear to act with some autonomy. This has also led to some interesting contradictions. For instance, during the 1960s, through its magazine *Women of China*, the Women's Federation emphasized women's role in the home, 'as a homemaker, wife, and mother' (Holly and Bransfield 1976: 371). During the Cultural Revolution this approach was shown up as counter-revolutionary and the Women's Federation was banned 'pending reorganisation and election of a new leadership' (Holly and Bransfield 1976: 371). It was re-established in the early 1980s, coinciding with the introduction of a new Marriage Law. Since then, the Women's Federation at a national level has taken part in debates and activities concerning violence against women and encouraged debate about women's position in Chinese society, albeit with a somewhat conservative approach. In a number of localities the Women's Federation has also been involved in collation of information about domestic violence in different

provinces. The more innovative approaches to, and understandings of, domestic violence have, however, tended to develop from the new popular
organizations.

With the socio-economic reforms of the 1990s in China there has been
a loosening up in relation to certain types of non-governmental or popular
organizations. The build-up to the 1995 UN Conference on Women enabled
popular women's groups, addressing a whole range of women's issues, to
develop, often with UN and other international funding. Women from some
of the organizations explained that this was possible because these women's
organizations dealt with gender issues rather than 'political' issues and were
not therefore perceived as threatening to the state. These new popular organizations included the Beijing Women's Hotline, a telephone support service
for women, the Jinglun Family Centre – 'helping women increase their self-
value and equal rights' – and the Centre for Women's Law Studies and
Legal Advice, which is attached to the University of Beijing Law Department.[4]
Even though they developed with a more general remit, all of these groups
also provide support for women who have experienced male violence. The
statistics from the Beijing Hotline, for example, show that women have
increasingly rung to talk about their experiences of abuse at the hands of
their male partners, bosses or colleagues.[5] The popular women's organizations, despite their existence as non-governmental organizations have thus
managed to address women's experiences of male violence and create new
types of support and activities regarding this.

Women's experiences of male violence

Dialogue across countries and cultures enables us to examine the continuities and discontinuities, commonalities and differences regarding women's
experiences of male violence. It also allows us to re-examine the debates
and theorizing around violence and abuse by western feminists and others.
During the training for the Beijing and other hotlines, which I organized in
1997 and 1998, the workers and volunteers who participated provided very
detailed descriptions of the often grossly abusive experiences of the (largely
female) callers to the hotlines.[6] These included descriptions of women having their ears cut off by their male partners, their vaginas mutilated, and
being threatened and humiliated at home and at work.[7] In many respects
these experiences were similar to those of women in the UK, although the
descriptions were often more luridly detailed than tends to be the case in
discussions or interviews with women in the UK. Interestingly, given that
Chinese people are usually considered to be reluctant to talk openly about
sex or sexual matters (see Evans 1997), the participants were very candid
about sexual abuse.

Listening to women in China talking about violence and abuse was a
salutary lesson in how far removed from the notion of a continuum of
sexual violence policy, practice and much theory in the West has become.

That is, the continuum of sexual violence which 'includes and connects different forms of sexual violence and ranges of behaviour and levels of seriousness within each form' (Introduction, this volume). While western feminists may highlight the overlaps and complexities that exist regarding different forms of violence and abuse, most researchers and practitioners tend to separate out different forms of violence: physical, sexual, physical, emotional etc., resulting at times in a (misplaced) emphasis on only one of these forms. Thus much western research into domestic violence has focused solely on physical assaults by men against their female partners, leaving out the other abuses that women also experience. A hierarchy of abuse is often presented where physical violence is seen as having a much greater impact than, for example, emotional abuse, even if that is not backed up by what women who have experienced domestic violence themselves say (Hester *et al.* 1998). With regard to practice in the UK (as elsewhere in Europe and North America), work with women and children has also tended to develop separately, based on quite different theoretical approaches to child abuse and woman abuse – where woman abuse is more likely to be perceived in a feminist sense in relation to male power and control, while child abuse tends to be explained from more psychological or individualist perspectives (see Stark and Flitcraft 1997) – the work in Women's Aid refuges with both women and children being a notable exception (see Hester *et al.* 1998). Yet feminist analysis of women's and children's experiences of male abuse identifies the similarities in the power dynamics and the multifaceted nature of the abuses involved that stand out (Hester and Pearson 1998).

In the Chinese context there does not (as yet) appear to have been a comparable separation of violence and abuse into different forms, or into woman-abuse versus child-abuse. For example, both physical violence and sexual assault are talked about in an interrelated way with regard to domestic violence. What tends to be distinguished between are the locations of the abusive behaviour – that is, violence and abuse at home, at work, and on the street. Consequently, domestic violence usually involves anyone within a household. Drawing largely on Marxist analysis, explanations often relate violence against women to their (lesser) role in production rather than patriarchal power relations, although domestic violence is also seen as the husband's right. What tends to be missing in most Chinese explanations is a generalized gender analysis of domestic violence that is also echoed methodologically in the studies that have been carried out.

How much? – the Chinese research

There have been a number of studies in China looking at violence in the home and in relation to intimate relationships.[8] These include questionnaire surveys of both the general population and clinical samples, analysis of reported cases of marriage-related violence, and some interviews with victims of such violence. The studies reflect the Chinese analytical preoccupation with social stratification, related in particular to distinctions between rural and urban locations, occupation, educational attainment, age and sex/gender (but not gendered or patriarchal relations).

Sun Xiaomei, an academic at the Chinese Women's College in Beijing, reports on the investigation carried out by the Women's Federation and State Statistical Bureau in 1990. This questionnaire-based survey, which examined the social status of Chinese women in 21 provinces, also included 'the issue of wife beating' (Sun Xiaomei 1997: 1). Of the married female respondents, more than a quarter reported being beaten at some time by their husbands (0.9 per cent often, 8.2 per cent sometimes and 20.1 per cent occasionally; Sun Xiaomei 1997: 1). These figures are similar to those reported in British surveys (Mirlees-Black 1995), although the levels of reporting may not be comparable given the different degrees and nature of public debate in China and Britain. For instance, in contrast to the largely urban women who contact the hotlines, women in rural China have been found to be especially reluctant to talk about their experiences of abuse (Institute for Studies of Women 1993; quoted in Sun Xiaomei 1997: 2). In a further questionnaire survey of 2118 respondents in Beijing in 1994, carried out by the Beijing Society of Marriage and Family, 21.3 per cent of respondents 'admitted wife-beating' (Sun Xiaomei: 3).

There have been two surveys in Beijing specifically concerning domestic violence, one carried out by the Beijing Family Research Centre of the local Women's Federation (1997), and another under the auspices of the Beijing local police (via the Commission for Protection of Women's Rights, see Sun Xiaomei 1997).[9] The research used questionnaires, apparently based on a similar approach to the early versions of the Conflict Tactics Scale (Straus and Gelles 1980). One of the Chinese researchers with whom I spoke considered the work to be superficial, criticizing in particular the difficulty in ascertaining gender-related issues from the data.

The Beijing Family Research Centre report on domestic violence in Beijing was carried out with the help of academics from a number of institutions. The findings suggest that:

20 per cent of men are violent to their wives;
14 per cent of women are violent to their husbands.

The research looked at both physical and sexual violence. However, there were no separate questions for men and women about the frequency and strength of the violence, where it happened and why. It is therefore difficult to see whether men and women were using violence in a similar way, or whether (as western research has indicated) women are more likely to use violence as retaliation against already abusive male partners. Respondents were also asked about reasons for the violence, which were looked at in terms of age, education level and occupation, with most of the violence being found among workers and those educated to middle school level (who also constitute the largest sectors of the population).

In contrast, the report from the Commission for Protection of Women's Rights, based on cases reported to the Beijing local police, focused exclusively on husbands and wives, excluding anyone else who may be living in the household (children, relatives, etc.). Questions included how the violence occurred. The most common abuses were found to be 'hitting' and 'swearing' (50 per cent). Of those injured, 47 per cent sustained bruising, 12 per cent injuries such as broken bones and cuts (for example with a knife), and 0.84 per cent had severe wounds and cuts. Ninety per cent of the violence took place in the house. According to respondents no one else came to help the victim. The violence was deemed to have occurred due to a variety of individual or socially-induced causes: the bad temper of the abuser, because the wife talked too much, the stress of unemployment and economic problems, as a result of disagreement around children's education, housework, alcohol/drugs, third party (that is, adultery), and sex problems (for example because one of the partners is ill).[10]

Chang Xianye, based at the East China Institute of Political Science and Law, outlines the statistics provided from another study in Shanghai in 1992, carried out by the Committee for Protection of Women. In 1992, 3899 events of domestic violence were reported in Shanghai. 'Domestic violence' is here taken to mean any violence within a domestic context, and is not confined to spouses or those in an intimate relationship, although these form the bulk of the incidents. The reported incidents included:

conjugal violence (61.55 per cent);
conflicts between two generations (25.9 per cent);
other (12.9 per cent).

As in the Beijing study, workers accounted for most of the reported cases (63.5 per cent) while the unemployed accounted for 14.7 per cent.

Chang Xianye (1996: 152) stresses, however, that domestic violence is increasing among the educated and professional classes: 'in recent years, of the offenders of domestic violence, the proportion of cadres, teachers, physicians, technicians or even superintendents has tended to rise'. Another apparent trend identified in the data from Shanghai is that overall domestic violence has increased considerably in recent years. Thus,

> In 1990, of the 1581 people who submitted accusation reports to the Women's Federation of Shanghai, 29 per cent lodged complaints about domestic violence. But in 1991, and in 1992, the percentage rose to 33 per cent.
> (Chang Xianye 1996: 152)

Moreover, the reported violence was ongoing and serious. According to staff from the Women's Federation,

> none of those who appealed to them for help accused their husbands as a result of a single punch, kick, slap or pulling of the hair. Instead, they were very badly bruised, with eardrum danger, broken nose, fractured ribs or even kidney bleeding. They had no choice but to go there for help.
> (Chang Xianye 1996: 152)

The main reasons given by respondents in the Shanghai study for the domestic violence occurring are classified by Chang Xianye (1996: 153) as:

1 allegations of extramarital affairs – that is, 'third person problems' (32.2 per cent);
2 losses in gambling (26.2 per cent);
3 feudal thoughts of male authority and supremacy; and
4 'A very few people are abusive, savage, and violent in their nature, cruel even to their family members'.

Contextualizing Chinese explanations of violence against women

Explanations and understandings of violence against women provided by the Chinese are very clearly situated in relation to social change and differing notions of gender in both contemporary and historical Chinese society. Three periods are usually identified as being of particular relevance: the 'bad' feudal pre-Communist period (up to 1949) with its 'traditional' views of gender relations, the establishment of a Communist society from 1949–78, and the period of reform since 1978, which has seen the introduction of market economics.

During the pre-Communist, feudal period, the innate superiority of men to women was stressed, and women were legally owned by men through marriage. This period saw the Chinese practice of binding girl children's feet, supposedly to make (in particular upper-class) women appear delicate and 'elegant', but actually rendering women unable to walk and in constant pain from their rotting feet. After 1949 the Chinese Communists were critical of the traditional discourse concerning gender. Women were now said to 'hold up half the sky', reflecting the more egalitarian approach. An important change was with regard to marriage, where a new law in 1950 supposedly outlawed marriage as a financial transaction between men, positing instead that partners would marry a freely chosen partner and form an equal partnership. This fitted both within the Marxist approach that equality between men and women would be attained through full participation in (non-household) production, and also with the government's need 'to secure a stable source of labour to contribute to the official programme of socio-economic transformation' (Evans 1997: 121).

In reality, while there has undoubtedly been a move towards greater equality, this has involved an emphasis on men's participation in the workplace and a dual role for women in both workplace and domestic sphere (Milwertz and Qi 1995; Milwertz 1996). Crucially, the Communist Party did not criticize patriarchal relations but economic relations. Thus, underlying discourses and structural inequalities concerning gender remained, if transformed by a greater emphasis on equality between people. The androgynous Mao suits may also be seen, within this framework, as merely a symbol of apparent 'people equality' which masked women's ongoing inequality and sexual exploitation by men.

The period of reform and development of a 'socialist market economy' since the end of the Cultural Revolution has seen increasingly rapid change in many aspects of Chinese society. This has included the development of non-state enterprises without the 'iron rice bowl' guarantee of a job for life, associated housing and welfare support which some of the urban population had previously enjoyed. It has led to a greater reliance on the family for support (see Palmer 1995). This period has shown up new fragilities and tensions in male–female 'equality', highlighting the structural inequalities and gendered 'biologistic' discourses of patriarchy. Thus, while workers generally have faced increasing vulnerability in the market place, it is women as a group who have been the most vulnerable and most liable to experience unemployment: 'Twice as many women as men have lost their jobs as a result of structural reorganisation of work places' (Women's Research Institute 1996: 2). Various economic activities primarily involving the exploitation and violation of women have also reappeared, such as prostitution and the abduction, kidnapping and sale of women for wives. New Chinese legislation has been brought in, in the attempt to deal with these infringements of 'women's rights and interests' (Law for Protecting Women's Rights and Interests 1992; see Li Shoufen and Cui Jianxin 1996).

It is argued that the reappearance of these exploitations and violations of women are both a result of 'feudal' leftovers (especially in rural areas), and the tensions created by the economic reforms (especially in cities). Many suggest that the reforms appear to be increasing the degree of violence against women, including domestic violence. As Chang Xianye has argued, 'The worrisome trend is that with the social economy developing, the number of cases involving domestic violence has risen year by year' (1996: 152), although of course this may merely be a product of the more public debate about such violence (Wang Xingjuan in Milwertz and Qi 1995).

In explaining violence against women in both rural and urban settings many Chinese writers apply an evolutionary approach, presenting 'backward' individuals as the problem – because they are not yet 'developed' or educated enough, because they are yet to become used to the pace of the reforms. As Sun Xiaomei (1997: 4) explains in relation to the cities:

> domestic violence is a by-product of the economic growth which quickens the tempo of life, arousing a psychological tension in people who are yet to become accustomed to it.

This does not, however, answer the problem of why violence against women in highly 'developed' and educated populations such as Britain or even Scandinavia have not dissimilar levels of domestic violence to that documented in China. Within the evolutionary approach it is also women (rather than their male abusers) who may end up being blamed for the violence they experience:

> While city residents are drawing higher and higher incomes along with the development of the reforms, those private business owners and

executives of foreign-funded enterprises have become wealthy. These people often spend huge sums of money on feasting, gambling and women. *Domestic violence is often the outcome when their ways of pleasure seeking arouses the resentment or opposition of other members of their families, their wives in particular.*

(Sun Xiaomei 1997: 4; my emphasis)

Thus violence against women is merely considered a temporary difficulty which will eventually be overcome by the evolution of the means of production, as reflected by Yang Dawen, from the Institute of Law at the People's University, who, talking about the impact of the socio-economic changes of the 1990s, explains that:

Fundamentally speaking, such [economic reform] changes are good for women's liberation. However, we must know that as some measures in the reform remain incomplete, there will occur some temporary difficulties in protecting women's rights and interests, because women as a group remain weak compared to men.

(Yang Dawen 1996: 10)

Societies facing rapid change, as is the case in China, are especially likely to show up the underlying tensions and conflicts that exist regarding cultural expectations of gender and male–female relations, and to illuminate how former patriarchal parameters may become reconstituted (Walby 1990; Hester 1992). As I have argued elsewhere, male violence against women is likely to be an important feature in 'patriarchal reconstruction' (Hester 1996). It is therefore interesting in relation to the Chinese context to address both the issue of 'patriarchal reconstruction' and the possible role of male violence within this.

An alternative explanation of the increase in violence against women in China, incorporating the notion of patriarchal reconstitution, might therefore theorize the increased economic difficulties faced by women, and the increase in certain forms of violence against them as both a means and result of male–female conflict in a period of uncertainty and change. As has been the case in other periods and in other places, in male–female conflict around resources and the developing shape of society, existing gendered blueprints and discourses are drawn on to construct and reconstruct patriarchal inequalities such that patriarchy continues (Hester 1992 and 1996).

Action against domestic violence – the 'official' approach

The All China Women's Federation in its close association with the Chinese Communist Party may be seen to represent the 'official' view on domestic violence. Xu Weihua, a senior lawyer based in the Department for Women's Rights of the All China Women's Federation, reiterated the type of explanations regarding violence against women already outlined. She saw feudal ideas as the underlying problem, and consequently domestic violence as a much greater problem in the countryside. Usually it is men who beat up women, in particular rural, uneducated men. Domestic violence is thus seen to occur in China because traditional views of housework result in quarrels when men do not want to help; because men drink or gamble; because some men become rich and establish what the Chinese call third person relationships (that is, a relationship with someone outside the marriage). Xu Weihua explained that the All China Women's Federation works to counter domestic violence, and stresses that it is of great importance to raise women's quality of life and enhance self-protection in order to do so.

The Women's Federation favours what they see as an 'active' way of dealing with domestic violence (as opposed to the 'passive' approach of hotlines), which draws on the Federation's four slogans for women of:

self-respect;
self-reliance;
self-confidence;
self-improvement.

The Federation has consequently decided on two main approaches:

- encouraging women to use legal instruments to protect themselves once violence has occurred; and
- encouraging a social mood where husband and wife can get on in a harmonious atmosphere.

While both the Constitution and the Marriage Law state that men and women are equal, violence none the less happens, and the Women's Federation therefore proposed and took part in the drafting of the legislation concerning Protection of Women's Rights and Interests in 1992. Some representatives of the Women's Federation present this legislation in a very positive light, suggesting that as a result of the new law and its enforcement (for instance, via 'women's courts' specializing in the protection of women's rights and interests), 'all serious crimes in this area have been resolutely tracked down and severely punished by the judicial departments and their spread or development effectively checked' (Ding Lu 1998: 1). However, the law is in practice not very easy for women to use. As Xu Weihua indicates in an article, the law is there, but 'the problem of law enforcement still exists':

> In particular, we must not treat cases that involve domestic violence against women as everyday domestic affairs. These cases should be accepted and tried by law, and the perpetrators should be punished by law.
>
> (1996: 168)

Indeed domestic violence is not included as a specific crime within the law on Protection of Women's Rights and Interests. It appears that while the 1992 Protection of Women's Rights and Interests law has made some difference, in practice it is too weak. Ma Yinan (1997), for example, pointed to the Commission for Protection of Women's Rights report, which showed up the lack of faith people have in the courts and the police. The report indicated that lawyers and judges will not tend to intervene unless the violence is deemed very extreme, with some judges giving only a few hours prison for a 'light' or 'middle range' injury. Judges are perceived as very far removed from people generally, and are thought not to care, especially where injuries appear light. Ma Yinan suggested that the police also need more powers to deal with the perpetrator as well as a change in their thinking. If the police are called, they just say 'you shouldn't do this' and do nothing further. If a woman goes to the police to say that her husband is threatening to kill her, they merely tell her to go back home and call again when the man is being violent to her. The 1992 Protection of Women's Rights and Interests Law also needs to specify involvement of agencies such as the police, which is not currently the case.

The Women's Federation's second strategy against domestic violence – encouraging a 'harmonious atmosphere' – can be done in a number of ways. Xu Weihua talked about the 'five good families' as a part of this. It is what she termed 'a very traditional programme' which includes respect for the old and the young, getting on with ones' neighbours, and protecting the environment. She stressed that in the Chinese character spirituality is as important as material life, and 'five good families' reflects this.

Another important way of creating a 'harmonious atmosphere' and dealing with domestic violence involves an economic approach. Xu Weihua described how international donations for enterprise development may be used to provide small amounts of credit to women so that they can raise angora rabbits. Angora wool is profitable, and where this scheme has been implemented the women's income increased from 300 to 2000 yuan per month (from approximately £23 to £140). The idea was that increasing their income raised the women's status in the eyes of their husbands and led to respect. Underlying the programme were also a variety of other incentives to curtail violence and conflict. Thus, in order to get the credits the women had to attend a Women's Federation meeting every 10 days where they were taught to raise rabbits and about the Protection of Women Law. Other criteria required that: the women had to help three or more families develop alongside themselves; they get on well in the family; and the men must not be violent to their wives. If the husbands continued to be violent then the women lost their entitlement to credit and involvement in the project.[10] This 'rabbit approach' to domestic violence, while ingenious, does not, however, tackle men's violent behaviour as such, and instead places responsibility for the containment of the violence on the women who happen to be on the receiving end.

Other action against domestic violence – legal remedies

Ma Yinan, also a founding member of the Centre for Women's Law Studies and Legal Advice in Beijing, stressed the centrality of divorce reform in order to support women experiencing domestic violence (1997). She argued that reform of divorce law and legal practice is needed to enable women to leave a violent relationship more easily. In China, as in many countries, there is great emphasis on keeping the family together. The Marriage Law from 1980 emphasizes emotional breakdown as the grounds for divorce. Divorce is thus possible, but in practice difficult to obtain, and may lead to a woman feeling she has failed or lost face in the eyes of the community. Pan Jianfeng, from the University of Beijing Law Department, points out that this is because 'non-legal' factors may take precedence:

> Non-legal factors, such as social ethics, traditional ideas, public opinion and possible consequences that may occur after divorce cases have been settled, will also have a certain influence on the court when it makes decisions.
>
> (1996: 106)

In reality, it means that divorce is even harder to obtain for women than for men, yet it is women who are most likely (as in western countries) to be the ones petitioning for divorce.

Currently there are many pressures relating to divorce which force the woman to stay in the violent relationship. For instance, the courts do not take violence into account the first time a woman applies for divorce, and she is usually refused. She can ask again after six months – but the intervening period is the most dangerous time for the woman, with a high likelihood of an increase in the violence. In situations where the woman leaves, the application for divorce is administered by the authorities where the man has residence (and vice versa if the man leaves). Thus if the woman leaves, it works to the man's advantage. Not infrequently women are further abused or even killed when they return to the man's area to sort out the divorce. (The Women's Legal Advice Centre get a lot of calls about this problem.) It means that many women decide not to proceed with the divorce. Property and money are jointly owned by husband and wife, although with the man often controlling it in practice. If the woman does not obtain a divorce, she will have no access to the money held jointly with the man. It is only after the divorce that the court rules what money the man should give to the woman, although that is no guarantee that she will obtain her share.[11]

It should also be noted that in China access to the law is not free, and lawyers and the court process have to be paid for. In order to take a domestic violence case to court a woman will need verification of any injuries by a hospital; however access to hospitals costs money. Ma Yinan explained that women who are taken to hospital may say that the man should pay, however, men often refuse to do so. The woman's work unit pays if the injury happens at work, but not for injury in a domestic setting.

Other action against domestic violence – refuges

While feminists in many western countries have argued for, and have established, refuges so that women may leave violent male partners and obtain a place of safety, refuges are often considered inappropriate in China. The All China Women's Federation, alongside the Communist Party, have tended to argue against the establishment of refuges, partly as these are seen to break up the family.[12] Instead, mediation tends to be suggested as the way forward, although this is increasingly seen as 'not enough for women seriously hurt by marriage-related violence' (Sun Xiaomei 1997: 6).[13] As refuges or similar organizations cannot exist without some form of official support or formal registration, it has consequently been difficult to sustain attempts at developing refuges. Resourcing is a related problem. Resourcing of 'adequate' refuge provision in a country the size of China is in any case extremely problematic. As Ma Yinan (1997) explained:

> It would be useful to have refuges in China, but they are very expensive and difficult to administrate. There could be official refuges, but the government do not have the capacity or will to set them up. Some people would like to set up refuges, but have no money. In general refuges would not be the solution because they would need a tremendous number across China.

None the less, there have been a small number of attempts at setting up refuges. The first women's refuge in China was the 'New Sun Marriage Service Centre for Women', set up in September 1995 in Wuhan City (obviously timed to coincide with the UN Women's Conference). Chang Xianye (1996: 156) describes it as follows:

> In a 200-square meter room, the founder of the refuge, Chang Xianfeng received within a month 12 women victims from Sichuan and Hubei and had phone conversations with many women.

In this instance, the local Women's Federation did support the refuge and provided a woman lawyer specializing in women's rights and interests, in order to help with divorce cases concerning the women contacting the refuge. A further refuge was set up, independently from the authorities and 'totally by civil efforts', in Shanghai. The idea was to provide 'temporary protection, meals, accommodation, hairdressing, health care and legal counselling for women in intense domestic conflicts'. However, the centre failed through lack of formal support. The authorities were not prepared to provide registration for the centre 'as such a centre was unprecedented in China' (Chang Xianye 1996: 156).

In Beijing, the Jinglun Family Centre also attempted to set up a refuge, but it proved both politically sensitive and too expensive. Chen Yiyun, the director of the centre, explained that domestic violence cases are generally expensive because women need health care, a place to stay, and a lawyer (none of which are free). Instead, attempts to set up alternative ways of supporting women have been tried. For instance, the centre ran a hotline specifically for domestic violence for a few years (from 1994) in conjunction with the National Trade Union, the Beijing Trade Union and the *Worker's Daily* newspaper (*Gongren Ribao*). There is an emphasis on use of community organizations and mediation. Women are advised to go and stay with their mother or other relatives, and report to the police where necessary. The difficulties for the centre of doing individual work with women who have experienced domestic violence has led to an emphasis on preventative work – especially discussion about the issues in schools and in public exhibitions using specially produced cartoons as a focus. This work is also aimed at boys and men.

Other action against domestic violence – hotlines

The Beijing Women's Hotline was the first of the growing number of telephone counselling services increasingly dealing with issues concerning domestic violence and other violence against women. The development of hotlines has been possible due to the exponential growth in use of telephones in China, especially mobile phones. In 1998, hotlines were at last given official recognition by the Communist Party and seen as providing a useful social service with regard to the 'mental health of the nation'. This should make their existence more secure.

Despite their popularity, hotlines may be problematic. It was clear from the training sessions I organized that there are tremendous differences in the nature and quality of service provided by different hotlines. While a few lines, such as the Beijing Hotline, have invested much time in training and skill development, others lag behind. Some 'hotlines' may also have been set up to exploit the growing market for pornography. Generally, hotlines have been free, but this does not necessarily apply to the newer lines.

Zhang Lixi and Li Hongtao from the Chinese Women's College emphasized that research is needed regarding the level and quality of the service provided by hotlines. They were concerned that hotlines often lack a gender perspective and merely tell women to be beautiful for their husbands. As a result, women may end up being hurt twice – once by her husband and then again by the counsellor. Women are at times told the wrong thing, for example, 'that there is no difference between the genders', or 'that all men are bad', or even 'that women should be obedient to men'. Instead, Zhang Lixi and Li Hongtao thought it an important principle to enable women to make their own decisions – as is also the basis of feminist support services in Britain. These are issues which have begun to be discussed, for example by the Beijing Women's Hotline as part of their training.

Conclusion

This chapter has taken a very brief look at perspectives and activities in China concerning violence against women, and domestic violence in particular. It has only been possible to skim the surface of what is a rapidly developing area of research, debate and activity. None the less, the experiences in China allows us to critically reflect on theory development, policy development and practice in Britain, for instance, the separation of women's and children's experiences of violence and abuse and the fragmentation of the 'continuum' of abusive experiences in recent policies and practice. The Chinese experience also allows us to re-examine the direction feminist support services have developed in the West, such as the emphasis on refuge provision.

Notes

1 'Women hold up half the heaven' was one of Mao's social liberation slogans (Rai 1992: 21).
2 For a discussion of some of the gendered contradictions of 'socialist androgyny' see Evans (1997: 134–43).
3 This interest has been echoed by a number of further conferences in China, including a conference on domestic violence in Beijing organized by the Chinese Women's College and the Chinese Psychological Association in autumn 1997, and a Sino-European conference involving the All China Women's Federation and the European Union in Beijing in autumn 1998.
4 The Beijing Women's Hotline is now called the Maple Women's Psychological Counselling Centre, Beijing.
5 There have also been developments in Shanghai and other areas of China, but I am focusing primarily on the developments in Beijing.
6 The training ran for 10 days in 1997 and 1998, with over 100 participants from Beijing Hotlines (mainly the Women's Hotline) and a further 40 participants from 32 hotlines across 11 provinces.
7 Cecelia Milwertz has pointed out to me that there was a much-publicized case of a woman worker whose husband cut off her ears. The case was pursued by the Women's Committee of the Trade Union and played an important part in highlighting domestic violence in China. The instance relayed by the training participants may thus have been a copy-cat incident, or in some other way may have featured prominently because of the previous publicity.
8 This chapter gives an overview of some of the studies, but is not exhaustive as new research is in process.
9 The Commission for Protection of Women's Rights is a government-related committee.
10 Much violence was reported to be triggered/caused by disagreements about children's education, apparently because a lot of hope is placed on the one child.
11 Ma Yinan; personal communication with the author.
12 This programme appears to be based on the format of the campaign of 'Knowledge and Competition' aimed at rural women, which was introduced in 1989. This aimed to make women literate and to learn poultry farming skills, thus augmenting their ability to compete. An important aspect was also to strengthen women's social standing both in the community and at home through their increased earnings and education (Milwertz and Qi 1995: 45).
13 The CCPs view of the family has changed over time, with criticism of the family during the revolutionary period – where collectivism was seen as more important, but now with increasing emphasis on the role of the family as provider of stability, welfare and other support (Palmer 1995).

14 China has a very long tradition of use of mediation in family and community disputes. By comparison to mediation in Britain where 'neutrality' of the mediator is considered key, Chinese mediators tend to be more directive and are likely to tell domestic violence perpetrators to stop their abusive behaviour.

References

Bulbeck, S. (1998) *Reinventing Western Feminisms: Women's Diversity in a Post-colonial World*. Cambridge: Cambridge University Press.

Chang Xianye (1996) On domestic violence against women and countermeasures to fight it, in Ma Yinan (ed.) *Women and the Law*. Beijing: University of Beijing and British Council, China.

Croll, E. (1983) *Chinese Women Since Mao*. London: Zed Press.

Ding Lu (1998) Position and role of women's federations in the development of women's human rights. Paper to Sino-European seminar, organized by the All China Women's Federation and the European Union, Beijing, September.

Evans, H. (1997) *Women and Sexuality in China*. Cambridge: Polity.

Hester, M. (1992) *Lewd Women and Wicked Witches: A Study of the Dynamics of Male Domination*. London: Routledge.

Hester, M. (1996) Patriarchal reconstruction and the early modern witch-hunts, in J. Barry, M. Hester and G. Roberts (eds) *Witchcraft in Early Modern Europe: Culture and Belief*. Cambridge: Cambridge University Press.

Hester, M. and Pearson, C. (1998) *From Periphery to Centre: Domestic Violence in Work with Abused Children*. Bristol: Policy Press in association with Joseph Rowntree Foundation.

Hester, M., Pearson, C. and Harwin, N. (1998) *Making an Impact – Children and Domestic Violence. A Reader*. London: Barnardos in Association with Department of Health.

Holly, A. and Bransfield, C.T. (1976) The marriage law: basis of change for China's women, in L.B. Iglitzin and R. Ross (eds) *Women in the World: a Comparative Study*. Santa Barbara, CA: Clio Books.

Li Shoufen and Cui Jianxin (1996) Protection for women's rights and interests by means of criminal law, in Ma Yinan (ed.) *Women and the Law*. Beijing: University of Beijing and British Council, China.

Ma Yinan (1997) Personal communication, Beijing, October 1997.

Milwertz, C.N. (1995) *Accepting Population Control: The Perspective of Urban Chinese Women on the One-Child Family Policy*. Copenhagen: Nordic Institute of Asian Studies.

Milwertz, C. (1996) *Accepting Population Control: The Perspective of Urban Chinese Women on the One-Child Family Policy*. London: Curzon Press.

Milwertz, C. and Qi Wang (1995) *Fra Maosko til Laksko* [*From Mao Shoes to Patent Leather Shoes*]. Copenhagen: Kvindernes U-landsudvalg.

Mirlees-Black, C. (1995) Estimating the extent of domestic violence: findings from the 1992 British Crime Survey. *Home Office Research Bulletin*, 37: 1–18.

Mohanty, C. (1991) Under western eyes: feminist scholarship and colonial discourses, in C. Mohanty, A. Russo and L. Torres (eds) *Third World Women and the Politics of Feminism*. Bloomington, IN: Indiana University Press.

Palmer, M. (1995) The re-emergence of family law in post-Mao China: marriage, divorce and reproduction. *The China Quarterly*, 141: 111–34.

Pan Jianfeng (1996) Non-legal factors that affect the decisions of divorce cases, in Ma Yinan (ed.) *Women and the Law*. Beijing: University of Beijing and British Council, China.

Rai, S. (1992) Watering another man's garden: gender, employment and educational reforms in China', in S. Rai, H. Pilkington and A. Phizacklea (eds) *Women in the Face of Change.* London: Routledge.

Stark, E. and Flitcraft, A. (1997) *Women at Risk.* London: Sage.

Straus, M., Gelles, R.J. and Steinmetz, S.K. (1980) *Behind Closed Doors: Violence in the American Family.* Newbury Park: Sage.

Sun Xiaomei (1997) The cause of violence in Chinese families and its prevention. Paper to conference on domestic violence, organized by the Chinese Women's College and the Chinese Psychological Association, Beijing, October.

Walby, S. (1990) *Theorising Patriarchy.* Cambridge: Polity Press.

Women's Research Institute (1996) *Annual Statistical Report on the Women's Hotline.* Beijing: Women's Research Institute.

Xu Weihua (1996) Preventing domestic violence against women, in Ma Yinan (ed.) *Women and the Law.* Beijing: University of Beijing and British Council, China.

Yang Dawen (1996) Legislation for women – review and prospects, in Ma Yinan (ed.) *Women and the Law.* Beijing: University of Beijing and British Council, China.

Theorizing commonalities and
difference: sexual violence, law
and feminist activism in
India and the UK

Jill Radford

This chapter revisits the theme of commonalities and differences in women's experiences of sexual violence. It compares legal, community and feminist responses to sexual violence in the UK and India. The starting point was December 1993 when Rights of Women (ROW) responded to an invitation to participate in a workshop on Women and Law, organized by the British Council and the National Law School of India.[1] Its central objective was to contribute to the protection of women's rights and interests by facilitating the enactment and effective implementation of the appropriate legislation. Its specific objective was to examine the law and its administration in relation to prostitution, 'indecent representations of women', rape and sexual assault, with a view to either strengthening them and/or suggesting alternative legislative proposals aimed at securing the effective delivery of gender justice.

The structure and organization of the workshop was interesting and relevant for UK feminists working around sexual violence and law, who since the elections of 1997 are exploring ways of working with a new and less hostile government (see Kelly and Humphreys, Chapter 2, this volume):[2]

> Unlike the conventional pattern of drafting legislation in the government departments, the attempt here has been to seek community and consumer perspectives on the social problem and then to structure the statute in simple comprehensible style, looking at alternative policy perspectives . . . In the process public education of law is accomplished along with the legislators' education of public opinion. For the cause of gender justice, the process appears to be more relevant than ever before.
>
> (Menon 1993)

In terms of organization the workshop was split into two forums: a less formal activist and academic workshop in Bangalore, and a formal one in

New Delhi where participants included senior members of the Indian government and judiciary. In our report to the British Council we commented on how much we had learnt from this imaginative law-making process. Specifically we noted:

> [In Bangalore] we were able to meet and engage in discussion with a wide range of activists, legal scholars and researchers . . . The workshops were informative, constructive and characterised by lively debate as women from a range of perspectives, different regions of India, Bangladesh and Sri Lanka took part . . . In the more formal atmosphere . . . of New Delhi, it was interesting to meet and hear senior representatives of legal and governmental institutions. It was impressive for us to witness senior figures engaging so seriously in these consultative processes.
>
> (Radford and Rupal 1994)

In both venues, time was given to each of the workshop themes: sexual assault, prostitution and pornography. Plenaries were held in the mornings where formal presentations were given by activists, senior politicians, lawyers, judges and police officers from different states of India, and international guests. These sessions provided background context, detailing the issues themselves and problem areas of law and the criminal justice process. Afternoons were comprised of focused seminars. Participants divided into committees who worked line by line on the legislative drafts. It was here particularly that experience of the operation of UK law became relevant.

Issues in international collaboration

Participating in this workshop, as well as being a memorable life experience, raised issues salient to debates in feminist methodology and standpoint in the context of collaborative international research and activism. As illustrated above, it also facilitated learning about different ways of working for law change. It felt empowering to see activists, academics, practitioners and politicians working to a common purpose.

Collaborative working can provide new insights into epistemological and ontological questions: what counts as knowledge; whose knowledge counts; how we know what we know; and demonstrate just how much we don't know. Within activism, it is recognized that working for changes that can make a difference to women and children requires knowing and understanding the issues: feminism recognizes the salience of personal experience when drawn on in reflexive and contextualized ways; while for academics the starting point is a literature review. On this occasion, however, time constraints precluded prior knowledge gathering; neither networking with feminist activists in India nor accessing relevant literature was possible. In relation to published work, First World bias has produced a situation where 'international' usually relates to North America, so little research pertaining to sexual violence in India was then accessible in the UK.

This absence also reflects the different social conditions in which research is undertaken and knowledge created. India is a diverse country. Its extremes of wealth and poverty are greater than in the UK. Higher education is well developed and there are long-established women-only universities, but literacy rates amongst women remain low (Sarkar 1997). In India, much of the work on violence against women has been conducted by voluntary sector women's organizations and was little known outside the country. Subsequent to, and possibly as an outcome of the workshop, more texts on women, sexual violence and the law have been published by Indian researchers. Contrarily, almost all of our background reading was post rather than prior to the workshop. The latter part of the chapter introduces this literature. It is quoted extensively as a way of enabling Indian feminist scholars, lawyers and activists to have a presence in this discussion.

Although underprepared in terms of background knowledge, there were some reassurances for us as guest participants. Rita Rupal is of Indian origin and had visited India frequently, but had no previous experience of working on legal issues there. Second, our brief made clear that our contribution would provide knowledge of relevant law and feminist activism in the UK. At one level this remit was straightforward. Since the mid-1970s feminists in the UK have critiqued law and legal practice relating to rape. The failings of law and limited nature of reforms secured to date are widely recognized (see for example Jeffreys and Radford 1984; Tempkin 1987; Smart 1995; Lees 1996) and Rights of Women had first-hand knowledge of its impact on women. Of more concern was how this input would be received. The invitation had been accepted in the spirit of global feminism, but it could also have been characterized by echoes of colonialism. Sharing expertise and experience with Indian sisters could be read as progressive, supportive and exciting; alternatively, through the shades of the Raj, as arrogant and imperialist. Despite this ambiguity, the prospect of meeting and working with feminist activists, and for me, seeing India for the first time was appealing.

Cross-cultural working can provide new experiences and construct new identities through the changed relationship to the sociocultural context. Although expected, the experience and feeling of 'otherness' linked to race and culture was new for me. One of its more confusing aspects was the frequency with which I felt completely out of control, failing to make sense of what to everyone else appeared straightforward. On the first day of the workshop I was seriously out of my depth. My usual cues for political networking were missing, and I could not read those present. As English was the language of the workshop, there was no need for interpreters, but its different usage and diversity of accents meant there were entire sessions I could not follow. I found the feminist activists, though at times even this required help. On occasions I almost confused them with fundamentalist activist women, although as discussed later, this might be partly explained by developments in Indian politics.

Collaborative working also highlights differences and commonalities in feminist political struggles. Women across the globe in many different ways have organized to name, raise awareness of, respond to and campaign against sexual violence since the 1970s. An outcome has been the formal recognition by the United Nations of violence against women and girl children as a violation of human rights. This collaborative effort, as demonstrated at the Beijing Conference and Platform of Action (1995), revealed issues of similarity and difference within a global problem of sexual violence.

The chapter proceeds by exploring continuities and differences in the nature, forms and extent of rape, the legal response, and women's activism in India and the UK. It is not a full scale comparative study, more a starting place for a longer and more collaborative project. More emphasis is placed on the Indian context as readers may be more familiar with the UK situation. Although the workshop also addressed prostitution and pornography, for reasons of space, only rape and sexual assault are addressed here.

Commonalities in the nature and extent of rape

In her treasurable book on the history of feminist activism in India, Radha Kumar provides a summary of the nature and extent of rape and sexual assault. She identifies rape as one of the most common and most under-reported crimes against women (Kumar 1993: 128). This has clear parallels with UK experience (see Lees 1996). There are also continuities in under-standings: 'sexual assault is one of the ugliest and most brutal expressions of masculine violence towards women . . . it reveals a great deal about the social relations of reproduction' (Kumar 1993: 128).

In India, as in the UK, having named the problem and analysed its nature and extent, feminists discussed visions of change and strategies for achieving it. Feminists in both countries sought justice and protection for women and children and an end to sexual violence, conceptualized, not as short versus long term, but as simultaneous goals. Kapur and Cossman (1996) note that Indian feminists adopted legal strategies as one attempt at improving the conditions of women's lives. As in the UK, this involved campaigning for changes in law, initiating public debate, raising awareness and providing legal services. Yet in both countries, the patriarchal nature of law has produced contradictions:

> The contemporary women's movement's engagement with law has been highly contradictory. On the one hand feminist activists have success-fully campaigned for reforms to a broad range of criminal and civil law; on the other hand legislative enactments often fell short of the demands of the movement. While the law reform campaigns succeeded in raising awareness of violence and discrimination against women, the legislative enactments seemed unable to live up to the promise of stemming this violence and discrimination.
>
> (Kapur and Cossman 1996: 66)

As the authors explain, the limited reforms led to disillusion with legal campaigning, but given the power of law, few were prepared to relinquish it as a site of struggle. This ambivalence was reflected at the workshop. The committee charged with redrafting the sexual assault laws prefaced its draft bill with a qualification:

the committee has been continuously conscious of the limited ability of law to provide a complete remedy to the problem of rape. As the law is subject to the interpretation of judges and lawyers, legislation on its own cannot be a solution. Working within these limitations, the committee has not sought to draft a comprehensive solution, but to write the experiences of women and minor children into law. Our endeavour has been to ensure that our collective experiences are inscribed into the law, rather than have our individual accounts disbelieved and dismissed in the court room.

(Committee for Redrafting Sexual Assault Law 18 on behalf of the National Commission For Women, New Delhi, 1993)

The contradictory nature of law has produced parallel debates in the UK where some feminists, recognizing its inherently patriarchal nature, consider it too compromised an arena to campaign for change. Others however recognize its patriarchal power but continue to see law as a necessary and legitimate arena of struggle. Arguing in favour of a transformative approach to law change, Liz Kelly and I have written:

it is specifically because [patriarchal] power relations are enscripted into the assumptions, concepts and categories of law itself that a more profound level of change, than amending existing law, is required if the legal discourse and practice is to recognise the material realities of oppressed and traditionally excluded groups.

(Radford and Kelly 1995: 198)

India's colonial history left a legacy of English law containing very similar assumptions regarding women's nature and sexuality. At the workshop clear parallels emerged in discussion of the legal definition of and responses to rape. A briefing paper summarized the situation in 1993:

The enforcement system has proved to be weak and uncertain against the rapists. Victims are often denied justice because of difficult standards of proof and lack of supportive services. Sentencing in rape cases has belied the expectations of law makers and women as a class felt let down by the legal system as a whole.

(Menon 1993)

A positive outcome of feminist activism was the appointment of a Committee by India's National Commission for Women to redraft the sexual assault law. Following extended discussions with the women's movement, this committee presented a draft bill, 'The Prevention of Sexual Violence Against Women and Children' for discussion at the workshop. Its preamble named a series of problems in existing law and legal practice: the definition of rape, consent, the admissibility of previous sexual history, poor medical evidence and sentencing practice. These issues are familiar to feminist campaigners in the UK where the current Campaign to End Rape has demanded a full investigation of the attrition rate, a changed definition of consent, and the introduction of specialist prosecutors to deal with rape and sexual assault.

A closer examination of the objectives and rationale underpinning the Indian proposals for a new sexual violence law reveals further parallels, despite differences in detail:

> existing definitions of rape, molestation do not adequately address the various types of sexual assault in terms of women's experiences nor do they adequately express the gender specificity of such crimes; existing law does not address child sexual abuse . . . [and] contains . . . serious contradictions which may inhibit women as well as children from reporting crimes of sexual assault and effective exercise of law . . . do[es] not adequately take into account the seriousness of sexual assault against women and particularly minor children.
>
> (Committee for Redrafting Sexual Assault Law 1993)

Most of these points have direct parallels with problem areas of law and legal practice in the UK where it is now acknowledged that the rape law and criminal process is in crisis, with convictions occurring in only 8 per cent of reported cases (Home Office 1996). This is not only a cause of concern for feminists but also for police spokespersons like Detective Superintendent Stephanie Yearnshire (1997).[3] A specific difference exists in relation to child sexual abuse, which is not criminalized in Indian law. In England and Wales it is outlawed but rules of evidence are complex and prosecutions rare, so the reality is not so different. Rape in marriage is not criminalized in India, but it was not outlawed in UK statute law until late 1994.

The provisions of the draft Indian Bill reflected the problems identified. It contained a comprehensive definition of sexual assault which specifically included child sexual assault; measures to ensure sensitive, speedy and effective prosecution, by reforming the prosecution process, police investigative practice, forensic procedures and court practice; positive measures to acknowledge the sensitive and gender-specific nature of sexual assault; and structures to make the criminal justice system accountable to women and minor children for its treatment of crimes of sexual assault (Committee for Redrafting Sexual Assault Law 1993).

As Kapur and Cossman (1996: 85) note, these recommendations go further than earlier reforms. The broad definition of sexual assault, extended to include all non-consensual sexual activity between adults, challenged established ideology underpinning rape law. The recommendations represent an integrated approach to law change by including all stages of the criminal justice process from police response, prosecution policy, to law and legal proceedings. They went beyond reforms to the letter of the law by identifying and addressing the culture of disbelief which characterized both legal discourse and public opinion. This broad approach has more in common with the comprehensive proposals made, for example, by the Irish National Task Force on Violence Against Women (Office of the Tánaiste 1997) than the limited, piecemeal approach to law reform in the UK. As the present (late 1990s) crisis in UK rape law and legal process illustrates, a fragmented approach to reform can only have a marginal impact.

However in India, as Kapur and Cossman (1996: 85) subsequently reported, the initial outcome of this law-making process was disappointing, as the National Commission refused to take up the Bill, even though it had received enthusiastic support from women's organizations. Consequently, it is not appropriate to engage in an analysis of all its provisions but given parallels with present UK campaigns, discussion of the connected issues of previous sexual history evidence and consent is of interest.

Previous sexual history evidence

The committee's draft bill included unequivocal provisions to exclude previous sexual history evidence because:

> This evidence has been used repeatedly by judges, the defence and the investigating agencies to discredit the victim and acquit the offender or lower the punishment. Evidence of the complainant's conduct, character and sexual history is invariably used to discredit the testimony of the victim and imply that she must have consented.
>
> (Committee for Redrafting Sexual Assault Law 1993)

This analysis reveals continuities with feminist critiques of sexual history evidence in the UK and the rest of Europe. The recommendations also parallel reforms which have been introduced in Canada and some states of Australia and advocated by feminists in many European countries including the UK (Tempkin 1987).

Consent

In India consent was highlighted by feminists campaigning against custodial and police rape in the 1970s and 1980s. Kapur and Cossman (1996: 60) reported that the women's movement challenged the prevailing social and legal discourse where consent was presumed from absence of physical injury and always if the woman was characterized as of 'loose' morals. This campaign led to an amendment in 1982, which categorically stated that consent was not relevant in cases of custodial rape (Kapur and Cossman 1996: 61). Although the context of rape in police or military custody is specific, and one where the notion of consent is completely unreasonable, this amendment was significant in categorically excluding it.

Similar measures to limit consent have occurred in relation to war rape. In her 'Dispatches from the front line', Sarah Maguire (1997/8: 4) documented the successful feminist struggle for rape to be recognized as a war crime with tight evidential rules governing consent:

> at the ad hoc tribunals, if a man wants to raise consent as an issue, he has to show why, and the burden is upon him to establish that consent really is a relevant issue.

Noting that even in the conflict in former Yugoslavia, rape was largely carried out by known men, Maguire made connections with rape in other contexts, arguing that if consent can be so qualified in one context it can be in any. In India, as Agnes (cited by Kapur and Cossman 1996: 61) documented, the elimination of consent in custodial rape had little impact because the same assumptions regarding women's sexuality continued to underpin the prosecution of cases.

The Indian Committee identified consent as the most important factor in a rape trial given the legal culture of disbelief and its uniqueness to rape. They questioned its necessity but interestingly concluded that removing consent would ultimately work against women's interests as they would be forced to rely on circumstantial evidence, for example, physical injuries, to prove that sexual assault had occurred. This would effectively reintroduce consent on terms more advantageous to the accused (Committee for Redrafting Sexual Assault Law 1993).

The alternative preferred by the committee was 'radical revision', the inscription into law of 'a woman's understanding of lack of consent'. Consent was redefined as 'an unequivocal voluntary agreement of the woman to engage in the sexual activity in question' (Committee for Redrafting Sexual Assault Law 1993). The radicalism of this proposal lies in its attempt to construct law on women's, rather than men's, understandings. Consent is thereby transformed into an active concept embodying women's agency.

This new definition was followed by an indicative list of circumstances where consent arguments were to be prohibited. Perhaps as a product of committee compromise, these seem less radical and closely parallel traditional definitions of rape by force, intimidation or fraud, found in many European countries. Cultural specificity is reflected in two further exclusions: misleading the woman that the man is her husband, and when consent is expressed by someone other than the woman herself. Both involve exploitation of marriage, including child marriage, and courtship customs. While reflecting the south-east Asian context, they stand in some tension against the radicalism of the committee's stated aims, illustrating the contradictory nature of law and law reform.

Consent was further discussed at the workshop. It was suggested that an amendment requiring consent to be explicitly expressed might tighten these provisions. This has parallels with the 'positive consent' model adopted in the sexual assault codes of Antioch College, Ohio in the USA (1991, 1996). In the UK, discussion of this initiative subsequently led to the Campaign to End Rape's proposal to shift the onus of proof of consent to the defence. Similar provisions have been introduced in Victoria, Australia. The strength of this approach is that it spotlights the defendant's actions, rather than complainant's behaviour, so making previous sexual history and character evidence redundant.

Differences within continuity

This comparative engagement with legal discourse has revealed a surprising degree of continuity in rape law and legal practice, debates in feminist jurisprudence and activist approaches to legal transformation. These parallels seem all the more remarkable when contextualized historically and against the wider culture and sociopolitics of the two countries.[4]

Alongside these commonalities are significant differences in the forms and meaning of rape in India. These have also shaped its legal definition, responses to it, and the historical contexts in which it became a public and political issue. Radha Kumar (1993: 128) identified 'the enormous number of forms' of rape recognized in India: 'landlord rape'; 'rape by those in authority'; 'caste rape', where caste hierarchy is invoked in the rape of lower caste or outcast women; 'class rape'; police rape; and unrecognized in Indian law, rape by family members, rape of minors and rape of prostitutes. There are resonances with UK law in some but not all these forms. In terms of meaning, Indian feminists recognize that rape is an issue of gender justice and about power and control of women by men, but its meaning is also informed by other power relations which have influenced the history of rape as a public and political issue. This is illustrated in their recognition as legal categories.

A different history

Historian Mushirul Hasan (1997) identified three dominant themes of south Asian historiography: colonialism, nationalism and communalism. Although it is impossible to summarize the history of a subcontinent in three words, they seem helpful in understanding the context in which rape emerged as a public issue. Radha Kumar's review of 'the agitation against rape' reveals a long history dating back to pre-Independence, nationalist struggles against colonialism:

> By the end of the nineteenth century . . . the issues of rape and racism were interlinked . . . nationalists were beginning to use rape as an example of imperialist barbarism, it was clearly seen as a violation of community – or national – honour, rather than an act of violence against women. Rape, it seems was a taboo subject, nameable only when committed by outsiders.
>
> (Kumar 1993: 37)

In 1947, independence or partition, as Hasan (1997: 50) noted, led to 'one of the largest migrations in world history with an estimated 12.5 million people being displaced and many hundreds of thousands killed'.[5] Urvashi Butalia (1995: 61) documented the use of sexual violence in this conflict:

The story of Partition, the uprooting and dislocation of women was accompanied by the story of the rape, abduction and widowhood of thousands of women on both sides of the newly formed borders.

These atrocities occurred in the context of violence between Hindu and Muslim communities and left a heritage of communalist violence as Sarkar and Butalia (1995: 6) record:

The partition of India, and the communal violence that accompanied it, provides a most immediate referent in recent violence against the Muslim community in India today. Perhaps the most emotive issue that communalists have been able to manipulate into their agenda of aggression, revenge and retribution for past wrongs, was the rape and abduction of women during and following on the partition.

Context and meaning

This history of colonialism, nationalism and subsequently communalism, had a major impact on how rape emerged as a public issue. As Agarwal (1995: 31) argued in his discussion of rape as a recurring symbol and reality in communal violence, this context produced a shift of meaning:

In a collective context, rape becomes an explicit political act, in the context of an organised aggression it becomes a spectacular ritual, a ritual of victory – the defilement of the autonomous symbol of honour of the enemy community.

Rape in the context of communalism resurfaced in the 1970s' 'mass agitation against rape' (Kumar 1993) when again landlord and police rape became central focuses. Specific incidents generated massive public outcry. For example, Kumar (1993) records a gang rape of a woman by police officers in 1978 in Hydrabad. The woman's husband was also killed, and 22,000 people took his body to the police station in protest. Telephone wires were cut and the building stoned. Armed police fired on the crowd killing nine people and injuring many more. A 'Hydrabad bandh' (the closing of all services) ensued, a curfew declared and the army was called in. The agitation was only repressed with the promise of a commission of enquiry into the rape. Kumar reports this was not an isolated occurrence.

Public reaction to rape on this scale is unimaginable in the UK. Understanding it requires further engagement with Hasan's (1997) third theme. Communalism seems to be the flip side of 'community', predicated on ethnic and/or religious conflict. It is a complex concept:

Communalism has been defined as a discourse based on the belief that because a group of people follow a particular religion, they have as a result, common social, political and economic interests. It is a discourse that attempts to constitute subjects in and through community attachment, particularly through religious community . . . Through communal discourses subjects come to understand the world around them as . . . based on the conflict between religious groups; Indian society is understood as fractured by the conflict between these groups. This community identity becomes the basis for social, economic and religious demands.

(Kapur and Cossman 1995: 84)

It is also a controversial concept, as Agarwal makes clear:

The misplaced conceptualisation of communalism solely within religious intolerance and socio-economic collision leads most liberal commentators to see a communal riot as just a riot, while to the participants or to the abettors, every riot is actually a battle in the unfinished war, not between two religious communities but between two racially defined nations.

(Agarwal 1995: 32)

Although 'communalism' is specific to India, it has been an issue of concern amongst feminists and progressive political groups in the Asian communities in the UK, as Pragna Patel has documented:

We came together to form an anti-communal organisation, the Alliance Against Communalism and for Democracy in South Asia. The aim was to support anti-communalist forces in India who were facing an uphill struggle in turning the tide of sweeping Hindu nationalism, and to prevent communalism from breaking out in our communities in Britain.

(Patel 1997: 266)

Parallels with the use of sexual violence in communalist conflict can be identified in the use of sexual violence in ethnic and civil conflict in former Yugoslavia, which has been subject of some western feminist analysis (for example MacKinnon 1993; McCollum et al. 1994; Maguire 1997/8). A central theme in these discussions is the need to make and analyse connections between 'routine and everyday rape' and rape in the context of civil conflict. This perspective takes issue with media accounts which treated the latter as unique war-time atrocities. In making these connections, feminist analysis identifies another dimension in the continuum of sexual violence; between rape in so-called 'peace', and rape in the context of communal or civil conflict and war. It illustrates how the hatred of the-other-the-enemy, is expressed through and transformed into the hatred and violation of women.

Kumar (1993) illustrates how feminists in India have also striven to make connections, rather than adopt a fragmented approach which conceptualizes communal rape as a discrete phenomenon. One thread of the analysis developed by Kannabiran and Kannabiran (1995) turns on how, within communalism, women's bodies are taken to represent the community, making a violation of a woman also a violation of a community. This has specific implications in terms of identity politics. These authors locate two modes of identity construction, both predicated on sexual violence:

First through the rape of women of minority or subordinated groups – religious as well as caste groups – which is also the rape of the community to which the woman belongs. The justification for this act of violence is provided by demonstrating the 'inherent immorality' of the community and its individual members. This is also an assertion of difference and separateness and a reinforcement of the aggressor's position . . . The second way in which identity is constructed through the allegation by the dominant group of the rape of and aggression on their women by men of minority communities, an allegation which serves to justify dominant caste/community hegemony, by demonstrating 'lack of character' of minority men who show scant respect for women. This affects the perception of minority women as women who by virtue of belonging to 'characterless' men become women without character.

(Kannabiran and Kannabiran 1995: 122)

These writers identify processes of classification, segregation and surveillance of women on the basis of caste and community to distinguish those accepted as 'normal' from the 'abnormal', both within and between the classifications. Those who are perceived as outside the norm are seen as undeserving of protection. This is applied not only to individual women, but also to the communities they inhabit.

Women and the new fundamentalism

Communalism and communalist conflict has a long, if intermittent and violent history in India, shaping women's identities and giving a broader meaning to rape. This may help explain the different ways in which rape has surfaced historically as a public issue. It also presents complex dilemmas for contemporary feminist activists. Explication of this requires understanding of the recent growth in right-wing Hindu fundamentalism, Hinduvta, and its construction of women as militant activists, heavily implicated in communal violence. This recent and large scale involvement of women in communal violence has generated shock waves amongst Indian feminists as Sikata Banerjee and Sarkar and Butalia note:

Violent feminine action, although not unheard of, is not very common in India. Indeed in the past, reports of female involvement in violent situations in India have emphasised their peace keeping role.

(Banerjee 1995: 217)

Politically and methodologically this assertive participation of women in right wing campaigns, pulled many of our assumptions into a state of crisis for we have always seen women as victims of violence rather than its perpetrators and we have always perceived their public, political activity and interest as a positive liberating force . . . we . . . have before us a large scale movement among women of the right who bring with them informed consent and agency, a militant activism.

(Sarkar and Butalia 1995: 3–4)

Banerjee theorizes this 'feminization of violence' as an outcome of the constitution of the New Hindu Woman by the Hinduvta. This was achieved through the construction of a discourse which cleverly balanced patriarchal traditionalist ideologies of familialism and communalism, which venerate women as mothers of Hindu sons, with postmodernist discourses which emphasize identity, agency and strength:

The constitution of the new Hindu Woman – a woman who may be educated, and who may work outside the home, a woman who is strong and powerful inside her family and her community – is still a woman constituted through traditional discourses of matri shaki, as mother and wife; and of Sita, as chaste, pure and loyal. The new Hindu woman is strong, but she is strong in restoring the glories of an ancient past . . . a past . . . reconstituted through communal discourse. A strong Hindu woman is essential for the constitution of a strong Hindu society.

(Kapur and Cossman 1995: 106)

Similar processes constitute Muslim women's identity, depicted as 'subservient' and 'other' by the Hindu right:

This Muslim woman is also the product of a paradoxical mix of traditional and modern discourses. But unlike the Hindu woman, she is neither respected as mother, nor is she the subject of rights. Saving Muslim women from their oppression becomes the justification for not respecting the practices and beliefs of the Muslim community, and indeed for subordinating this community to Hindu rule.

(Kapur and Cossman 1995: 106)

As Kapur and Cossman (1995) argue, the discursive strategy of the Hindu right is skilfully constructed to strike at the heart of identity. Through an elision of community and familial ideologies the private and public spheres are merged, facilitating women's entry into the political arena as wives and mothers of sons, through a notion of female power that glorifies these roles. Community and gender become mutually constituting; women are constituted in and through community and community in and through women's identity, sexuality and gender. This construction of female power is illusory and partial, but strategically deflects attention from the subordinate position of women within the community. Sarkar and Butalia (1995: 9) describe how the communalist parties:

firstly persuade women to see themselves as legitimate, equal and valued participants in public and even political demonstrations of Hindu fervour and faith, and secondly, the careful erasure of boundaries between the home and the world, private and public spaces, religion and politics through ceremonial enactments of familiar household rituals transforms and reinscribes the public Hindu cause as a deeply felt and experienced private wrong that every woman, irrespective of her caste and community origins, will willingly nurse in her heart.

The Hinduvta Right mirrored feminism in eliding the private and public spheres, but drew women into activism in the familial role of mothers. As several commentators (Kumar 1993; Agnes 1995; Banerjee 1995) have pointed out, the Hindu Right has never critiqued patriarchal power, and consequently can offer only a limited notion of emancipation:

> This new woman could come out on to the streets with as much ease as the men from the community to avenge their wrongs. And in this action she had the blessings of the party and community leaders. Hence women found this role not only exciting but also more comfortable than one which involved protesting against a violent husband or rapist from within the community. In this latter role they would not have the protective mantle of the party nor the blessings of community elders.
>
> (Agnes 1995: 140)

By erasing the boundary between public and private, the discourse of the Hindu Right also expanded the definition of familial rape to include rape by men of the community, reinforcing its taboo or unspeakable status. In contrast to the increasing invisibility of rape by men of the community, communal rape became increasingly visible, celebrated in ritualized spectacle. Through this discourse the Hinduvta encouraged women into activist protest against rape, into violent action.

While the emergence of a violent movement of far-right women activists has alarmed feminist activists, Agnes (1995: 140) has noted a further danger in the Hinduvta's construction of the modern Hindu woman as an 'angry, rebellious "new Durga" – a destroyer of evil', in its superficial similarity to feminist heroes. This adoption of feminist imagery is compounded by the Hindu Right's appropriation of feminist style, symbols and slogans:

> Through a process of selection, Hindu communal forces usurped the external usages popularised by the feminist movement such as protest marches, and road blocks . . . But what was even more distressing was that women from communal organisations mouthed slogans coined by the women's movement . . . [We are the women of India, not delicate flowers but smouldering embers] while leading demonstrations during the riots.
>
> (Agnes 1995: 141)

The apparent similarities between the two movements created a need to specify the central ideological differences:

> There are . . . important differences between the two: while the women's movement challenges notions of women's domination within the family and society, the ideology of Hinduvta places women squarely in the home and propagates a patriarchal model.
>
> (Sarkar and Butalia 1995: 7)

Banerjee, speaking of Shiv Sena, a Bombay Hindu communal party, identifies key differences in the political goals:

> The Shiv Sena . . . encourages women to come out and shout slogans which emphasise feminine power. But, unlike feminists, the Sena is harnessing this power not to challenge the patriarchy but to ferment communal hatred.
>
> (Banerjee 1995: 226)

Confusingly, also like the fundamentalist religious Right in the West, the Hindu Right has successfully mobilized women's activism on issues of sexual violence, representation and pornography, and prostitution. As in previous agitations against rape, however, this is from a fundamentalist, religious and communalist standpoint. In the context of pornography and representation, for example, the Shiv Sena objects to 'obscenity' as insulting to the purity of a woman's role within the family, which contrast with feminist critiques of pornography 'as embedding women further in the cycle of male domination which also shapes and includes the role of women in the family' (Banerjee 1995: 226).

Agnes (1995: 141) notes that in a similar manner feminist protests against media representations of women as sex objects and in derogatory and subservient roles, were hijacked:

> In the hands of the communal forces the issue took a dangerous turn and somehow got pulled into another communal campaign aimed at curtailing freedom of speech and expression on secular issues.

The implications for feminist politics of the mass mobilization of women by communalist parties are worrying. As well as articulating their theoretical distance from fundamentalism, feminists have responded to the threat by exploring the appeal of communalism, particularly for poorer and slum-dwelling women. Several elements have been identified: the positive identity of women as strong, a sense of belonging, and the provision of material, cultural and spiritual support at grass-roots level. Banerjee (1995: 229) suggests these can inform strategies for countering communalism:

> feminists should construct direct and meaningful relationships by living and working in the slums as the Shiv Sena has done to create the trust necessary for grass roots mobilisation. Indian feminists must reclaim the political space the Shiv Sena has encroached upon to provide a positive alternative to the fundamental message of violence and hatred this organisation is spreading.

Although the growth of the Hindu Right has been rapid and is expanding from its traditional northern base into the South, it is not yet ideologically dominant.[6] Rather, according to Kapur and Cossman (1996), it is involved in a discursive struggle politically, culturally and economically and significantly for this discussion at the level of law. These authors, both contributors to the workshop, have documented the struggle in which women's relationship to law has been contested in a range of legal concerns, including personal law, *sati*, employment and civil rights. While at one level the workshop was about facilitating gender justice in relation to sexual violence, it was also a site of ideological struggle between feminism and fundamentalism.

Conclusion

Central to holding feminist ground in this discursive struggle over legal definitions of sexual violence, was an awareness of the continuities between the different forms of sexual violence. Of particular importance is the analysis of continuities between communal rape and rape by men from within the community and/or family. At a theoretical level this adds new dimensions to the continuum of sexual violence. For example, the elision of the boundary between family and community expands what is considered to be the private sphere where rape is a taboo issue. This transforms western conceptions of public/private and stranger/familial rape from dichotomies into dimensions of the continuum. This theorization of commonality and continuity between the different forms of rape enabled feminists to hold on to the recognition of rape as embodying the power relations of gender and sexuality as well as communalism. This can provide common ground for feminists to come together across communal divisions to challenge sexual violence. The feminist insistence that women's identities are multidimensional, constructed through the power relations of gender and sexuality as well as community, is central to the task of challenging the populist discourse of the Hindu New Right. These two issues mark limitations of fundamentalist discourse, and feminists in India hope they may facilitate a shift away from the negative discourse of Hinduvta towards a secular feminist analysis which recognizes that sexual violence represents a violation of the human rights of all women.

Notes

1 Rights of Women is a feminist legal project based in London. Rita Rupal and I attended this Workshop held in Bangalore and New Delhi, India, January 1994.
2 In opposition, the Labour Party produced *Peace at Home* (1995), a consultation paper on the elimination of domestic violence and sexual violence, in which it committed itself to 'review and strengthen the law in relation to rape and sexual assault' (Labour Party 1995: 13).
3 In 1999 the Home Office, recognizing the force of feminist criticisms, established a committee to review the law on sexual offences.
4 A similar argument about commonality and difference in feminist activism against gender violence is made by Kelly (1998) in her discussion of a range of women's projects working with survivors of sexual violence in Calcutta.
5 In 1947, the Indian Independence Act was passed, confirming the partition of India and the dominion status of both India and Pakistan.

6 The winning of the General Election of 1997 was a significant moment for the fortunes of the BJP, a Hindu communalist party which appeals to high castes.

References

Agarwal, P. (1995) Savarkar, Surat and Draupadi, in T. Sarkar and U. Butalia (eds) *Women and Right-Wing Movements: Indian Experiences*. London: Zed Books.

Agnes, F. (1995) Redefining the agenda of the women's movement within a secular framework, in T. Sarkar and U. Butalia (eds) *Women and Right-Wing Movements: Indian Experiences*. London: Zed Books.

Antioch College (1991, 1996) Sexual offence prevention and survivors' advocacy program, in *Antioch College Survival Handbook*, http://www.antioch-college.edu/survival/html/sopsap/html.

Banerjee, S. (1995) Hindu nationalism and the construction of woman: the Shiva Sena organises women in Bombay, in T. Sarkar and U. Butalia (eds) *Women and Right-Wing Movements: Indian Experiences*. London: Zed Books.

Butalia, U. (1995) Muslims and Hindus, men and women, in T. Sarkar and U. Butalia (eds) *Women and Right-Wing Movements: Indian Experiences*. London: Zed Books.

Hasan, M. (1997) Partition: the human cost. *History Today*, 47(9) September: 47–53.

Home Office (1996) *Criminal Statistics: England and Wales*. London: HMSO.

Jeffreys, S. and Radford, J. (1984) Contributory negligence or being a woman? the car rapist case, in P. Scraton and P. Gordon (eds) *Causes for Concern: British Justice on Trial*. Harmondsworth: Pelican Books.

Kannabiran, V. and Kannabiran, K. (1995) The frying pan or the fire? engendered identities, gendered institutions and women's survival, in T. Sarkar and U. Butalia (eds) *Women and Right-Wing Movements: Indian Experiences*. London: Zed Books.

Kapur, R. and Cossman, B. (1995) Communalising gender: engendering community: women, legal discourse and the saffron agenda, in T. Sarkar and U. Butalia (eds) *Women and Right-Wing Movements: Indian Experiences*. London: Zed Books.

Kapur, R. and Cossman, B. (1996) *Subversive Sites: Feminist Engagements with Law in India*. New Delhi: Sage.

Kelly, L. (1998) Between contexts and continents: feminist activists in South Asia are making connections between forms of sexual violence. *Trouble and Strife*, 37, Summer: 12–22.

Kumar, R. (1993) *The History of Doing: An Illustrated Account of Movements for Women's Rights and Feminism in India, 1800–1990*. New Delhi: Kali for Women.

Labour Party (1995) *Peace at Home: A Labour Party Consultation Document on the Elimination of Domestic and Sexual Violence Against Women*. London: Labour Party.

Lees, S. (1996) Unreasonable doubt: the outcomes of rape trials, in M. Hester, L. Kelly, and J. Radford (eds) *Women, Violence and Male Power: Feminist Activism, Research and Practice*. Buckingham: Open University Press.

McCollum, H., Kelly, L. and Radford, J. (1994) Wars against women. *Trouble and Strife*, 28, Spring: 12–18.

MacKinnon, C. (1993) Turning rape into pornography: postmodern genocide. *Ms*, 4(1) August/September.

Maguire, S. (1997/8) Dispatches from the front line. *Trouble and Strife*, 36, Winter: 2–5.

Menon, M. (1993) Programme. Workshop on Women and Law, National Law School of India University, Bangalore, 3–5 January.

Office of Tanáiste (1997) *Report of the Task Force on Violence Against Women*. Dublin: The Stationery Office.

Patel, P. (1997) Third wave feminism and black women's activism, in H.S. Mirza (ed.) *Black British Feminism*. London: Routledge.

Radford, J. and Kelly, L. (1995) Self-preservation: feminist activism and feminist jurisprudence, in M. Maynard and J. Purvis (eds) *(Hetero)sexual Politics*. London: Taylor & Francis.

Radford, J. and Rupal, R. (1994) *Rights of Women*, unpublished report from Rights of Women.

Sarkar, T. and Butalia, U. (1995) *Women and Right-Wing Movements: Indian Experiences*. London: Zed Books.

Sarkar, T. (1997) Women in South Asia: the Raj and after. *History Today*, 47(9) September: 54–9.

Smart, C. (1995) *Law, Crime and Sexuality: Essays in Feminism*. London: Sage.

Tempkin, J. (1987) *Rape and the Legal Process*. London: Sweet & Maxwell.

Yearnshire, S. (1997) Revictimisation. *Police Review*, 18 July: 16–19.

Index